# WALKINGVANCOUVER

VICTORIA | VANCOUVER | CALGARY

john lee

# WALKINGVANCOUVER

**36** strolls to dynamic neighborhoods, hip hangouts, and spectacular waterfronts

Published in the United States of America by Wilderness Press

Published in Canada by Heritage House Publishing Co. Ltd.
#108 – 17665 66A Ave., Surrey, BC V3S 2A7
www.heritagehouse.ca

**LIBRARY AND ARCHIVES CANADA CATALOGUING IN PUBLICATION**

Lee, John, 1969–
    Walking Vancouver: 36 strolls to dynamic neighborhoods, hip hangouts, and spectacular waterfronts / John Lee.
Includes index.

ISBN 978-1-894974-90-5
    1. Walking—British Columbia—Vancouver—Guidebooks. 2. Vancouver
(B.C.)—Guidebooks. I. Title.

FC3847.18.L433 2009      917.11'33045      C2009-904145-6

Editor: Gail Buente
Cover design: Jacqui Thomas
Maps: Scott McGrew

FRONT-COVER PHOTO: View of English Bay and the West End by Jacqui Thomas
FRONTISPIECE: Marine Building, Burrard Street, by John Lee
BACK-COVER PHOTOS (CLOCKWISE FROM TOP): Alan Chung Hung's *Gate to the Northwest Passage* in Vanier Park by Noel MacDonald; Capilano suspension bridge by John Lee; Vern Simpson's *Gassy Jack* with the flatiron Hotel Europe in background by John Lee; a perfect latte at Elysian Coffee by John Lee
INTERIOR PHOTOS: John Lee except for pp. 25, 27, 41, 125, 143, 149, 151, 169 by Noel MacDonald

Printed in Canada

Heritage House acknowledges the financial support for its publishing program from the Government of Canada through the Book Publishing Industry Development Program (BPIDP), Canada Council for the Arts, and the province of British Columbia through the British Columbia Arts Council and the Book Publishing Tax Credit.

SAFETY NOTICE: Although the publisher and the author have made every attempt to ensure that the information in this book is accurate, they are not responsible for any loss, damage, inconvenience, or injury that may occur to anyone while using this book. You are responsible for your own safety and health while following the walking trips described here. Always check local conditions, know your own limitations, and consult a map.

*For my Dad,*
*who taught me all about the value of walking everywhere.*

*Stanley Park totem pole*

# acknowledgments

After more than 10 years as an adopted Vancouver local, there are hundreds of individuals who have contributed their valued insider input to the selection, stories, and asides contained herein. Most of those conversations have taken place in shady corners of the Railway Club or the Irish Heather (in its older, shadier incarnation). I would especially like to thank Dominic Schaefer, Glenn Drexhage, and Peter Mitham for joining me on many of these beery nights. And for this project in particular, I'd also like to send my thanks to Noel MacDonald for his sterling photography work on seven of these walks; Ryan Ver Berkmoes for hooking me up with Wilderness Press in the first place; and Roslyn Bullas . . . mostly for her patience.

# author's note

Having rushed countless times along many of the streets covered in this book, it's been a real pleasure to slow down, lift my gaze above foot level and finally find out the stories behind them. Barreling along Robson, Georgia, Granville or Hastings on a frantic, chore-laden quest, you barely notice what's around you, but this project has enabled me to do just that. I'll certainly never see the city in the same light again. And that, of course, is the point: this book is an opportunity for readers across the Lower Mainland to rediscover the metropolis they thought they knew.

Luckily, Vancouver is a walking town. There are 36 sidewalk-tested strolls in this book. They cover all the city's key districts as well as some exotic out-of-town locales like the North Shore, New Westminster, and Steveston. All the routes are easily accessible by public transit and are designed so you can go at your own pace: feel free to speed walk along any route or turn a short stroll into a half-day amble with coffee breaks, shopping stops, and a long, leisurely dinner—there are handy pit stop recommendations throughout.

Right, what are you waiting for? It's time to hit the streets, unpeel a few layers of unexpected history, and dive into neighborhoods you haven't properly looked at for years. Make sure you bring your curiosity, always look above the main level on every building and, since this is the Wet Coast, consider packing a rain jacket—you'll thank me in the end.

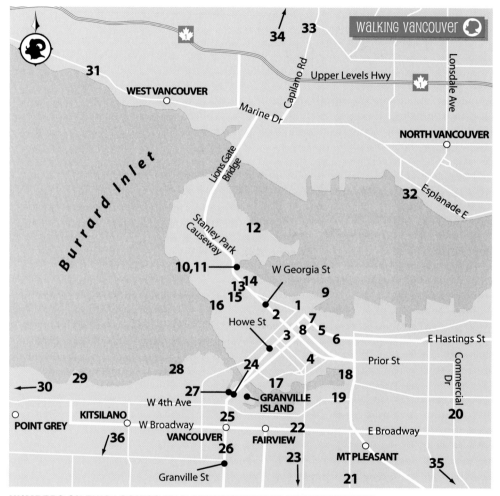

NUMBERS ON THIS LOCATOR MAP CORRESPOND TO WALK NUMBERS.

# TABLE OF CONTENTS

# INTRODUCTION

Unless you've lived in Vancouver for more than 200 years, hitting the streets in the city you thought you knew almost everything about can trigger some eye-opening surprises, and raise more than a few questions.

For example: Why is the cenotaph located in what's now called Victory Square? Where did the first Greenpeace protest launch from? Who died in the old Hotel Georgia? Where is there a marker for the first official visit by a U.S. president, and why is it a memorial? Which much-loved building was once the Canadian headquarters of the Ku Klux Klan? Where is the city's best hotdog stand? Just how many time capsules are hidden in this city, anyway? And, of course, which are the best bars to visit on a merry trawl around Gastown?

Slip on your (preferably waterproof) walking shoes, tuck this book into your backpack, and you're on your way to finding out the answers. Just remember one key maxim: slow down and you'll likely enjoy it a whole lot more.

Burrard Pl

Thurlow St

start

Waterfront Rd W

Burrard St

Hornby St

W Cordova St

Melville St

Howe St

W Hastings St

W Pender St

Water St

finish

Seymour St

Dunsmuir St

Richards St

Robson St

Granville St

Homer St

W Georgia St

Hamilton St

0 100 200 300 yards
0 100 200 300 metres

# 1 DOWNTOWN: arts & architecture

BOUNDARIES: **W. Hastings St., Burrard St., W. Georgia St., Howe St.**
DISTANCE: **½ mile/¾ kilometre**
DIFFICULTY: **Easy**
PARKING: **There is an underground parkade at 999 W. Hastings St.–the entrance is on the east side of Burrard. There's also underground parking at Canada Place, a short walk away.**
PUBLIC TRANSIT: **The Burrard SkyTrain station is on the west side of Burrard St., just past the intersection with Dunsmuir St. Buses 22, 44, and 98 B-Line also stop along Burrard.**

The heart of Vancouver's latter-day central business district radiates from the W. Hastings St. and Burrard St. intersection. This is where the city's main bank and corporate headquarters colonize the mirrored glass skyscrapers, sucking in thousands of office workers every weekday—in fact, the area is a virtual ghost town on weekends. But aside from the business of making money, this downtown stretch is also home to some unexpected architectural and artsy features that many Vancouverites pass by every day without even noticing. This walk is all about seeing these familiar streets in a different scratch-beneath-the-surface light. In the process, you'll come across hidden stained glass windows, historic reminders of near-forgotten buildings, and landmark hotels with surprisingly colorful stories to tell.

● **Start at the spectacular Marine Building on the northwest corner of W. Hastings and Burrard Sts. Completed in 1930, when its 321-foot/98-metre height made it the British empire's tallest building, it vies with City Hall as Vancouver's finest Art Deco structure. In fact, it almost became the new City Hall when the Great Depression reduced the number of available tenants for the tower and its desperate owners tried to sell it to the city. Spend some time here perusing the exterior's lavish depictions of streamlined ships and trains, alongside aquatic motifs like seahorses, lobsters, and disembodied boat hulls. Inside, it's even more elaborate. Check out the decorated brass elevator doors (and their inlaid wood interiors), the Technicolor stained glass windows, and the sumptuous polished floor depicting signs of the zodiac. Renovated in 1999, the heritage-designated structure is now an office building.**

- Strolling south on the right side of Burrard St., cross over W. Hastings St. and then W. Pender St. You're now among the city's flagship bank headquarters. Just past the W. Pender intersection, you'll come to the *Fountain of the Pioneers.* An abstract bronze water feature by George Tsutakawa, an artist who created more than 60 public fountains in Japan and North America, it was installed in 1969. When the piece was cleaned in 2003, its newly sparkling, gold-hued look made many people notice it for the first time.

- Continue to the intersection with Dunsmuir St. and cross over to the other side of Burrard. Half a block up the slightly sloped incline, you'll come to a slender park space on your left that's a tranquility respite for area office workers. Backed by a granite-faced waterfall and bristling with hanging flower baskets, it's a surprisingly quiet spot that manages to defuse the rumble of the buses idling nearby.

- Maintain your southward uphill stroll and you'll soon come to Christ Church Cathedral on your left. Nestled incongruously among the area's towers, it's the city's most attractive heritage church. But rather than heading for the main entrance, duck through the doorway of the vestibule at the first corner you come to. Once inside, swivel around 180 degrees, and you'll face a fantastic, three-paneled stained glass window. Designed by Edward Burne-Jones in 1905, it was crafted by the famed William Morris Company and has many of the rich, resonant color highlights for which Morris himself was well known. Follow the signs inside the cathedral and head up the steps into the magnificent nave.

- Exit the church from the main entrance at the corner of Burrard and W. Georgia Sts. Stroll east along W. Georgia and check out the exterior of Cathedral Place next door. The 1929 skyscraper originally here was particularly well known for three statues of First World War nurses—one on each of the building's visible corners—that graced the 10th story, a tribute from its architects to the nurses who cared for them during the war. When the tower was slated for demolition in 1989, a campaign to save the statues for the new building was launched. However, they proved too difficult to preserve and replicas were made, this time placed a few floors lower, for enhanced visibility.

- Past Cathedral Place, turn left onto Hornby St. Half a block down, on your left, climb the short flight of steps to the new Bill Reid Gallery of Northwest Coast Art.

## Back Story: Vancouver's Favorite House of Worship

The city's oldest church, Christ Church Cathedral was the site of the first Anglican service in 1889, when the unfinished building was little more than a brick shed. In fact, uncharitable locals nicknamed it the "Root House." The Canadian Pacific Railway (original owners of the plot of land where the church stood) were unhappy with the ugly building, claiming it was detrimental to the sale of other plots in the area. With the threat of eviction hanging over it, the congregation launched a major fundraising drive and plans were soon in place for a grand new building. Dedicated in 1895, the beautiful Gothic Revival structure, complete with its stunning hammer beam ceiling and kaleido-scope of stained glass, soon became the city's favorite downtown house of worship. Surprisingly, the cathedral's now-celebrated Douglas-fir flooring and its elaborate cedar ceiling were covered over in the 1950s: the ceiling was obscured with "fashionable" Tudoresque panels, while modern linoleum covered the old hardwood floor. By the 1970s, the congregation had decided to demolish the cathedral entirely in favor of a smart new modern structure. Locals protested, the building was added to the city's heritage preservation list and, following extensive renovations in 1995 and 2003, it's become a beloved favorite of both religious and non-religious Vancouverites.

Dedicated to the work of the Haida First Nation's most revered artist—one of Reid's bronzes adorns the back of Canada's $20 bill—the gallery is a compact labyrinth of carvings, jewelry, and paintings surrounded by contextualizing video displays and touch-screen computers. The Great Hall is a highlight: head to its second level for a face-to-face view of a towering totem pole and a 26 foot/8.5 metre bronze frieze of intertwined creatures on the opposite wall.

● Re-trace your steps along Hornby to the corner of W. Georgia. Cross east over Hornby and enter the Pendulum Gallery. One of Vancouver's most unlikely art spaces, the lobby of the HSBC Building here has been transformed into a free-entry art space where regularly changing exhibitions enliven what would otherwise be a bland stretch of teller counters. There's a little café here and the immense open space is dominated by a permanent artwork: a mammoth steel pendulum created by Alan Storey that swings silently overhead.

- Continue east along W. Georgia and the next building on your left is the brick-built Hotel Georgia. Undergoing a dramatic transformation that will see it paired with a soaring glass tower, the property was built in 1927 and has a colorful past. Celebrity guests have included Elvis Presley, the Rolling Stones, and the Beatles, although presumably not at the same time. Known as a chic party lodge, unlike the more sedate Hotel Vancouver nearby, this was where Errol Flynn died of a heart attack in 1959, allegedly after spending his final week propping up the hotel's bars.

- Cross south over W. Georgia at Howe St. The Vancouver Art Gallery lawn in front of you is the city's main public rallying space and is frequently used for political protests. In its center is a large, mosaic-lined fountain installed in 1966 to mark the centenary of the uniting of Vancouver Island and British Columbia. Peruse the exterior of the Art Gallery behind. Designed by Francis Rattenbury, the architect responsible for many landmark Victorian- and Edwardian-era BC buildings, this grand 1907 structure was originally the Provincial Law Court. Although the gallery entrance is on the other side of the building, this is its more handsome face, complete with Trafalgar Square-style lions flanking a sweeping staircase topped by Neoclassical ionic columns.

- Head west along W. Georgia and cross over to the other side of Hornby. Stroll half a block south on Hornby and turn right into the side entrance of the gargoyle-topped Fairmont Hotel Vancouver. Griffins Restaurant is on your immediate left (the buffet is recommended, especially for seafood fans). Alternatively, follow the carpeted corridor westward. On your left, just before the lobby, you'll see historic photographs depicting the property's construction—this was the city's third Hotel Vancouver building—as well as the 1939 visit of King George VI and Queen Elizabeth.

- Exit the building through the main entrance onto W. Georgia and turn left toward the Burrard St. intersection. Embedded in the sidewalk a few steps along, you'll find a colorful mosaic depiction of local bandleader Dal Richards. His swinging orchestra used to hit the hotel's stage five nights a week, and the twinkle-eyed nonagenarian legend still performs concerts throughout the city. Conclude your stroll here with a coffee at the one of the nearby java stops.

## POINTS OF INTEREST

**Marine Building** 355 Burrard St.

**Christ Church Cathedral** 690 Burrard St., 604-682-3848

**Bill Reid Gallery of Northwest Coast Art** 639 Hornby St., 604-682-3455

**Pendulum Gallery** 885 W. Georgia St., 604-250-9682

**Vancouver Art Gallery** 750 Hornby St., 604-662-4719

**Fairmont Hotel Vancouver** 900 W. Georgia St., 604-684-3131

## route summary

1. Start at the northwest corner of W. Hastings and Burrard Sts.
2. Head south on the right side of Burrard.
3. Cross W. Hastings and W. Pender Sts.on Burrard.
4. Cross over to the left side of Burrard at Dunsmuir St.
5. Continue south on Burrard to the W. Georgia St. intersection.
6. Turn left onto W. Georgia.
7. Turn left along Hornby St. for half a block.
8. Return north along Hornby to the W. Georgia intersection.
9. Cross east over Hornby on W. Georgia.
10. Continue east on W. Georgia.
11. Cross south over W. Georgia at Howe St.
12. Head west along W. Georgia to Hornby.
13. Cross west over Hornby on W. Georgia.
14. Head south half a block on the right side of Hornby.
15. Enter the Fairmont Hotel Vancouver.
16. Exit the hotel via the main entrance and turn left.
17. Continue west on W. Georgia to the intersection with Burrard.

*Fairmont Hotel Vancouver, reflected in downtown office block*

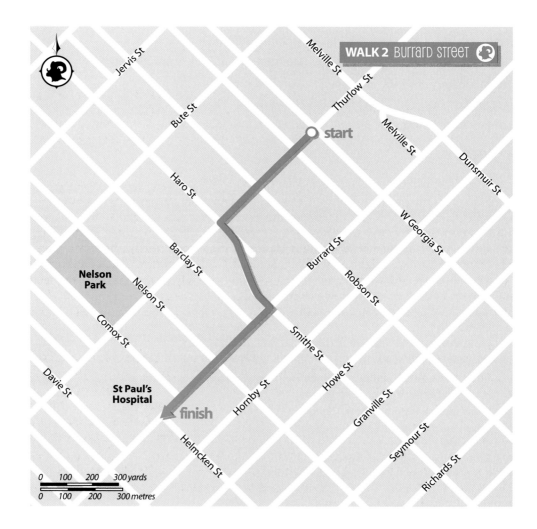

start

finish

Jervis St

Bute St

Haro St

Barclay St

Nelson St

Comox St

Davie St

Nelson Park

St Paul's Hospital

Melville St

Thurlow St

Melville St

Dunsmuir St

W Georgia St

Burrard St

Robson St

Smithe St

Howe St

Hornby St

Helmcken St

Granville St

Seymour St

Richards St

0  100  200  300 yards

0  100  200  300 metres

# 2  Burrard Street: a Tale of Two Towers

BOUNDARIES: **W. Georgia St., Thurlow St., Burrard St., Helmcken St.**
DISTANCE: **½ mile/¾ kilometre**
DIFFICULTY: **Easy**
PARKING: **There's a parkade in the 1300 block of Alberni St., a short walk from the Shangri-La Hotel. Alberni also has metered street parking for several blocks.**
PUBLIC TRANSIT: **The Burrard SkyTrain station is a five-minute walk south of the Shangri-La. Buses 22 and 44 stop on nearby Burrard St. and bus 5 stops a couple of blocks away on Robson St.**

Burrard is one of those busy downtown thoroughfares that locals pass along frequently without really noticing. Even the street's name barely elicits a response, unless you happen to know your early British naval history. For those who may have forgotten or who actually have a life: the street is named after Sir Harry Burrard, whose moniker was originally appended to the nearby inlet by his friend Captain George Vancouver. Luckily, the naming took place before his marriage, or we might be walking Burrard-Neale St. today. If he could miraculously arrive on the street aboard a time-traveling SkyTrain, probably he'd smack his forehead in incredulity, before tucking into a nori-covered hotdog from the city's best Japanese dog stand and catching a movie at the giant multiplex across the street. With Burrard-Neale in mind, look at this familiar street with an outsider's curiosity.

● **Begin at the southwest corner of W. Georgia and Thurlow Sts, craning your neck as skyward as humanly possible. Completed in early 2009, the 61-story Shangri-La is Vancouver's tallest tower and dominates the surrounding shops and office buildings. The 659-foot/201-metre glass box comprises a luxury hotel (the first North American branch of the Asia Pacific Shangri-La chain) topped with swanky condos on the upper floors, where the priciest "penthouse estate" had an initial listing at $15 million. To get an idea of your new neighbors, swing by the nearby high-end stores: there's a Burberry shop on the building's ground level, a pricey Urban Fare supermarket next door and, spreading east along Alberni St., a string of platinum card hangouts including Tiffany and Hermés.**

- Cross over Alberni and head south on the right side of Thurlow St. Within a minute or so, you'll come to Joe Fortes Seafood & Chophouse, one of Vancouver's most popular dine-outs. The oyster bar and rooftop patio are especially celebrated. Budget noshers should drop by at lunch for the $10 Blue Plate Special (the heaping Cobb salad is recommended). The restaurant is named after a legendary Jamaican immigrant who arrived in the city in 1885, later becoming Vancouver's first unofficial lifeguard. Dedicated to his adopted community, this well-loved character taught generations of local children to swim.

- Cross clamorous Robson St. and continue south on Thurlow. At the next intersection, turn left along Smithe St. and follow its curve past the fire hall on your right. A little farther along is Le Crocodile, the city's finest French restaurant. Behind its unassuming half-curtained windows, this immaculate eatery has been satisfying loyal, in-the-know locals for two decades. Consider coming back for dinner to tuck into one of the classic dishes: filet de boeuf grillé is recommended. The headwaiter here, complete with an almost clichéd heavy French accent and a white napkin permanently draped over his bent arm, adds to the Parisian ambiance.

- If you're salivating, continue east along Smithe and you'll soon roll up at the best hotdog stand in town. For a city justly famous for its dining scene, Vancouver's street food options are woeful, but it's worth saving your budget-level appetite for Japa Dog. The Japanese-flavored menu here includes the Misomayo, a turkey smokie with miso sauce; the Terimayo, served with shreds of nori and teriyaki sauce; and the Oroshu, a bratwurst with daiko, green onions, and soy sauce. Consider trying all three, just like TV chef Anthony Bourdain did when he filmed a segment here. Or you could emulate Ice Cube who, according to the stand's gallery of photos, has eaten here 10 times. Sadly, Steven Segal only dropped by once.

- Cross here to the other side of Burrard St. and you can wash down your dog with a quick beer at the Winking Judge pub on the corner. This is a Brit-style, welcoming little watering hole: there are few traditional-style taverns like this in Vancouver any more, so this one was an instant novelty when it opened in 2008. The regulars here are after-work office slaves and barrel-bellied solicitors from the city's legal profession: the Provincial Law Court is just a couple of blocks away. Sip on a cold one, then try to resist the lure of the sherry trifle on the pub classics menu.

- Cross over Smithe here and continue south on the left side of Burrard St. The Scotiabank Cinema on your left is the city's largest multiplex. Unless it's raining and you fancy sitting down for a couple of hours, keep walking. On your right, across Burrard, is the former YMCA building. A sandy-colored 1940s structure with some Art Moderne architectural flourishes, its façade was preserved in the new condo tower now occupying the site.

- Continue south on the left side of Burrard and you'll soon come to one of Vancouver's best, yet most neglected, Modernist buildings. The Dal Grauer Substation, designed by Ned Pratt, was a symphony of public art and utility when it opened in 1954. Part of the BC Electric downtown grid, the machinery and staircases of the interior were revealed by a spectacular floor-to-ceiling exterior of colored glass panels, created by contemporary artist B.C. Binning. The impression was of a living Mondrian painting. When a 1980s fire damaged the building, the panels were replaced with gray Plexiglas, giving the structure a faceless, monolithic look. Plans to restore its original esthetic have stalled several times over the years.

  The substation was such a success that an adjoining building was commissioned from the same architects. Next door's BC Electric tower, now known as "Electra," mirrors the feel of the substation. Check out the building's lower level mosaic of blue, black, and green tiles (also designed by Binning). BC Electric, now called BC Hydro, moved out in 1995 and the heritage-designated structure—the city's best Modernist skyscraper—now houses condos and offices.

- Turn your back on Electra and cross to the right side of Burrard. This Nelson St. intersection probably has more heritage buildings than any other downtown crossroads. Ahead of you on the northwest corner is the handsome gray stone visage of the First Baptist Church. The cornerstone of the Gothic Revival building, dominated by its large tower and steeply gabled roof, was laid in 1910 and it's housed a busy downtown congregation ever since. The church, which replaced a wooden original, was gutted by fire in the 1930s. It was restored by Charles Bentall, a wealthy church-goer and prominent local developer.

- Cross over to the other Nelson St. corner and you'll be face-to-face with an even bigger house of worship. St. Andrew's Wesley United Church opened its heavy wooden doors in 1933. Climb the steps and slip inside and you'll find a Medieval-Gothic-style interior with a high-ceilinged nave, deep transepts, and soaring leaded and stained glass windows. Alongside its active pastoral role (you'll likely see the homeless camped outside on most mornings), St. Andrew's has also become an atmospheric music venue in recent years. Several choirs are based here, there's a "jazz vespers" service every Sunday afternoon, and visiting performers from Bryan Adams to Billy Bragg have graced the pulpit with concerts.

● Re-cross to the left side of Burrard. Hogging the block from Nelson to Helmcken St. is the Wall Centre complex, complete with frenetic fountains, a landscaped garden, and the giant One Wall Centre tower. Completed in 2001, this elliptical glass spike was Vancouver's tallest building until the Shangri-La surpassed it in 2009. Housing a 733-room Sheraton Hotel and splashy condos (including one rumored to be owned by action movie star Jean-Claude Van Damme), the 48-story tower is 491 feet/150 metres tall but it's more infamous locally for its two-tone glass exterior. Due to an argument with the city over the look of the finished structure, the builders were made to change the glass they were using partway through the project. The tower now has darkened mirror glass on its lower floors and clear glass on its upper floors.

● Continue south on Burrard and turn right over the crosswalk at the Helmcken St. intersection. St. Paul's Hospital will be rising ahead of you. This old red-brick site has a long history. Built by the Montreal-based Sisters of Providence Catholic order in 1894, it quickly grew from its original 25-bed facility to more than 500 beds by WWII. The Sisters remained involved in the running of the hospital until the late 1960s, when the first lay administrator was hired. St. Paul's is famous for its annual festive display of Christmas lights on its Burrard St. exterior. Duck inside to treat your blisters here or weave back along Burrard for a coffee pit stop.

# POINTS OF INTEREST

**Shangri-La** 1128 W. Georgia St., 604-689-1120

**Joe Fortes Seafood & Chophouse** 777 Thurlow St., 604-669-1940

**Le Crocodile** 909 Burrard St., 604-669-4298

**Japa Dog** northwest corner of Smithe St. and Burrard St.

**Winking Judge** 888 Burrard St. St., 604-684-9465

**Scotiabank Theatre** 900 Burrard St., 604-630-1407

**Dal Grauer Substation** 950 Burrard St.

**Electra** 970 Burrard St.

**First Baptist Church** 969 Burrard St., 604-683-8441

**St. Andrew's Wesley United Church** 1022 Nelson St., 604-683-4574

**Wall Centre** 1088 Burrard St., 604-331-1000

**St. Paul's Hospital** 1081 Burrard St., 604-682-2344

# route summary

1. Start at the southwest corner of W. Georgia and Thurlow Sts.
2. Head south on the right-hand side of Thurlow, crossing Alberni and Robson Sts.
3. Turn left along Smithe St. to the intersection with Burrard St.
4. Cross over to the other side of Burrard.
5. Head south on the left side of Burrard.
6. Cross to the other side of Burrard at Nelson St.
7. Cross over Nelson and re-cross to the left side of Burrard.
8. Continue south on the left side of Burrard.
9. Cross back to the right side of Burrard at the Helmcken St. intersection.

*St. Andrew's Wesley United Church*

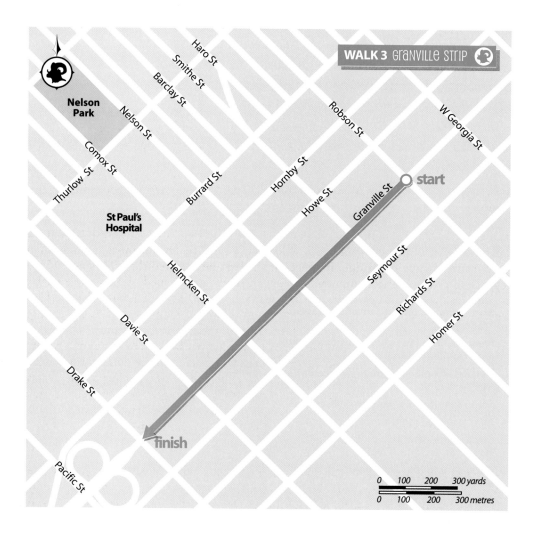

Haro St

Smithe St

Barclay St

Robson St

W Georgia St

Nelson
Park

Nelson St

Comox St

Hornby St

Howe St

Granville St

start

Thurlow St

Burrard St

St Paul's
Hospital

Seymour St

Helmcken St

Richards St

Davie St

Homer St

Drake St

finish

Pacific St

0      100     200     300 yards

0      100     200     300 metres

# 3 Granville Strip: Nightlife Ghosts of Yesteryear

BOUNDARIES: **Robson St., Granville St., Drake St.**
DISTANCE: **½ mile/¾ kilometre**
DIFFICULTY: **Easy**
PARKING: **There's an underground parkade beneath the Pacific Centre, accessed at the southeast corner of Robson and Howe Sts. There's also metered street parking on much of Granville and on the side streets along its length.**
PUBLIC TRANSIT: **Buses 4, 7, 10, 16, and 17 stop on Howe St., parallel to Granville. The SkyTrain stops at Granville station, under the Bay department store at the corner of W. Georgia and Granville.**

The city's central nightlife hub, known as the "Granville Strip" by locals and "Granville Entertainment District" by city planners, who clearly need to get out more, stretches from Robson St. to the Granville Bridge. Its neon-lit golden age spanned the 1940s and 1950s, when legions of Vancouverites came here to spend their hard-earned weekly wage partying at clubs and restaurants and catching the latest silver-screen flicks. The area declined in the 1960s; with entertainment options spreading out across the city, the strip lost its rep as the only place in town to have a good time. Stores moved in (including a smattering of sex shops at the southern end) and many of the original venues closed. In the 1970s, a stretch running north from here was transformed into "Granville Mall," a plain-Jane, concrete-accented pedestrian walkway, leaving the south end to languish. In recent years, city planners have encouraged a return of neon signs in the area, aiming to recall the halcyon years. A second makeover project was launched in late 2008 to underline this drive. Strolling the strip today, you'll find plenty of latter-day clubs and bars, alongside several reminders of the area's glamorous past.

● Starting at the corner of Robson and Granville Sts, check out the giant TV screens and oversized store signs adorning the northeast corner. These were encouraged as part of a new policy to restore neon signage to the strip—although they're not quite as romantic as the old hoardings that once winked at passers-by. If you fancy a brew, nip into the Lennox Pub on the southeast corner. This narrow, wood-lined bar has

## Back Story: Orpheum Echoes

Opened in 1927, the Orpheum Theatre was originally part of a chain of Chicago-based vaudeville houses—all called "Orpheum"—that welcomed famously diverse acts from around the world. With almost 3,000 seats, it was also one of the largest theatres in Canada at the time. The stars who have performed here over the years include Bob Hope, B.B. King, Harry Belafonte, Jay Leno, Shirley MacLaine, and Victor Borge—around the stage door on Seymour St., there's a series of wall plaques recognizing international legends who have repeatedly hit the Orpheum stage. In the 1970s, the aging venue was about to be turned into a multiscreen cinema complex when public outcry con-vinced the city to step in and buy the theatre, transforming it into a new civic concert hall. After a complete restoration, the Orpheum reopened in 1977 and early visitors were reminded of what a gem they had in their midst. Inspired by the Spanish Baroque school, the building's domed, multi-arched interior is a feast of sumptu-ous marble and plaster decoration. Now designated a National Historic Site, the Orpheum is the home of the Vancouver Symphony Orchestra and continues to host leading musical acts from around the world. It also hosts highly recommended backstage ghost and heritage walks during the summer months.

been here since 2000 and has a wide selection of on-tap beers including Guinness and Strongbow. Join the throng for a broadcast Canucks game, or head for the upstairs snug for quieter quaffing.

● Continue south along Granville's left-hand sidewalk. This short stretch used to house cinemas, an independent bookshop and a legendry German bakery but in recent years, it's been colonized by trendy boutiques. Consider unleashing your credit card at the Puma or Adidas stores. Alternatively, you can gaze for free at the sidewalk. This doesn't make you crazy, it just means you're perusing a series of small granite discs otherwise known as the BC Hall of Fame's Starwalk. Not quite as glamorous as the Hollywood version, the regional stars honored include Diana Krall, Chief Dan George, and Randy Bachman. The nearby Orpheum Theatre has a wall of photos covering all 158 inductees.

Once you've finished staring at the ground, look up at the Commodore Ballroom, stretching over the top of several storefronts above you. Vancouver's favorite mid-sized music venue, it opened in 1929 and was dripping with Art Deco flourishes—many carefully restored in an extensive renovation several years ago. While contemporary live acts frequently storm the stage here, it's not hard to squint a little and recall the feel of the old place, with its stepped perimeter seating, sparkling mirror-backed sidebars, and expansive ballroom dance floor. This famed floor was originally underlaid with horsehair to add extra bounce: it's been replaced with rubber in recent years. Count Basie, Cab Calloway, the Dead Kennedys, Nirvana, U2, and the Police have all played here.

- A few steps from the Commodore's ground level box office, check out the Orpheum. Its giant heritage neon sign, cascading from the top of the building, is an evocative reminder of those that used to crowd the skyline here.

- If it feels like time to shake your thang, head across Granville St. to the Plaza Club. A movie theatre for many years, the Plaza was transformed into a nightclub and live music venue in 1998. It's arguably the best of several clubs crowding this end of the strip—its larger rival is the Caprice on the next block. The Plaza's club nights draw a generally young crowd but its live music roster is eclectic enough to lure a more diverse group.

- Cross over Smithe St. and return to the left side of Granville. A few steps south you'll come to the handsome, yet paint-peeled Vogue Theatre, the strip's other great heritage venue. Built in 1941 in the Art Moderne style—check out the streamlined accents on its prow-like neon signage—this was a purpose-built movie house: vaudeville had already been replaced by film just a few years after the Orpheum opened. The Vogue remained an independent movie theatre until the 1980s. Changes in ownership and varying amounts of renovation since have left its future in limbo, but renewed interest in local heritage makes it unlikely it will disappear.

- If you need to wet your whistle at this point, cross over Granville and check out the right side of the 900 block. There are several bar choices here, including Speakeasy and Caprice Lounge, but the sleek, brick-lined Granville Room is recommended. This compact bar is popular among weekend nightclub crawlers taking a cocktail breather from the area's dance floors. There's also a surprisingly wide array of international bottled lagers.

● If you're hung up on retro, though, continue south until you reach the **Templeton.** An authentic evocation of a 1950s diner, this narrow eatery comprises cozy vinyl booths on one side and a long, chrome-accented counter on the other. But while there are jukebox terminals on the tables and period postcards encased on the counter tops, the menu here rises above standard greasy spoon fare. There are lots of organic and locally sourced ingredients, and vegetarians have plenty of options. On Monday nights free movies are screened above the serving area.

● Cross back over to the left side of Granville and continue south. You're now at the seedier end of the street, among the sad array of grubby sex shops. You can expect to be discreetly offered soft drugs by wandering peddlers. But you haven't entered a culture-free zone: cross Davie St. and then Drake St. On the southeast corner of Granville and Drake—marked by a magnificent neon saxophone—stands arguably the strip's most historic performance venue. Built in the 1880s as a bunkhouse for Canadian Pacific Railway employees, the **Yale Hotel** was far enough from the center of town to survive Vancouver's infamous 1886 fire. A neighborhood pub and live music venue ever since, it's become one of Canada's best blues bars, featuring live music nightly. Over the years, the Yale has hosted legendary performers like John Lee Hooker and Clarence "Gatemouth" Brown. It's a great spot to kick back, grab a beer, and end your Granville Strip trawl.

COMMODORE

# POINTS OF INTEREST

**Lennox Pub** 800 Granville St., 604-408-0881

**Commodore Ballroom** 868 Granville St., 604-739-4550

**Orpheum Theatre** 884 Granville St., 604-665-3050

**Plaza Club** 881 Granville St., 604-646-0064

**Vogue Theatre** 918 Granville St., 604-688-1975

**Granville Room** 957 Granville St., 604-633-0056

**Templeton** 1087 Granville St., 604-685-4612

**Yale Hotel** 1300 Granville St., 604-681-9253

# route summary

1. Start at the northeast corner of Granville and Robson Sts.
2. Staying on the left side of Granville, cross Robson.
3. Continue south on Granville, crossing over to the right side opposite the Orpheum Theatre.
4. Cross back to the left side of Granville at the next intersection.
5. Continue south on the left side of Granville.
6. Cross back the right side of Granville at the 900 block.
7. At the Helmcken St. intersection, re-cross to the left side of Granville.
8. Continue south on the left side of Granville, passing the intersections with Davie St. and Drake St.

*Commodore Ballroom*

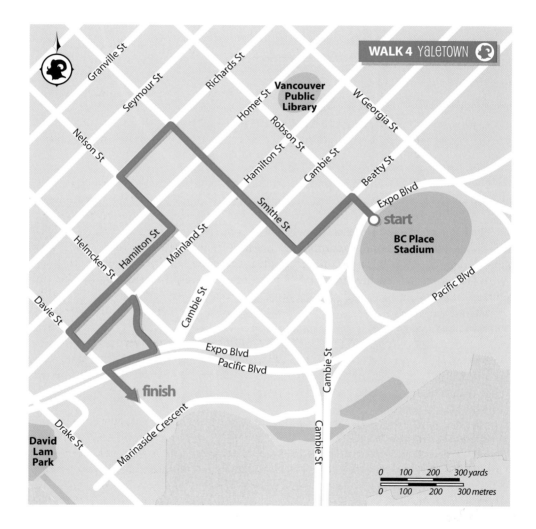

Granville St

Seymour St

Richards St

Homer St

Nelson St

Robson St

Hamilton St

Cambie St

W Georgia St

Beatty St

Vancouver
Public
Library

Smithe St

Expo Blvd

start

BC Place
Stadium

Helmcken St

Hamilton St

Mainland St

Davie St

Cambie St

Pacific Blvd

Expo Blvd

Pacific Blvd

Cambie St

finish

Drake St

Marinaside Crescent

Cambie St

David
Lam
Park

| 0 | 100 | 200 | 300 yards |
| 0 | 100 | 200 | 300 metres |

# 4 Yaletown: Vancouver's Brick-Built SoHo

**BOUNDARIES:** BC Place Stadium, Richards St., Davie St., Pacific Blvd.
**DISTANCE:** 1 mile/1½ kilometres
**DIFFICULTY:** Easy
**PARKING:** There's a parking lot in the 600 block of Cambie St., a short walk from BC Place. There's also metered street parking in the streets near the stadium.
**PUBLIC TRANSIT:** SkyTrain's Stadium station is a short walk from BC Place, while Canada Line trains stop at the Yaletown-Roundhouse station at Davie and Mainland Sts. Bus 15 stops on nearby Cambie St.

Yaletown looks totally different from any other Vancouver neighborhood. Created almost entirely from red bricks—both the buildings and elevated sidewalks here are brick-faced—the area was filled with railway sheds and storage warehouses in the 1880s after the Canadian Pacific Railway relocated its operations from the pioneer settlement of Yale in BC's rugged interior. Along with the name, the imported workers brought their hard-drinking ways with them and Yaletown soon became a no-go nook for anyone who preferred not to have a fist fight with their beer. When the trains left a few decades later, the area was quickly colonized by squatters and fell into rapid disrepair, only to be completely scrubbed up and reclaimed as part of the site for the giant Expo '86 world exposition. After the event, the area, complete with its character-packed heritage status, became Vancouver's version of SoHo. The old brick warehouses were reappointed and transformed into chichi shops, restaurants, and apartments and the elevated loading docks became its sidewalks. Today, Yaletown is a compact treat for strollers, with plenty of pit stops and colorful historic reminders. We'll launch our walk on the fringes of the area, with a little sporting dalliance.

● You'll start your Yaletown-area weave at BC Place, the city's biggest sporting venue. As well as being home of the CFL's BC Lions, this is the venue of choice for the kind of music acts that like to pack in crowds of up to 60,000: Madonna and the Rolling Stones have strutted their stuff here in recent years. The stadium's air-supported fabric roof—at 10 acres/4 hectares, it's the largest of its type in the world—hit the headlines in 2006 when it deflated, sending icy water cascading into the interior. Since patched up, the venue hosts the opening and closing ceremonies for the 2010

Olympic and Paralympic Winter Games, after which its dodgy lid will be replaced with a slick new retractable model.

- Exit the stadium precinct west, crossing over Expo Blvd. Then cross over to the west side of Beatty St. Head south downhill on Beatty. About half way down on your right, you'll come to Dix BBQ & Brewery. An ideal spot for a heaping lunch, this popular drinking hole is beloved of carnivores who drop by en masse to slaver over southern-style pulled pork and velvet-soft brisket. And don't forget the beer: one of the city's handful of brewpubs, Dix serves its own heady tipples as well as brews from favored local producers like North Vancouver's Red Truck Beer Company.

- If your liquid lunch hasn't got the better of you, continue south along Beatty to the next corner, then turn right up Smithe St. Head west over Cambie St. and on your right is Artworks Gallery, a popular exhibition space where everything is for sale. Nip inside and check out the array of landscape, abstract, and photography works.

- Continue west on Smithe, crossing Hamilton St. and passing Fire Hall Number 8 on your right. On the corner of the next block, you'll pass Subeez Café, one of Vancouver's favorite nighttime haunts. The dark interior of this cavernous spot is atmospherically lined with giant, half-melted candles. Make a mental note to come back in the evening for a chatty meal with friends or to join the martini scrum around the small bar. On balmy summer nights, the narrow patio here is usually packed to the gills.

- Maintain a westerly direction as you stroll up the slight incline and take the next left along Richards St. This thoroughfare has been transformed over the last decade with a forest of glass condo towers—a far cry from the rooming houses and railway-worker cottages that used to be here. Even the sidewalks have been beautified: check out the leaf prints artfully pressed into the cement.

- Cross to the right side of Richards and continue southward to the intersection with Nelson St. On the corner here you'll find the free-entry Contemporary Art Gallery, a small public exhibition space focused on local and international modern works. Photography is usually well-represented here and it's well worth a few minutes to nip in and see what's on the walls.

## CeLeBraTING SPORTING HeROeS

After perusing the stadium's exterior, consider ducking inside to the BC Sports Hall of Fame, accessed via Gate A. One of the city's small museum gems, this smashing little exhibition space is lined with memorabilia from decades of regional and international sporting achievement. There are strips here from long-forgotten teams as well as medals from local heroes who triumphed in past Olympic Games. There's also plenty for children to do, including races, basketball practice, and lots of push-button shenanigans. The museum's most poignant gallery honors national legend Terry Fox, the young Port Coquitlam cancer sufferer whose one-legged 1980 Marathon of Hope run across Canada ended abruptly after 143 days and 3,339 miles/5373km when the disease spread to his lungs. Fox died the following year but his achievement is marked by a large memorial outside the stadium, across from the foot of Robson St. The shiny steel interior of the walk-through archway, designed by architect Franklin Allen, is etched with a large image of Fox and a map tracing the route of his trek. When Fox started his run, he received very little attention, but by the time he was forced to stop, the entire country was behind him. Every year since his death, fundraising runs have been staged across Canada and around the world in his honor. The Terry Fox Foundation estimates that, to date, these have raised more than $400 million for cancer research.

● Turn east down Nelson and, after two blocks, turn right onto Hamilton St. This is your introduction to the brick-lined heart of old Yaletown. Also keep your eyes peeled for the remnants of old rail lines embedded in the asphalt of the roads here. Head up the ramp along Hamilton's right-hand sidewalk and at the end of the block you'll come to Blue Water Café on your right. An exemplar of the kind of stylish regeneration that has taken place here, this is one of the city's most popular restaurants. Seafood fans come for its delectable Pacific Northwest approach to regional catches, as well as its Japanese-style raw bar, renowned as one of Vancouver's top sushi joints.

● Cross over Helmcken St. and continue south along Hamilton. Among the designer shops and precious boutiques lining this stretch, you'll spot the Mini car dealership, an indicator of Yaletown's yuppie provenance. Take the next turn left along Davie St.

and stroll down the hill. On your right is the Opus Hotel, one of the city's favorite boutique sleepovers. Its mod rooms include the kind of swanky features only rich people view as standard, including mini oxygen canisters that allegedly enhance metabolism: of course wealth is no guarantee of intelligence. The hotel's guests have included Michael Stipe, Robert De Niro, and Harrison Ford and its on-site coffee shop is a handy place for a java stop.

- Fully wired, continue south down Davie and take the next left along Mainland St., the other brick-lined Yaletown thoroughfare. Continue north along Mainland and on your left you'll soon come to the tiny Chocoatl, a boutique confectionary store where a little over-indulgence goes a long way. There's a small seating area here where you can sip on some hot chocolate and indulge in a choc-dipped marshmallow or two. But takeout is your best bet: scoop up a bag full of bars and bonbons and pretend you're taking them home for the kids.

- Backpack bulging, continue north along Mainland to the end of the block. At the corner is the Yaletown Brewing Company, the area's favorite brewpub. If you have time, nip inside. On its left is the narrow, brick-lined bar where you can sup on brews like Mainland Lager and Frank's Nut Brown; on the right is the large restaurant area where pub classics are served—the cappicola and mushroom pizza is recommended. The patio here is always packed on sunny evenings, so arrive early if you'd like an outside perch to watch the designer-dressed locals cruise by.

- From here, cross over Mainland into the parking lot opposite the pub. Stroll east through the lot and the little park adjoining it. Within a minute or two, you'll come to Pacific Blvd. Turn right along Pacific, then turn left along Davie St. Ahead on your right is one of the city's best historic sites. Enter the Roundhouse Arts & Recreation Centre and visit the handsomely preserved Canadian Pacific Railway locomotive number 374. This is the steam engine that pulled the first transcontinental train into Vancouver on May 23, 1887, symbolically unifying the nation. Its museum home is now staffed by volunteers from Squamish's West Coast Railway Heritage Park. Save time to check out the fully restored 1888-built train turntable outside. One of the city's oldest structures, this is an ideal spot to conclude your Yaletown exploration.

# POINTS OF INTEREST

**BC Place** 777 Pacific Blvd., 604-669-2300

**BC Sports Hall of Fame** 777 Pacific Blvd., 604-687-5520

**Dix BBQ & Brewery** 1871 Beatty St., 604-682-2739

**Artworks Gallery** 225 Smithe St., 604-688-3301

**Subeez Café** 891 Homer St., 604-687-6107

**Contemporary Art Gallery** 555 Nelson St., 604-681-2700

**Blue Water Café** 1095 Hamilton St., 604-688-8078

**Opus Hotel** 322 Davie St., 604-642-6787

**Chocoatl** 1127 Mainland St., 604-676-9977

**Yaletown Brewing Company** 1111 Mainland St., 604-688-0064

**Roundhouse Arts & Recreation Centre** 181 Roundhouse Mews, 604-713-1800

*Yaletown's brick-lined sidewalks*

## route summary

1.  Start on the west side of BC Place Stadium.
2.  Cross west over Pacific Blvd. and head though the Terry Fox arch.
3.  Turn left along Beatty St.
4.  Continue south on Beatty.
5.  Turn right along Smithe St.
6.  Continue west along Smithe for four blocks.
7.  Turn left onto Richards St.
8.  Turn left along Nelson St. for two blocks.
9.  Turn right along Hamilton St. for two blocks.
10. Turn left onto Davie St.
11. Take the next left onto Mainland St.
12. Opposite Yaletown Brewing Company, head east through the parking lot and adjoining park.
13. Turn right along Pacific Blvd..
14. Turn left and head east along Davie St.

*Restored rail sheds at the*
*Roundhouse Arts & Recreation Centre*

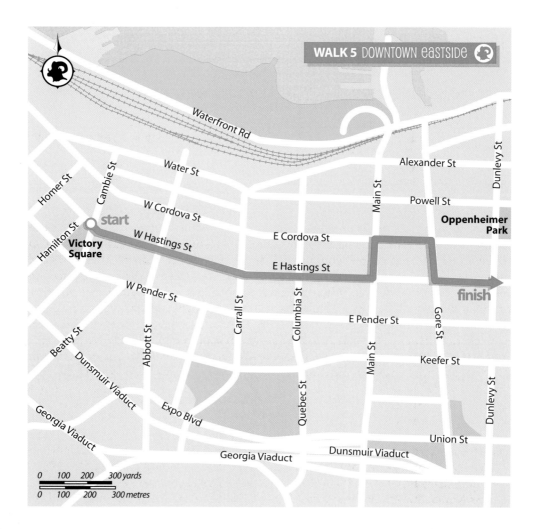

Waterfront Rd

Water St

Alexander St

Dunlevy St

Homer St

Cambie St

W Cordova St

Main St

Powell St

**start**

**Oppenheimer Park**

Hamilton St

W Hastings St

E Cordova St

**Victory Square**

E Hastings St

**finish**

W Pender St

Carrall St

Columbia St

E Pender St

Gore St

Beatty St

Abbott St

E Pender St

Main St

Keefer St

Dunsmuir Viaduct

Expo Blvd

Quebec St

Dunlevy St

Georgia Viaduct

Georgia Viaduct

Dunsmuir Viaduct

Union St

| 0 | 100 | 200 | 300 yards |
| 0 | 100 | 200 | 300 metres |

# 5 DOWNTOWN EASTSIDE: VANCOUVER'S "OTHER" NEIGHBORHOOD

BOUNDARIES: **Cambie St., E. Hastings St., E. Cordova St. Dunlevy Ave.**
DISTANCE: **¾ mile/1¼ kilometres**
DIFFICULTY: **Moderate**
PARKING: **There is a parkade at the southeast corner of W. Pender and Cambie Sts, close to Victory Square. There is also metered street parking along Cambie St.**
PUBLIC TRANSIT: **The 10 and 16 buses stop at dozens of points along W. and E. Hastings St. and are your main link with the downtown core.**

A surprisingly short walk from the city center and often referred to as Canada's poorest postal district, Vancouver's gritty Downtown Eastside comprises several blocks of once-handsome brick buildings long past their best. Centered on E. Hastings St., this skid-row thoroughfare was once the city's most genteel commercial strip but has been a no-go area for decades, with a multitude of social problems transforming its character. Despite the poverty, noisy construction clamor shows that change is beginning to come to the district that time forgot. Strolling the streets today, you'll find the initial shoots of this gentrification mixed with many reminders of the area's vibrant past. Look beyond the paint-peeled façades and moldy shutters of long-closed buildings and you'll see landmark historic banks, stores, and theatres as well as a "living museum" of heritage neon, the last remnants of a time when Vancouver was lined with flickering signs advertising its businesses. A word about safety: strolling the Downtown Eastside is not for those of a nervous disposition, but crimes against visitors remain rare here. Street smarts are essential, so stay on the main thoroughfares (especially avoid the back alleys) and keep your wallet well-hidden.

● **Start your trek in the heart of "Vansterdam," the two-store clutch of counter-culture businesses just before the intersection of W. Hastings and Cambie Sts. Nip inside the friendly Cannabis Culture Headquarters (CCHQ), signified by the oversized marijuana leaf paintings adorning its exterior. Home of the BC Marijuana Party, it serves to demystify, educate, and promote legal use of certain drugs: there's a kaleidoscope of glass bongs and racks of quality hemp clothing for sale, plus a tiki-themed café at the back for hanging out with your new buds.**

● A few steps east along W. Hastings St., you'll have your first taste of the grand buildings that once lined this area, originally the city's main financial and commercial district. One of Vancouver's most attractive heritage structures, the curve-topped 13-story Dominion Building was one of the tallest in the British Empire when completed in 1910. Initially the local headquarters of the Toronto Dominion Bank, its handsome red-brick exterior is now protected, while interior is home to a mishmash of offices and small businesses.

● Step across W. Hastings here to take photos of the towering Dominion Building and you'll come across Victory Square. Original site of an old courthouse, this is where locals signed up for active service in World War I. After the courthouse was moved, the area became a park and, in 1924, a cenotaph was built to honor the region's war dead. Now the site for Vancouver's main Remembrance Day services, the austere three-sided granite obelisk here is surrounded by a crescent of streetlamps topped with reproductions of the tin hats soldiers used to wear. Even though the park is a year-round 24-hour-a-day hangout, the memorial is respected and poppy wreaths laid here are never disturbed.

● Cross over Cambie St. next and continue east along W. Hastings St. into the heart of the Downtown Eastside. You'll immediately notice the increase in marginalized locals, many hanging around street corners or scoring deals in back alleys. But change is coming: on your left, the site of the old Woodwards department store—a landmark, multistory shop that thrived here for decades—is being transformed into a giant development of new housing, shops, and a university campus. Its arrival is touted as a major catalyst for regeneration. Immediately opposite, you'll see just how much work still needs to be done: the block of weathered, boarded-up former restaurants and retail outlets is like a row of broken teeth.

● Continuing east, cross Abbott St., passing the stale-smelling dive bars. Keep your eyes peeled: the leveling of decrepit flophouses and refurbishment of ancient structures here is uncovering some of the area's history for the first time in years and you might see suddenly revealed old advertisements painted directly onto brick walls decades ago. You'll also spot some of Vancouver's best old neon signs, still winking their invitations to passers-by decades after their 1950s heyday. Among the finest is at Save-on-Meats on your left, where a jaunty pink pig holds up a big loonie. This historic butcher shop closed in early 2009 but hopes are high that the sign will be preserved by new tenants.

● Continue east to the intersection with Carrall St., where W. Hastings becomes E. Hastings. Don't linger at Pigeon Park, a grubby corner where the area's sketchiest residents hang out day and night. Instead cross Carrall and head to the right-hand side of E. Hastings to check out the colorful seahorse-shaped neon sign of Only Seafoods Café, a legendary fish restaurant that was closed in 2009. Its sign, so far, remains intact. Keep the pace fairly swift here and stroll briskly uphill. For another snack option, drop into the Radio Station Café, on the left-hand corner of E. Hastings and Columbia, named for Co-op Radio, the volunteer community station upstairs that's been a neighborhood fixture since the 1970s. Enjoy your java and a muffin while you peruse the goings on outside the windows—you'll likely see industrious locals dragging giant sacks of cans and bottles to the nearby recycling center.

● The café is a sign that businesses are beginning to return and thrive in this area. In fact, nip south along Columbia St. for half a block and you'll find one that may indicate a bright commercial future. Occupying an old barbershop, Wanted—Lost Found Canadian is the kind of cool, artsy store often found in much trendier Vancouver neighborhoods. Dedicated to recycling, artist-owner Susan Schroeder transforms baseboard wood planks into cute collage blocks covered with butterfly prints, and vintage wool blankets into bird-shaped coin purses and artful new cushions. She's always happy to chat about the challenges of the area and why she thinks things are slowly improving.

● Returning to E. Hastings, turn right and within a few steps you'll come to the site of the old Pantages Theatre. Built in 1907 at the height of Vancouver's love affair with vaudeville, it had later incarnations as City Nights movie house and Sung Sing Theatre. Plans are afoot to give it yet another life. Across the street, you'll spot the handsome, if worn, signage of the Balmoral Hotel. Originally an upscale inn, it's not recommended as accommodation now, but its renovated ballroom has been colonized by Vancouver hipsters and cool up-and-coming indie bands.

● Continuing uphill, you'll soon come to the Main St. intersection and, on your right, one of Vancouver's handsomest heritage buildings. The entrance often obscured by a regular coterie of dodgy characters, the old Carnegie Library now acts as the area's main community center. This is not a corner where you'll want to stay for long, but do look for the splendid stained glass window of Shakespeare, Spenser, and Milton, a reminder of the days when this grand sandstone edifice, built in 1903 with funds given by U.S. industrialist Andrew Carnegie, was the city's first public library and also the site of the original Vancouver Museum.

● Since you're not lingering here, turn left along Main St. and head north to the large police station building. Cross to the other side of Main, then make a right on E. Cordova St. The police officers wandering around here will likely make you feel a little easier about that expensive camera nestled in your backpack, but that's not the reason for coming here.

● Continue walking east on E. Cordova and, on your right, you'll soon come to arguably the city's best off-the-beaten-path attraction. Occupying a spooky former coroner's building, the Vancouver Police Centennial Museum uses archival photos and eye-opening artifacts to illuminate the city's crime-fighting history. Head up to the second floor galleries and you'll come face-to-face with confiscated homemade weapons, counterfeit currency and a mothballed autopsy room that's not for the faint-hearted. It includes stainless steel dissection tables, surgical tools, and a wall of glass-encased tissue samples including brain slivers and bullet-wounded hearts. The museum also offers an excellent summer walking tour that delves deeper into the area's murky crime history.

● After the museum, keep going east on E. Cordova and check out the preserved old firehall at the intersection with Gore Ave. Built in 1906, this handsome red-doored, brick edifice was the city's leading fire station for decades, quelling blazes across the region. In 1975, the firemen moved out and the Firehall Arts Center was born, becoming one of Vancouver's most enduring and successful venues for avant-garde theatre and dance productions. Its season starts in the fall and its clientele are usually among Vancouver's most artsy: you can rub shoulders with them in the brick-lined lobby bar.

● Stay for a show or turn right and head south for one block to E. Hastings. Turn left onto E. Hastings and stroll for one block, crossing over Dunlevy Ave. Consider a brewpub beer at Pat's Pub in the Patricia Hotel here. You can toast your day in the city's grungiest neighborhood before hopping back on the number 10 bus outside. You'll be back in the heart of Vancouver's more salubrious downtown district within a few minutes.

## POINTS OF INTEREST

**Cannabis Culture Headquarters** 307 W. Hastings St., 604-682-1172

**Dominion Building** 207 W. Hastings St.

**Victory Square** cnr of W. Hastings St. and Cambie St.

**Save-On-Meats** 43 W. Hastings St., 604-683-7761

**Pigeon Park** cnr of W. Hastings St. and Carrall St.

**Radio Station Café** 101 E. Hastings St., 604-684-8494

**Wanted–Lost Found Canadian** 436 Columbia St., 604-633-0178

**Pantages Theatre** 152 E. Hastings St.

**Carnegie Centre** 401 Main St.

**Vancouver Police Centennial Museum** 240 E. Cordova St., 604-665-3346

**Firehall Arts Centre** 280 E. Cordova St., 604-689-0926

**Pat's Pub** 403 E. Hastings St., 604-255-4301

*Downtown Eastside wall painting*

## route summary

1. Start on W. Hastings St., just before the intersection with Cambie St.

2. Cross on W. Hastings St. to Victory Square.

3. Cross east on Cambie St. and continue east along W. Hastings St.

4. Continue east along W. Hastings St. and cross to the other side at the intersection with Carrall St.

5. Continue east along E. Hastings St. and turn right onto Columbia St.

6. Return to E. Hastings St. and turn right, continuing east to the intersection with Main St.

7. Turn left on Main St. then take the next right onto E. Cordova St.

8. Continue east on E. Cordova St. to the intersection with Gore Ave.

9. Head south one block on Gore Ave. and turn left on E. Hastings St.

*Heritage neon sign in the Downtown Eastside*

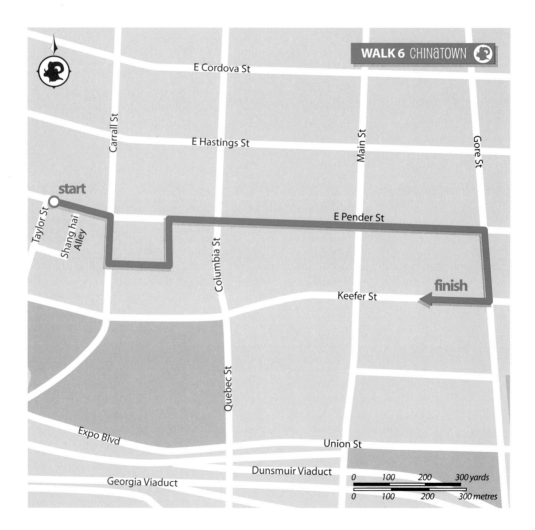

start

finish

E Cordova St

Carrall St

E Hastings St

Main St

Gore St

Taylor St

Shang hai Alley

E Pender St

Columbia St

Keefer St

Quebec St

Expo Blvd

Union St

Dunsmuir Viaduct

Georgia Viaduct

0       100       200       300 yards

0       100       200       300 metres

# 6 CHINATOWN: TECHNICOLOR HISTORY STROLL

BOUNDARIES: **Taylor St., W./E. Pender St., Gore Ave., Keefer St.**
DISTANCE: **½ mile/¾ kilometre**
DIFFICULTY: **Easy**
PARKING: **There's a parking lot at W. Pender's International Village shopping mall near the Chinatown Millennium Gate. There's also metered street parking along W./E. Pender.**
PUBLIC TRANSIT: **Buses 19 and 22 run along Pender St., 8, 10, 16, and 20 roll along adjoining W./E. Hastings St. SkyTrain Stadium station is also nearby**

One of North America's largest Chinatowns is also one of Vancouver's oldest and most storied neighborhoods. While latter-day Asian immigrants are now more likely to call Richmond home, this is where the earliest Chinese settled in the 1880s. Most came for jobs in BC's sawmills, canneries and railway construction. Soon a colorful and clamorous enclave of shops, businesses, theatres and rooming houses sprang up where the predominantly male populace lived—due to a controversial head tax on Chinese immigrants, few could afford to bring their families along. With such a high concentration of single men, Chinatown soon gained a reputation for brothels and opium dens. Many Vancouverites disapproved, though some secretly continued to patronize the illicit attractions. Not all attacks were verbal: a concerted effort by groups organized to drive them out sometimes erupted into violence. Strolling Chinatown today, you'll find plenty of reminders that this is arguably Vancouver's most intact heritage neighborhood—plus a full menu of bustling stores and eateries.

● You'll start on W. Pender St., near the intersection with Taylor St. The Chinatown Millennium Gate looming over you here was inaugurated by Prime Minister Jean Chrétien in 2002. It stands on a site first occupied by a flag-covered wooden gate built to mark the 1912 Vancouver visit of Canada's Governor General, the Duke of Connaught. The new gate contrasts bare concrete pillars with an elaborately painted upper section topped with a traditional flare roof. The characters inscribed on its eastern side implore visitors to "Remember the past and look forward to the future." Check out the stylized lions flanking the site: each gaping mouth used to contain a polished marble ball. They mysteriously disappeared soon after the gate's inauguration.

● Walk east under the gate and you'll immediately notice red-painted street lamps (some topped with ferocious golden dragons), rows of pagoda-topped old buildings and street signs adorned with Chinese characters. On your immediate right is Shanghai Alley. While it seems like a quiet backstreet today, this was once a clamorous Chinatown enclave, home to hundreds of single men domiciled in cheap lodgings. The self-contained thoroughfare had its own shops and restaurants and its vibrant nightlife was centered on a large 500-seat auditorium called the Sing Kew Theatre.

● After peering down Shanghai Alley, continue east on W. Pender. On your right, you'll come to the Sam Kee Building, one of Chinatown's most famous structures. Gaze into the windows here and you'll see framed newspaper clippings showing that this slender construction has been recognized by the *Guinness Book of Records* as the world's narrowest building. At only 6 feet/2 metres wide, it's hard to argue the point. It was built in 1912 when a public road-widening project expropriated all but a slender strip of a lot owned by merchant Chang Toy (aka Sam Kee). Rather than let it go to waste, the stubborn businessman built this narrow structure. The green glass rectangles studding the sidewalk are remnants of a public steam bath built below the street.

● Just past the Sam Kee Building, turn right along Carrall St. Half a block down on your left, you'll come to the entrance of the Dr. Sun Yat-Sen Classical Chinese Garden. A team of 52 artisans was flown in to build this stunning landscaped enclave in 1986, creating an exact Ming-style formal garden. Named after the first president of the Republic of China, it's a tranquil labyrinth of traditional pavilions, mini-courtyards, covered walkways, and bridge-traversed ponds alive with koi and bobbing turtles. If you have time, take the guided tour that illuminates the deep meaning behind the garden's multifarious features.

● Alternatively, if you're on a budget, stroll east past the entrance. A little farther along the wall you'll find a circular doorway leading to a free-entry public park built on similar principles. While not nearly as elaborate as the main attraction, this garden has its own pavilion, limestone features, and a lily-pad-strewn pond.

● Once you've had your serenity fix, head back into the concrete courtyard fronting both gardens. Check out the imposing, militaristic bust of Dr. Sun Yat-Sen here, then stroll north across the square toward what's now E. Pender St. Before you get there, peruse the discreet bronze frieze recessed into the scarlet wall tiles on your right. It recognizes the "blood, sweat, tears and toil" of the more than 10,000 Chinese railway workers "and all Chinese pioneers" who came to Canada during an earlier era.

● On E. Pender, you'll find another Chinatown gate rising above you, parallel with the street's southern edge. This one looks like the ghostly visage of a traditional bright painted gate and that's not far from the truth. The elaborate red, gold, and green construction that fronted the China Pavilion at Expo '86 was donated to the city and moved to Chinatown after the event. Designed as a temporary structure, it soon began to crumble and efforts to secure restoration funding failed. It was demolished in 2001, but in 2005, a replacement was donated by Guangzhou, Vancouver's Chinese sister city. Constructed with pale marble pillars and topped with carved white panels, it's an unusual, almost spectral, alternative.

● Stroll east along E. Pender. This stretch of Chinatown includes some of the area's best-preserved historic buildings, many of which housed the merchants and cultural establishments that once drove the district's micro-economy. On your right, just past Columbia St., you'll soon come to the slender green- and red-brick Chinese Benevolent Association building. Opened in 1904, this organization distributed welfare to the area's destitute and even housed a small hospital for a few years. Echoing classic Southern Chinese architecture of the period, the building's deeply recessed balconies protect from lashing rainstorms—a handy feature in Vancouver, too.

● E. Pender gets a little steeper here but continue east along the right side of the street. You'll notice that new developments are emerging, while many of the old buildings still have busy shops and eateries occupying their lower floors. You'll soon come to one of the best of these. A perfect pit stop on your walk, the cheap-and-cheerful New Town Bakery has a busy takeout operation at the front. Peruse the racks of unfamiliar treats and pick-up a baked barbecued pork bun or two for the road.

● Continue up E. Pender and your next intersection is Main St. Expect to be accosted by a vagrant or two asking for spare change here. Cross east over Main and duck into the Ten Lee Hong Enterprises building on the opposite corner. One of the area's most famous traditional teashops, it's lined with aromatic leaf varieties, mostly imported from Taiwan and Mainland China. If your timing is right, you may get a choice of small free samples.

- Keep strolling east along E. Pender and you'll find yourself in Chinatown's main food-shopping area. Fronted by pyramids of dry fish, leathery red lychees, and spiky durian fruits, the grocery stores lining this strip are a visitor attraction in themselves. Expect a sensory explosion of salty barbecue aromas and loud Chinese banter, and make sure you duck into the shops and pick up a snack or two for later.

- Continue east to the next intersection, then turn right along Gore Ave. Stroll south for one block. You'll spot a handful of cottage vendors here selling everything from hand-knitted hats to unfamiliar backyard-grown vegetables to dried lizards splayed on sticks. At the next intersection, turn right down Keefer St. The shops here, from old-school apothecaries to garish trinket stores, are just as busy as those on E. Pender. This strip is the center of Chinatown's popular summertime night market when the street transforms into an alfresco bazaar of hawker food, live music, and tempting stalls on Friday, Saturday, and Sunday nights.

Conclude your Chinatown walk with dinner at Hon's Wun-Tun House, on the left-hand side of Keefer. Chinatown is stuffed with restaurants but this one has been a local favorite for many years. One of the first Vancouver restaurants to bring Hong Kong-style noodles to town back in 1982, it's since branched out and developed a bewildering array of good-value dishes. The room here is often stuffed with chattering locals and if you're not sure what to go for try the barbecued duck noodles with a side order of pork pot stickers.

## POINTS OF INTEREST

**Sam Kee Building** 8 W. Pender St.

**Dr. Sun Yat-Sen Classical Chinese Garden** 578 Carrall St., 604-662-3207

**Chinese Benevolent Association Building** 108 E. Pender St.

**New Town Bakery** 158 E. Pender St., 604-689-7835

**Ten Lee Hong Enterprises** 500 Main St., 604-689-7598

**Hon's Wun-Tun House** 268 Keefer St., 604-688-0871

# route summary

1. Start on W. Pender St., at the intersection with Taylor St.
2. Stroll east on W. Pender under the Chinatown Millennium Gate.
3. Turn right along Carrall St.
4. Stroll south for half a block on the left side of Carrall.
5. Turn left into the entrance for the Dr. Sun Yat-Sen Classical Chinese Garden.
6. Exit the garden into the courtyard.
7. Stroll north through the courtyard.
8. Turn right along E. Pender St.
9. Head east along E. Pender, on the right side of the street.
10. At the intersection with Main St., cross over and continue east on E. Pender.
11. Continue east on the right side of E. Pender.
12. Turn right along Gore Ave. for one block.
13. Turn right onto Keefer St.
14. Continue west on Keefer St.

*Dr. Sun Yat-Sen Classical Chinese Garden*

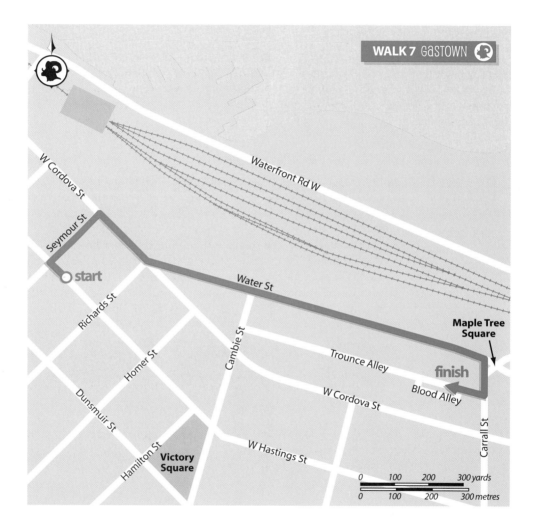

W Cordova St

Seymour St

Waterfront Rd W

start

Richards St

Water St

Homer St

Cambie St

**Maple Tree Square**

Trounce Alley

**finish**

Blood Alley

W Cordova St

Dunsmuir St

Carrall St

Hamilton St

**Victory Square**

W Hastings St

| 0 | 100 | 200 | 300 yards |
| 0 | 100 | 200 | 300 metres |

# 7 Gastown: Historic Shopping and Noshing

**BOUNDARIES:** **W. Hastings St., Seymour St., Water St., Carrall St.**
**DISTANCE:** **¾ mile/1¼ kilometres**
**DIFFICULTY:** **Easy**
**PARKING:** **There's a parkade on the south side of Cordova St, between Howe and Burrard Sts. and another at 165 Water St., where there's also metered street parking.**
**PUBLIC TRANSIT:** **SkyTrain and Canada Line trains stop at Waterfront Station. Buses 4, 7, 8, 10, and 16 stop near the Vancouver Lookout.**

Gastown is the place where the city began, even before it was called Vancouver. But despite its unrivalled historic provenance, this district of brick-lined streets and handsome heritage blocks was facing the wrecking ball just a few years ago. Not big on historic preservation in the 1950s, the city had merrily wiped out many of the ornate mansions and clapboard late-19th-century cottages that crowded the West End. Gastown faced a similar fate: after years of neglect, it had become an underused area where most locals never bothered to tread. Despite the dereliction, heritage-minded Vancouverites eventually managed to save the area, although only in recent years has it been fully reclaimed as a place where people want to hang out. Wandering the streets today, you'll find a neighborhood of historic buildings filled with artsy shops and independent restaurants—a far cry from the rough-and-ready pioneer days of "Gassy Jack" Deighton, the man who kick-started the original settlement.

- Get the lay of the land from Harbour Centre's Vancouver Lookout attraction, near the corner of W. Hastings and Seymour Sts. Still one of the city's tallest buildings at 581 feet/177 metres, its '70s-era observation deck was opened by Neil Armstrong, a man who knows a thing or two about heights. Access the deck via one of the glass-sided elevators and hang on to your ticket: it's valid for the day, so a panoramic sunset is also in the cards. Up top, guides will help you identify city landmarks, or you can do-it-yourself with plaques dotted around the glass-encased perimeter. Gaze east and you'll see a tree-lined street almost parallel with the old train tracks. That's Water St., the heart of Gastown.

- Pick up your stomach after the descent, and, once you leave the building, turn right along W. Hastings to the corner of Seymour. Turn north, head downhill and across

Cordova St. The stately, multi-columned edifice of Waterfront Station will be looming ahead of you. Built as the city's third Canadian Pacific Railway station in 1914, this is where generations of European immigrants arrived in Vancouver, after arduous trans-Atlantic boat treks and trans-Canada train journeys. The station was saved from demolition in the 1970s as part of the wider push to preserve Gastown. Still a transportation hub, it's now home to local services: SkyTrain, Canada Line, SeaBus, and West Coast Express.

Nip between the columns and check out the high-ceilinged interior. If you're a hungry train buff, veer to the right and enter Steamworks Transcontinental, a cavernous restaurant/bar lined with heritage railway posters. Muse on the long-forgotten golden age of rail travel as you tuck into a locally brewed beer and some grilled ahi tuna, the restaurant's menu highlight.

- Head along the station's east corridor and exit into the parking lot. Hang over the railings that overlook the waterfront here. Most of the original tangle of crisscrossed train lines are still below, now used for freight locomotives and the West Coast Express service that rolls in from Lower Mainland suburbs. On your left is Canada Place but crane right and you'll catch sight of the brick-built backs of some of the city's oldest buildings. Many of these were once warehouses and hotels for transient workers, although from the front, they now have modern shop façades.

- Exit the parking lot left onto Cordova St. then take the next left onto Water St. Now the city's most attractive heritage thoroughfare, it was almost lost to modern development in the 1960s, until heritage-minded locals drew a line in the sand and eventually triggered a plan to save the old buildings, many of which had been derelict for decades. The project took years to bear fruit and only recently has the area been fully revitalized. Glancing along Water St. today, you'll see a street like no other in Vancouver, complete with old-fashioned streetlamps, cobbled sidewalks, and dozens of preserved historic edifices.

- Strolling east down Water St., cross to the right-hand side and you'll soon come to Social at Le Magasin. One of the area's more recent preservations, this solid 1911 building hosts a three-part business: there's a cozy bar downstairs, a restaurant on the main floor, and a hidden butcher shop/deli out the back. Step up to the entrance and take the checker-floored corridor toward the back of the building. Peruse the restaurant ceiling on your left as you pass along the corridor: its ornate pressed tin design is the building's architectural heritage highlight. At the deli, consider ordering a charcuterie sandwich for the road.

- Returning to Water St., continue east and cross the road at the corner of Cambie St. You're now facing Vancouver's most-photographed attraction. A modern steam clock, it was designed and made by Vancouver horologist Raymond Saunders, who has built several more since; all act as public artworks in the cities where they reside. The clock is famous for marking 15 minute increments with toots from its steam whistles, powered from an underground steam heat system that also serves nearby buildings. (The mechanism for the clock itself runs on electricity.)

- Squeeze through the camera-wielding throng eagerly awaiting the next tooting symphony, cross over Cambie and continue east on Water St. After a few steps on your left is one of the best First Nations galleries in the city. Hill's Native Arts houses an intriguing menagerie of authentic masks, totem poles, and museum-quality jewelry, paintings, and artifacts, many created by BC's best Coast Salish artisans. Check out the chunky handmade Cowichan sweaters from Vancouver Island.

- A little farther along the street, also on your left, you'll almost miss the unobtrusive entrance to House of McLaren, a hangout transplanted from across the pond that's often teeming with misty-eyed Brits. While Scots roll in here for tailor-made clan kilts and attendant paraphernalia, other homesick U.K. expats drop by to stock up on reminders of home. Where else can you pick-up Tizer, Curly-Wurlys, tinned treacle puddings, and Marmite-flavored crisps?

- Continuing east, cross Abbott St. and on your left you'll come to John Fluevog Shoes. Typifying the trendy boutique stores that have begun colonizing Gastown, this is the flagship outlet of a Vancouver footwear designer whose hipster creations include modern reinventions of brogues and towering ladies boots that are more like art installations. The shop, a vast glass-sided fill-in cleverly created between two brick buildings, lures slavering shoe fans from around the world, including Madonna, who has a pair of pink Fluevog platforms.

## Back Story: How It All Began

Near the middle of what's now called Maple Tree Square once sat a waterfront saloon that was built in 1867 by "Gassy Jack" Deighton, a colorful pioneer who saw the need for a drinking hole to service the thirsty workers of the nearby Hastings Sawmill. Attracting an attendant string of squalid shacks, the rough, ramshackle area around the bar soon became known as Gastown. As the ad hoc settlement grew, the colonial administration decided to formalize it, creating the new town of Granville in 1870. Most people still called it Gastown, especially when Deighton opened a larger saloon nearby a few years later. In 1886, though, the town's name was officially changed to Vancouver and plans were laid for a larger city, encompassing the old Gastown/Granville area. Within a few weeks, a giant fire swept rapidly through the fledgling townsite, destroying around 1,000 mostly wooden buildings in less than an hour. When the reconstruction began, stone replaced wood—which explains why this area now has so many brick and rock buildings that can withstand fires, if not earthquakes.

Wrapped around the southwest edge of the Water and Carrall St. intersection, you'll find the red-painted Byrnes Block. Standing on the site of the second Deighton saloon, it was one of the first structures to be re-built after the 1886 fire and is the oldest Vancouver building still standing in its original spot.

At the end of Water St. you'll be facing Maple Tree Square, a handsome brick-paved intersection that's often regarded as the spot where Vancouver began. Ask the jaunty statue of "Gassy Jack" Deighton, set atop a whisky barrel, and he might, as his nickname implies, tell you a tale or two.

● Follow the curve of this building south along Carrall, and then take the first turn on your right. Named Blood Alley after the many butcher shops that resided here, this is one of the city's most intact historic streets and it has a spooky brick-lined ambiance. Continue west along here for a minute or so and you'll come to your final destination. Echoing the butchers that once colonized the area, Salt Tasting Room is a smashing hidden charcuterie restaurant where you can feast on plates of delectable meats and cheese along with glasses of wine at a large communal table.

## POINTS OF INTEREST

**Vancouver Lookout** 555 W. Hastings St., 604-689-0421

**Steamworks Transcontinental** 601 W. Cordova St., 604-678-8000

**Social at Le Magasin** 332 Water St., 604-669-4488

**Hill's Native Arts** 165 Water St., 604-685-4249

**House of McLaren** 125 Water St., 604-681-5442

**John Fluevog Shoes** 65 Water St., 604-688-6228

**Salt Tasting Room** 45 Blood Alley, 604-633-1912

## route summary

1. From the Harbour Centre on W. Hastings St., turn right down Seymour St.
2. Cross W. Cordova St.
3. Head east along W. Cordova.
4. Turn left along Water St.
5. Continue east along Water St.
6. Turn right along Carrall St.
7. Take the next right into Blood Alley.

*Gastown's iconic steam clock*

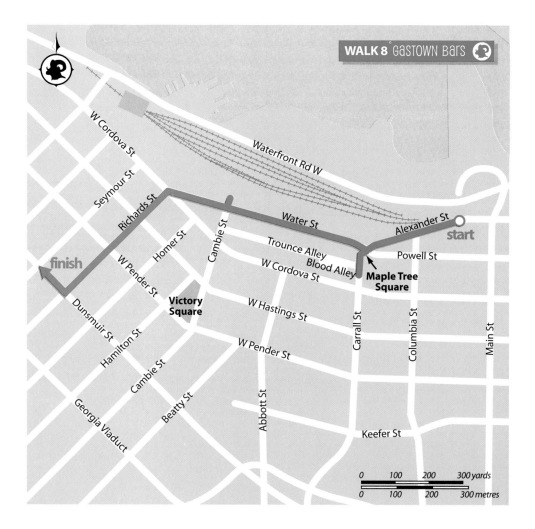

W Cordova St

Seymour St

Richards St

Waterfront Rd W

Homer St

Cambie St

Water St

Alexander St

**start**

Trounce Alley

Blood Alley

W Cordova St

Powell St

**finish**

W Pender St

**Maple Tree
Square**

**Victory
Square**

W Hastings St

Dunsmuir St

Carrall St

Columbia St

Main St

Hamilton St

W Pender St

Cambie St

Beatty St

Abbott St

Keefer St

Georgia Viaduct

0      100      200      300 yards
0      100      200      300 metres

# 8 GASTOWN BARS: PUB-CRAWLING IN THE OLD 'HOOD

**BOUNDARIES:** **Main St., Water St., Dunsmuir St., Seymour St.**
**DISTANCE:** **¾ mile/1¼ kilometre**
**DIFFICULTY:** **Easy**
**PARKING:** **There's a parkade at 165 Water St., where there's also metered street parking.**
**PUBLIC TRANSIT:** **SkyTrain and Canada Line trains stop at Waterfront Station. Buses 4 and 7 stop on nearby Powell St.**

When "Gassy Jack" Deighton arrived on the southern bank of Burrard Inlet in the mid-1800s, the main cargo in his boat was a much-protected barrel of whisky. The barrel is said to be the first stock he used to open his makeshift bar, a wooden shack that soon lured thirsty workers from the nearby Hastings Sawmill. Deighton's hostelry quickly became a fixture—presumably with a more regular stock of the hard stuff—and after several small businesses sprang up around it, the area became locally known as Gastown. Deighton himself would no doubt be delighted to learn that, well over a century later, the district that still bears his name remains the best spot in Metro Vancouver to grab a drink. While Gastown descended into disuse for many decades, recent years have seen its handsome stone and brick buildings refurbished and re-colonized with a host of atmospheric bars. Here then, for those who like a little guidance before launching on their own pub crawl, is a weave through the area's best drinking holes. Drink long and drink well and old Gassy Jack will be proud of you.

● Remember to pace yourself as you start at the long, brick-lined Alibi Room on Alexander St., near the intersection with Main St. Once a hangout for Hollywood North movie crews, the Alibi has reinvented itself in recent years as Vancouver's best bar for BC microbrew fans. There are usually around 18 regional ales on tap here, giving you the chance to taste-trip though treats like Hop Head IPA from Tree Brewing, Back Hand of God Stout from Crannog Brewing, and Lederhosen Lager from Swans Buckerfield's Brewery. The Old Yale Pale Ale is recommended for those who like smooth dark beer.

● Weave (hopefully not too much) west along Alexander St. This follows the trail that workers from the old Hastings Sawmill used to traverse (probably quite quickly) to get to Deighton's bar at the end of the day. Train lines still run parallel with the street here and there's a somewhat gritty, industrial feel to the area. A few steps past the Alibi Room on your right, you'll spot a new water pumping station that's been beatified with a public art façade: its three windows display installations representing the past, present, and future. The past display shows an evocative aerial photograph of old Gastown.

- Continue west along Alexander and within a couple of minutes you'll come to Maple Tree Square. On your right is Chill Winston, occupying an old 1898 warehouse building. On sunny afternoons or balmy summer evenings, this large bar and restaurant has one of the city's best and most lively patios. At street level overlooking the cobbled panorama of historic buildings, it's an ideal place to sip a cold one and have a chat.

- Cross to the other side of Alexander here and you'll be right in front of the Hotel Europe, a slender wedge of a building. Built in 1907, it's Vancouver's finest flatiron-style edifice and was originally expensively lined with marble, brass, and stained glass. It's had its ups and downs, but always retained a certain cool. For years it was a residential hotel, with an underground tavern popular with the alternative crowd. Its rooms now provide accommodation for social housing, art galleries, and antique shops.

- Cross over Powell St. and then stroll south up Carrall St. for half a block. You're now at the relatively new location of the Irish Heather, arguably Vancouver's favorite pub. Originally occupying an atmospheric brick-lined old spot across the street—its bathrooms were reputedly on the site of the city's first jail—the Heather was forced to relocate in 2008 due to seismic upgrading of its original venue. The wooden floors at the swankier new location are made from old Guinness barrels, the back bar (known as the Shebeen Whisky House) is a chatty snug, and the food is among the best gastropub fare you'll find anywhere in BC.

- Cross the road here and return north along Carrall St. Raise your proverbial glass to the barrel-mounted statue of "Gassy Jack" here, then nip behind him into Six Acres. This small, eclectic, but perfectly cozy bar manages to be the area's best hipster hangout without exhibiting a shred of pretentiousness. It's the kind of place where student-types and cool locals come to wax lyrical about Sartre over a bottle or two of quality beer—such as Hobgoblin, Oyster Stout, or Newcastle Brown Ale. The menu of shareable tasting plates is also excellent (the Sophia Loren meat and cheese plate is recommended). Six Acres is located in the Byrnes Block: built in 1866, it's the oldest Vancouver structure still in its original location.

- If you're still upright, continue along Carrall and turn left onto Water St. On your left, after a minute or two, you'll come to the Lamplighter. A bar and hotel in handsome red-brick that's been here since 1925, this was the first pub in Vancouver to officially serve alcohol to women. For years, the grungy bar was one of the area's favorite live music venues until it was taken over and refurbished in 2007. The new owners closed the budget hotel upstairs and made the place a little slicker: the dinged tables have been replaced and there's a sports bar feel, complete with TVs and pool tables.

- Continue west on Water St. and take the next turn on your right along Cambie St. Walk toward the train tracks and on your right you'll see the slender, easy-to-miss Black Frog. A favorite among in-the-know locals, this little drinking hole is off the tourist map, but it's well worth it if you're one of those pub fans that hates over-produced bar interiors. There are nightly drink specials here and the draft roster ranges from Alberta's Big Rock Traditional to BC's Russell Cream Ale and France's Kronenbourg. This is also a good spot to catch a live Canucks or Vancouver Whitecaps broadcast.

- Return to Water St. and turn right, continuing west on the slightly uphill stretch, then bearing right onto Cordova St. after a couple of minutes. On your right, occupying a building that looks like it was hewn from a single lump of rock, is Steamworks Brewing Company, one of the city's few authentic brewpubs. If you're hungry, tuck into the pub classics menu—this is a good spot for fish and chips and the pizzas are a permanent favorite. Downstairs is the intimate subterranean bar where there's usually a great pub atmosphere, especially on weekends. Of the five regular in-house brews on offer, Lions Gate Lager is the most popular but there are often additional seasonal treats like Dopplebock or Oatmeal Stout.

- With your whistle well and truly wetted, it's probably time to end your boozy city stroll. Cross over W. Cordova St. and head south on a bracing uphill stroll along Richards St. After three blocks, turn right onto Dunsmuir St. Just before the next corner on your right, you'll come to an easily missed doorway with a small sign marking the entrance to the Railway Club. Push through the heavy door and head up the grungy, carpeted staircase. If you're here before 7 p.m., admission is free. If not, you'll have to pay a cover charge of up to $10. Even if you have to pay, it's worth it: the "Rail" is Vancouver's most authentic old-style bar. Recalling well-worn English city pubs, the slim space comprises intimate tables for chatting and a narrow bar stocked with local drafts. The reason for the cover charge is the live music (from beat poets to metal rap) that hits the small stage nightly. Your crawl now over, you can sit back, sip your beer, and send a silent prayer of thanks to the man with the whisky barrel all those years ago.

## POINTS OF INTEREST

**Alibi Room** 157 Alexander St., 604-623-3383

**Chill Winston** 3 Alexander St., 604-288-9575

**Irish Heather** 217 Carrall St., 604-688-9779

**Six Acres** 203 Carrall St., 604-488-0110

**Lamplighter** 92 Water St., 604-687-4424

**Black Frog** 108 Cambie St., 604-602-0527

**Steamworks Brewing Company** 375 Water St., 604-689-2739

**Railway Club** 579 Dunsmuir St., 604-681-1625

# route summary

1. Start on the right side of Alexander St., just west of the intersection with Main St.

2. Head west along Alexander St. to Maple Tree Square.

3. After Chill Winston, cross south over Alexander St. and then over Powell St.

4. Stroll half a block south on Carrall St., on the left-hand sidewalk.

5. Cross to the other side of Carrall St.

6. Head north along Carrall and turn left along Water St.

7. Continue west on Water St., on the left-hand sidewalk, until you reach Cambie St.

8. Turn right along Cambie St. for half a block.

9. Return north along Cambie and turn right onto Water St.

10. Continue west on Water St., then bear right onto W. Cordova St.

11. Cross to the other side of W. Cordova and head south up Richards St.

12. Turn right along Dunsmuir St.

13. Continue west and stop just before the intersection with Seymour St.

*"Gassy Jack" Deighton*

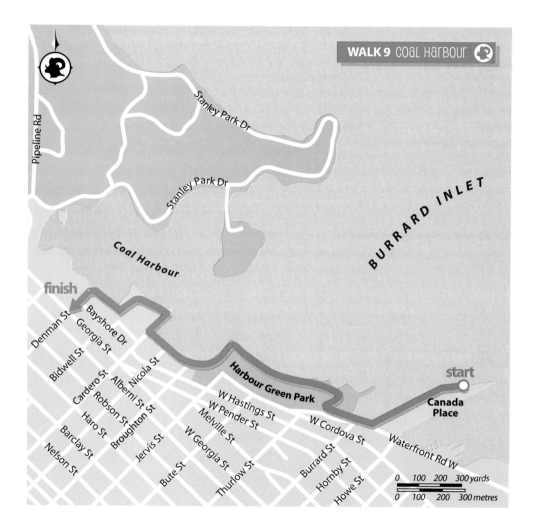

BURRARD INLET

Stanley Park Dr

Stanley Park Dr

Pipeline Rd

Coal Harbour

finish

Denman St

Bayshore Dr

Georgia St

Bidwell St

Cardero St

Nicola St

Alberni St

Robson St

Haro St

Broughton St

Barclay St

Jervis St

Nelson St

Bute St

W Georgia St

Thurlow St

W Hastings St

W Pender St

Melville St

Harbour Green Park

W Cordova St

Burrard St

Hornby St

Howe St

start

Canada
Place

Waterfront Rd W

0    100   200   300 yards
0    100   200   300 metres

# 9  coal Harbour: from Industrial Shorefront to Waterfront Idyll

**BOUNDARIES: Canada Place, Burrard Inlet, Harbour Green Park, Denman St.**
**DISTANCE: 1¼ miles/1¾ kilometres**
**DIFFICULTY: Easy**
**PARKING: There's a parkade at Canada Place and another at the Terminal City Club on the nearby 800 block of W. Hastings St. There's also some metered street parking on this stretch of W. Hastings.**
**PUBLIC TRANSIT: The Waterfront Sky Train station is a short walk from Canada Place.**

One of colonial BC's early explored areas, the southern banks of Burrard Inlet from Canada Place to Stanley Park (no, they weren't there at the time) is Coal Harbour, named after the streaks of coal that could be seen in the rock face from the water. But it's the shoreline's later industrialization that formed its distinctive character for many decades. This was the site of the sprawling Canadian Pacific Railway western terminus that stretched far along the waterfront—the rails stop short on the east side of Canada Place today. It soon attracted a gritty hive of cottage industries, many of them servicing the marine businesses swarming around the port. These included Boeing Canada's floatplane factory, the precursor of Coal Harbour's current armada of floatplane operators. While judicious infill moved the original shoreline north (it once snaked along the present route of W. Hastings St.) to its current location, these industries—whacked by the double-whammy of the Depression and WWII—eventually faded away and the port shrank east along the shoreline. Today's Coal Harbour is dramatically different. Forested with sparkling condo towers and a seawall promenade, this stroll makes for a relaxing waterfront amble.

● **Start at the watery northern tip of Canada Place's long promenade and drink in the panorama of Burrard Inlet complete with dive-bombing floatplanes, and the shimmering North Vancouver skyline against the looming Coast Mountains. While nature dominates the vista, this is also the traditional heart of Vancouver's industrious port: there's a forest of orange freight cranes to your right and a flotilla of mammoth commercial ships studding the water ahead. Canada's largest port now handles around $43 billion of cargo annually, trading with 90 countries, which explains the towering stacks of freight containers piled like giant Lego bricks.**

- Turn your back on the view and stroll along the western flank of Canada Place, with the water to your right. Ubiquitous on Vancouver postcards, this landmark building serves as a convention center and cruise ship terminal—you can expect one or two giant Alaska-run vessels to be parked alongside in summer. Constructed for Expo '86 and echoing the area's maritime provenance, the building is topped with five sail-shaped peaks: it's the city's version of Sydney Opera House. If the weather's friendly, strolling the promenade delivers unfolding views of Stanley Park and the Lions Gate Bridge, but if it's raining, nip inside to the IMAX theatre.

- Hit dry land at the end of the promenade and turn right. You'll spot the new convention center expansion building right ahead, rising like an undulating wave of glass from the shore. The project was beset with delays and budget problems, eventually costing more than double its original $400 million price tag. Presumably some of that was spent on the shaggy grass roof that cools the building in summer and insulates it in winter. Across the street is the city's main Tourist InfoCentre. If you want to visit Smithers (where the locals are officially called Smithereens) or anywhere else in BC, this is the place to grab a brochure.

- Continue west and follow the signs to the waterfront floatplane dock. Three airlines splash in here (including Harbour Air, the world's largest all-floatplane operator) and they service downtown Victoria and points around BC. These short hops are arguably the best way to see the region. Consider strapping-in for a 20-minute sightseeing tour and you'll have a birds-eye view of Stanley Park, the Southern Gulf Islands, and the region's ring of snow-capped mountains. Even if you're not boarding, it's worth watching a landing or two.

- Continue west from here and you'll hook up with the seawall. One of Vancouver's most attractive strolls, it was extended in the last few years—a final reminder that the old industrial Coal Harbour really isn't coming back. The unobstructed waterfront is on your right now and Harbour Green Park is on your left. In summer, its gentle, grassy slopes are covered with sunbathing workers from nearby businesses.

- Within a couple of minutes, you'll come to the park's main hangout on your left. Fronted by a fountain-spraying water feature that brings out the giggles in most kids, Mill Marine Bistro is an ideal landing place. Arrive early on particularly balmy days (it

## Back Story: Vancouver's Big Bang

The biggest disaster in Coal Harbour's history occurred at Pier B in March 1945 when the freight ship *SS Greenhill Park* suddenly exploded. Eight longshoremen were instantly killed and 19 others were injured—several local firemen summoned to fight the blaze were also hospitalized. The spectacular blast was felt across the city and hundreds of windows were blown out, with some downtown buildings left without a single unbroken pane. The local rumor mill quickly sprung into action. With Pearl Harbor still fresh in many minds, some Vancouverites were convinced the Japanese had flown in and bombed the vessel. While a later inquiry concluded that poor stowage of flammable materials had led to the explosion, not everyone was convinced and stories continued to circulate for years afterward.

fills up fast once 5 p.m. strikes) to ensure an outdoor table—it's one of the city's best patio views. While the food is of the standard pizza, sandwich, and burger variety, the beer selection includes choice tipples from local Granville Island Brewing. If it's hot, go for a Hefeweizen wheat beer.

- Back on the seawall and weaving west, continue to the corner of the small park. Here you'll find one of the city's most evocative public artworks. *Light Shed* by Liz Magor is a half-sized aluminum replica of one of the hundreds of little wooden sheds that teetered on piles here around a century ago. It's one of the few reminders of the area's working past. For an alternative reminder of its upper-class present, check the luxurious boats anchored just behind it in the marina. Usually the one parked right by the sculpture is the *Nova Spirit*, the biggest boat in the dock. This 150-foot/46-metre, arrow-shaped vessel is owned by BC billionaire Jimmy Pattison.

- After failing to board the boat for a closer look, follow the seawall to the left as it curves around the marina and its clutch of smaller but still fairly luxurious vessels. In the middle of the bobbing melee, you'll spot a string of three charming houseboats that arguably exhibit more taste than all the ostentatious boats surrounding them. If it's ice cream time, stop at the concession on the corner of the nearby Coal Harbour Community Centre.

• Curving west along the seawall, you'll pass a string of little shops footing the upscale condo towers that have risen here in recent years. Nestled among these half-empty stores you'll find *Sliding Edge*, a public artwork by Jacqueline Metz and Nancy Chew that includes a bronze figure seemingly about to jump from the top of a waterfall.

A few steps ahead on your right is Cardero's, the area's best restaurant. You can snag a leather armchair by the fire in the pub on the building's right half or aim for a table in the ritzier restaurant section on your left. The restaurant food—think Pacific Northwest treats—is pricier, but it has an excellent patio where you can catch the view. Before you leave, peruse some of the nautical memorabilia on the pub walls. If you only want a java, go across to Cafe Villaggio with its chunky wooden tables, giant cookies, and rocket-fuel Americanos.

• Continue west along the seawall and the **Westin Bayshore** hotel will be straight ahead. A classic posh sleepover, it was the temporary home of famous recluse Howard Hughes, who booked the top two floors for his entourage and himself for three months in 1972. Apparently, no one saw Hughes enter or leave the hotel: he brought his own chef to cook his favorite meals so he wouldn't have to nip out to the nearest Tim Hortons.

• Follow the seawall around the hotel, keeping one eye on the water for harbor seals and great blue herons. When you follow the wall south past Lift Bar and Grill, you'll also come to another reminder of the area's portside past. Under a metal canopy is a large brass bell that was found in the harbor during dredging and later inscribed with the names of characters and companies that worked the area. Evocative monikers like Olaf Stockland, Gim Tee Tong, Blue Band Towing, and Pacific Sea Bulldozers are the bell's colorful reminders of the past.

• Continue west along the seawall and you'll soon pass the dock used by Harbour Cruises. You can take one of their frequent tours of the harbor for a fish-eye view of the city and the port. They also offer tranquil dinner cruises that curve around Stanley Park, under Lions Gate Bridge and out to English Bay. After your return to shore, head south on Denman St., turn left onto W. Georgia, and stroll back downtown.

## POINTS OF INTEREST

**Canada Place** 999 Canada Pl., 604-775-7200

**Vancouver Convention Centre** 1055 Canada Pl., 604-689-8232

**Harbour Air** W. Waterfront Rd., 604-274-1277

**Mill Marine Bistro** 1199 W. Cordova St., 604-687-6455

**Coal Harbour Community Centre** 480 Broughton St., 604-718-8222

**Cardero's** 1583 Coal Harbour Quay, 604-669-7666

**Cafe Villaggio** 1506 Coal Harbor Quay, 604-687-6599

**Westin Bayshore** 1601 Bayshore Dr., 604-682-3377

**Harbour Cruises** North Foot Denman St., 604-688-7246

## ROUTE SUMMARY

1. Start at the northern waterfront tip of Canada Place.
2. Stroll south back to land along the west side of Canada Place.
3. Turn right along Burrard Pl. and follow the sign to the floatplane dock.
4. Follow the seawall west from the floatplanes.
5. Continue along the seawall to the western corner of Harbour Green Park.
6. Follow the seawall as it curves south and then west again from here.
7. Continue west along the seawall, past the right side of the Westin Bayshore.
8. Follow the seawall west to Harbour Cruises, just past the north foot of Denman St.
9. Stroll south up Denman and turn left onto W. Georgia St.

*Coal Harbour*

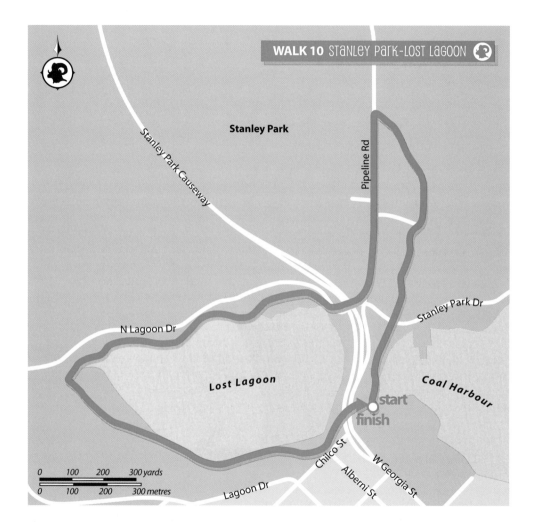

Stanley Park

Stanley Park Causeway

Pipeline Rd

Stanley Park Dr

N Lagoon Dr

Lost Lagoon

Coal Harbour

start
finish

Chilco St

W Georgia St

Alberni St

Lagoon Dr

0    100    200    300 yards
0    100    200    300 metres

# 10 STanLey Park: LOST en route to Lost Lagoon

BOUNDARIES: **Seawall, Pipeline Rd., North Lagoon Dr., Lagoon Dr.**
DISTANCE: **¾ mile/1¼ kilometre**
DIFFICULTY: **Easy**
PARKING: **There's a parking lot at the north foot of Denman St., near the park's W. Georgia St. entrance. There's also metered street parking on Alberni St., a five-minute walk away.**
PUBLIC TRANSIT: **Bus 19 stops near the W. Georgia St. entrance and at the Bus Loop in Stanley Park. Buses 240, 250, and 251 also stop near the W. Georgia St. entrance.**

The seawall promenade hogs all the attention but there's much more to Stanley Park than the sea-to-sky vistas famously radiating from its nature-hugging perimeter. In fact, despite being a dense 1,000-acre/400-hectare temperate rainforest of 500,000 cedar, fir, and hemlock trees, the park has been a bustling playground for Vancouverites since official opening day in 1888. While past attractions have come and gone or never quite materialized—including giant open air checker boards, a pair of polar bears, and a fast-abandoned plan to install animatronic dinosaurs—the city's favorite green space still has an aquarium, swimming pool, outdoor theatre, cricket oval, and four restaurants that are as popular as ever. And there are also plenty of off-the-beaten-path spots to check out, including secret statuary, several little-known memorials, and a couple of manicured landscaped gardens. So, strap on the daypack and plunge right into this interior walk for a rewarding, alternative take on Stanley Park.

● Starting on the seawall at the park's W. Georgia St. entrance, hop left across the path and head north up the bridge-like ramp rising ahead of you. Almost immediately, the crowds will disappear and you'll be surrounded by noble old trees. Continue to the end of the walkway and make a sharp right across the grass. Here you'll find a magnificent bronze statue of Robert Burns, looking down on the seawall joggers who probably don't even know he's there. Unveiled by British Prime Minister Ramsay MacDonald in 1928, its almost too-tall plinth is decorated on three sides with scenes from three of Burns' poems.

● Retrace your steps back to the end of the walkway and ahead of you is one of the most welcoming statues you'll likely ever see. Suitably encircled by trees, the 1960 bronze of Sir Fredrick Arthur Stanley—now known simply as Lord Stanley, he was Canada's Governor General when the park was dedicated to him and officially opened in 1888—stands here with its arms outstretched, atop a large declaration of the park's intent: "To the use and enjoyment of people of all colours, creeds and customs for all time." While he only lent his name to the park, Stanley also donated the original trophy that NHL hockey teams battle over to this day.

● Take the left-hand trail and wave goodbye to Lord Stanley. Like a microcosm of the rest of the park, this area is lined with indigenous and imported trees and plants. You'll spot hardy maples, spectacular flowering rhododendrons, and towering Douglas-firs. Look up between the needles and you'll likely see a floatplane or two droning past en route to Coal Harbour. Expect to be accompanied here by gray and black squirrels.

● Continue north through the trees, passing the small playground on your right, and you'll come to a fork in the path. Take the right-hand track toward the Malkin Bowl. Hidden in the foliage, this pretty, open-air auditorium was built by former Vancouver mayor W.H. Malkin in 1934 to honor his deceased wife. It took over a site originally occupied by the park's bandstand. Every summer, Theatre Under the Stars stages two musicals here, and the atmospheric venue is also used for concerts by indie bands like the Raconteurs and the New Pornographers.

At the rear of the theatre's grass seating area, you'll find one of Vancouver's most surprising hidden memorials. Flanked by a pair of doe-like bronze ladies representing the youth of Canada and the U.S., a gray granite monument recalls the 1923 visit by W.G. Harding—the first official visit to Canada by any U.S. president. Stopping off for only 10 hours on a trip from Alaska, he managed to take in nine holes at the Shaughnessy Golf Club. When Harding died just a week later in San Francisco, the Vancouver Kiwanis Club raised the funds for this elaborate memorial.

● Continuing north across the grass, ahead you'll see the classic Stanley Park Pavilion, an eye-catching reminder of Edwardian stone and wood-beam lodge architecture. Fronted by carefully coiffured gardens, it's one of the park's few surviving pre-WWI buildings and is now home to the casual Stanley's Park Bar and Grill. Its updated interior retains the spirit of the West Coast wood and stone look, while the menu is dominated by comfort-food favorites—including the rather dubiously named Lord

Stanley's Foot Long Frank. If it's balmy, grab a seat on the large deck. One of the best nature-bound patios in the city, it's an idyllic spot to sip a Granville Island Honey Lager or two.

- Head north past the pavilion and, on your right, you'll quickly arrive at two of the park's best kids' attractions. Opened in 1982, the Children's Farmyard is a domestic animal petting zoo with more than 200 species—don't try petting the llama, though. The adjacent Miniature Railway has been a fixture since 1964 when a hurricane swept through the park, creating a clearing of fallen trees that opened a space for the new train track. With tunnels and trestle bridges, the best times to climb aboard are Halloween, when the route is decked with spectral surprises, and Christmas, when the fire department stages its Bright Nights fundraising event, transforming the layout into a winter wonderland of fairy lights.

- Stroll west from the farmyard entrance and hook up with nearby Pipeline Rd., one of the park's main thoroughfares. Cross over and walk south along its right-hand side-walk and within minutes you'll come to the landscaped Rose Garden. First planted in 1920, this immaculate plot is home to 3,500 bushes and is a fragrant summertime highlight. While the garden flanks both sides of the road, stick to the right side and then pass along its gable-topped trellis walkway.

- Turn left at the end of the trellis and amble south downhill through the gardens until you reach a bridge. Duck under it and ahead of you will be the edge of Lost Lagoon. Originally part of Coal Harbour, this now freshwater pool was formed when the Stanley Park Causeway was built, slicing a section off the old harbor area. Originally envisaged as a formal garden, it's become an urban nature reserve and bird sanctuary in recent years. Turn right onto the trail that encircles the lagoon. You'll spot the foun-tain in the lagoon's center: built for the city's 50th anniversary in 1936, it operates in summer, while in winter it's turned off and strung with colored lights shaped like a Christmas tree.

Wandering west along the trail, keep your eyes on the lagoon to your left. A protected wetland just minutes from the city clamor, it's filled with the ecosystem essentials of hard-stem bulrushes and floating yellow lilies. It's the aquatic birdlife that makes the area special, though. Expect to see ducks and swans but also keep your eyes peeled for the magnificent sight of a great blue heron or two, often standing statue-still near the shoreline.

● After a leisurely stroll along this northern bank, cross the humpbacked stone bridge and follow the trail down the lagoon's southern side. There's less foliage here, apart from some giant weeping willows, but the bare shoreline is popular with basking ducks and Canada geese. After a few minutes, look out for the signpost directing you to the free-entry Nature House. A colorful and informed introduction to the park's delicate ecosystem, this little waterfront science center is run by friendly staffers and is lined with interpretive exhibits. The experts here stage weekly nature walks around the area (1pm every Sunday) as well as monthly Sunday bird strolls.

● Continue past the Nature House and along the lagoon's waterfront—this is traditionally the muddiest stretch of the trail. Within a minute or two, you'll meet up with W. Georgia St., across from where you started.

## POINTS OF INTEREST

**Theatre Under the Stars** Malkin Bowl, 604-734-1917

**Stanley's Park Bar and Grill** Stanley Park Pavilion, 604-602-3088

**Children's Farmyard** near Pipeline Rd., 604-257-8531

**Miniature Railway** near Pipeline Rd., 604-257-8531

**Nature House** Lost Lagoon, 604-257-6908

# route summary

1. Start on the seawall at the W. Georgia St. entrance and take the walkway ramp that runs parallel.
2. At the end of the ramp, turn right.
3. Return to the end of the ramp and follow the path north.
4. Take the left-hand path past the Lord Stanley statue.
5. At the next trail fork, take the right-hand path.
6. Continue north past Malkin Bowl and Stanley Park Pavilion.
7. Head west from the Children's Playground to Pipeline Rd.
8. Turn south along Pipeline.
9. Turn right along the Rose Garden trellis walkway.
10. Turn left through the garden to the Stanley Park Causeway bridge.
11. Head under the bridge and follow the trail counterclockwise around Lost Lagoon.
12. Cross over the small bridge and continue along the lagoon's southern shore.
13. Follow the sign to the Nature House.
14. Continue past the Nature House to W. Georgia St.

*Lost Lagoon*

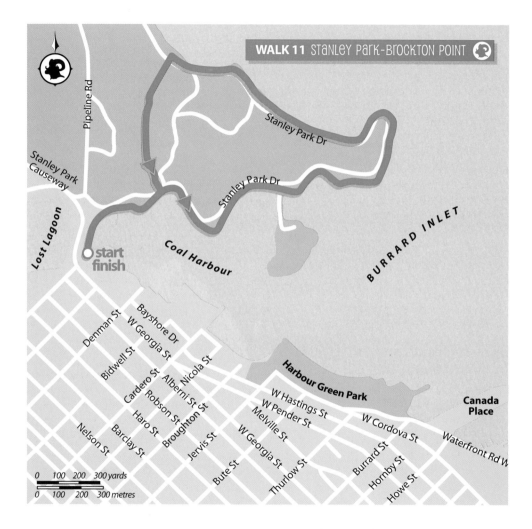

Pipeline Rd

Stanley Park Dr

Stanley Park Causeway

Stanley Park Dr

Lost Lagoon

BURRARD INLET

start finish

Coal Harbour

Denman St

Bayshore Dr

W Georgia St

Bidwell St

Nicola St

Cardero St

Alberni St

Robson St

Haro St

Broughton St

Harbour Green Park

W Hastings St

W Pender St

Melville St

W Cordova St

Canada Place

Nelson St

Barclay St

Jervis St

W Georgia St

Bute St

Thurlow St

Burrard St

Hornby St

Howe St

Waterfront Rd W

0    100    200    300 yards

0    100    200    300 metres

# 11 STanLey Park: Brockton Point Loop

BOUNDARIES: **W. Georgia St., Coal Harbour, Burrard Inlet, Lumberman's Arch**
DISTANCE: **2¼ miles/3¾ kilometres**
DIFFICULTY: **Moderate**
PARKING: **There's parking on this side of the park off Park Dr., just past the AAA Horse and Carriage departure point and also just behind Brockton Point Lighthouse.**
PUBLIC TRANSIT: **Bus 19 stops near the W. Georgia St. entrance and at the Bus Loop in the park. Buses 240, 250, and 251 also stop near the W. Georgia St. entrance.**

Stanley Park's main visitor attractions crowd the site's southeastern section, which is uncharitably shaped like a large boot kicking at the cruise ships passing by en route to Canada Place. In the park's early days, this area was teeming with leisure activities that illustrated the drive to combine planned outdoor pursuits with the rugged forest backdrop. This nature-based idyll included a large number of sports and leisure activities, ranging from boating to cricket and lawn tennis. While some of these facilities remain, the "Brockton boot" is now more likely to be crowded with tourists on their way to the totem poles, the park's most photographed landmark. In fact, the poles indicate the area's almost-forgotten past as a First Nations home: when the park was declared open in 1888, there were still First Nations families living near the shoreline. Strolling the area today, enjoy the seawall promenade and its sterling views of downtown and the North Shore, but keep your eyes peeled for quirky reminders of the park's colorful past.

● You'll start on the seawall near the W. Georgia St. entrance, with Coal Harbour curving ahead on your right. Follow the seawall around the water's edge and within a minute or two you'll see on your left one of the most recent additions to the park's assortment of landmarks and memorials. A reminder of the tumultuous 2006 storm that felled thousands of trees, the large and evocatively skeletal uprooted tree deliberately left here on its side shows just how powerful the tempest was. While some of the trees felled that night rotted into the forest floor and others were saved for premium construction planks, this remains as a stark memorial.

● Continue farther along the seawall and you'll soon come to the Vancouver Rowing Club on your right. Perched on piles above the water, this gable-roofed 1911

In the early morning of December 15, 2006, gale-force winds of up to 77 miles/125 kilometres per hour battered the Vancouver region, downing trees and power lines, and flinging debris around with ease. When dawn came, the locals looked to Stanley Park to check the damage. One of the worst storms in living memory had toppled an estimated 10,000 trees, leveled 110 acres/45 hectares of woodland, and thrown landslides across large sections of the seawall. Initially, it was difficult to assess just how much damage had been done because all the park's roads and most of its trails were blocked by debris. Dozens of park staff worked day and night for two weeks before the roads were cleared. Interior park trails took longer. And sections of the seawall—especially the exposed wind-whipped western side—were not rebuilt and opened to joggers and cyclists for almost a year. A public appeal raised much-needed funds from shocked locals to help pay for the restoration, but the storm reminded older residents of the last time the park was hit by a brutal tempest. In 1962, Hurricane Frieda raged though the area, clearing trees that had stood here for hundreds of years.

Tudoresque construction is one of the best examples of the park's early leisure facilities. The club—still active today, hence the regular canoes slicing through the waters here—was formed in 1889 by the merger of the Vancouver Boating Club and the Burrard Inlet Rowing Club. At the time, both clubs had their own floating clubhouses at the foot of Bute St. This impressive new building replaced them a few years later. If you can snag entry to the private bar inside, its floating waterfront deck offers one of the most idyllic city views.

● Ambling farther along the seawall as it curves left, you'll soon come to the park's Information Centre, a good spot to pick up a handy map of area highlights and buy an ice cream. Continue east along the seawall, though, and you'll quickly come to one of the park's most historic areas, located in the water on your right. Named Deadman's Island (although it's actually a peninsula) it's the site of the **HMCS Discovery** naval station. Its stately quietude masks an intriguing history: Deadman's Island was a traditional First Nations burial ground where the bones of the dead were placed in cedar boxes and set among the branches of the trees. European settlers later created their own cemetery here and it became the chosen burial site for smallpox victims. The spot was eventually taken over by the federal government and transformed into a naval station in 1944.

- As you round the next corner, crane your neck to the left and over your shoulder you'll see Brockton Point Cricket Pavilion. With its mountain backdrop making it arguably North America's most scenic sports venue, it's like stepping onto a 1920s English village green, especially when the players are out in their whites and spectators are fanned out on the grass, drowsily following the game. If you're a die-hard cricket nut, reflect on the fact that legends Don Bradman, Freddie Trueman, and Geoff Boycott have wielded their willow bats here over the years.

You'll likely see a clutch of tour buses parked ahead on your left. They herald a mini forest of colorful totem poles that every Vancouver visitor seems keen to photograph. The first poles were brought to Stanley Park in the 1920s from Alert Bay and they were initially situated a few hundred feet away at Lumberman's Arch as part of a plan to recreate an "Indian village" for tourists. Although the theme park idea was dropped, the pole collection stayed, moving to its current location in the 1960s. The original poles, suffering from years of weathering, were later moved to museums and those here today are 1980s reproductions. Several exquisite n-shaped "gateway" carvings were added to the site in 2008.

- Push through the tourists and return to the tranquility of the seawall. Continuing east, you'll soon pass alongside the bronze statue of North Vancouver sprinter Harry Jerome seemingly racing back in the opposite direction. One of Canada's most celebrated sporting heroes—he held six world records and was designated BC's "athlete of the century" in 1971—Jerome ran in three Olympics, bringing home a bronze from Tokyo in 1964. The prestigious Harry Jerome Track Classic, staged at Burnaby's Swangard Stadium, is held annually in his honor.

A few steps farther along, you'll come to the Nine O'Clock Gun, an 1816 English cannon housed in a cage at Hallelujah Point (named after the lively Salvation Army prayer meetings that used to be staged here). Blasted by automatic trigger at precisely 9 p.m.

nightly, it's a tradition that's been maintained for decades. In 2008, a group of home-work-avoiding UBC miscreants daubed the cannon with red paint.

- The seawall takes you north from here and within a few minutes you'll come to the squat red and white Brockton Point Lighthouse: the seawall actually passes through an archway underneath it. Get your camera out here for some of the best views across Burrard Inlet. Replacing an 1890 structure, the current lighthouse was built in 1914.

- After the lighthouse, the pathway takes you downhill and west alongside a narrow band of beach strewn with driftwood and pebbles. Ahead on your right you'll spot the mermaid-like visage of the *Girl in a Wetsuit* perched on a rock just offshore. A 1972 bronze by Elek Imredy, it recalls the much more famous statue in Copenhagen. While this lady is fully clothed in wetsuit and flippers, successive visitors often deem it necessary to dress her up—expect to see a hat or sweater keeping her warm on chilly days.

- Continuing west, you'll soon come to a waterpark and playground that's usually teeming with galloping kids in summer. Consider running through the fountains and sprinklers yourself before turning left and ducking under the concrete road bridge. The walkway here takes you into the grassy heart of the park and to one of the area's most popular picnic spots, Lumberman's Arch. The area is named for a clunky wooden log sculpture erected in 1952 to recognize BC's logging industry.

- The uphill southbound pathway through the trees soon delivers you to the popular Vancouver Aquarium: avoid peak hours in summer, when the queue often snakes around the building. Check out the playful otters floating on their backs and eating off their chests, drop by the eerily illuminated jellyfish tanks, and wave hello to the baby belugas born here in 2008 and 2009. Like many similar facilities around the world, the aquarium has adopted a more concerted conservation role in recent years—the park has come a long way since polar bears were exhibited nearby in concrete pens.

- Once you've had your aquatic fill, continue along the pathway south and peruse the Artists Corner where, in summer, local painters display their work. After you're done, continue south downhill for a couple of minutes and you'll soon be back on the seawall near where you started. Turn right and retrace your steps west toward the W. Georgia St. entrance.

## POINTS OF INTEREST

**Vancouver Rowing Club** 450 Stanley Park Dr., 604-687-3400

**Vancouver Aquarium** 845 Avison Way, 604-659-3474

## ROUTE SUMMARY

1. Start at the park's W. Georgia St. entrance.
2. Follow the seawall north into the park to the Vancouver Rowing Club.
3. Continue east on the seawall, passing Brockton Cricket Pavilion on your left and Deadman's Island on your right.
4. Continue east along the seawall, passing the totem poles on your left.
5. After the Nine O'Clock Gun, the seawall takes you north to Brockton Point Lighthouse.
6. After Brockton Point, follow the seawall west to the waterpark.
7. Turn left under the road bridge.
8. Follow the trail into the park, with the Vancouver Aquarium on your left.
9. Continue south past the aquarium and rejoin the seawall.
10. Turn right onto the seawall and follow it west to your original starting point.

*Statue of Harry Jerome*

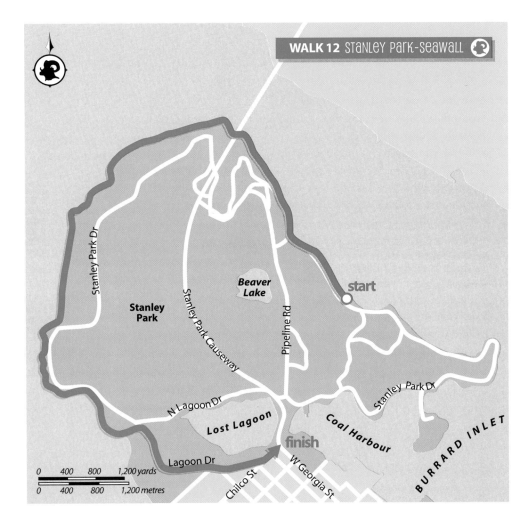

Stanley Park Dr

Stanley Park
Park

Beaver
Lake

Stanley Park Causeway

Pipeline Rd

start

Stanley Park Dr

N Lagoon Dr

Lost Lagoon

Coal Harbour

BURRARD INLET

finish

Lagoon Dr

Chilco St

W Georgia St

0      400      800      1,200 yards

0      400      800      1,200 metres

# STANLEY PARK: SURFING THE SEAWALL

**BOUNDARIES: Lumberman's Arch, Prospect Point, Ferguson Point, Lagoon Dr.**
**DISTANCE: 2¼ miles/4½ kilometres**
**DIFFICULTY: Moderate**
**PARKING: There's parking near Lumberman's Arch and at the nearby Vancouver Aquarium.**
**PUBLIC TRANSIT: Bus 19 stops at the Bus Loop in the park. Buses 240, 250, and 251 stop near the W. Georgia St. entrance.**

The Stanley Park seawall, the popular waterfront route from Coal Harbour around to English Bay, is approximately 5.5 miles/8.8 kilometres long and offers some of the region's best sea, sky, and mountain vistas. But while circling the entire park is a multi-hour hoof for most, this shorter, slightly more leisurely version takes you to some of the promenade's not-to-be-missed highlights. If you're feeling energetic, combine this walk with the Brockton Loop stroll and you'll have a full tour of the seawall. Also consider hopping on a bike or strapping on your rollerblades for a speedier circumnavigation. Taking almost 70 years to finish, the seawall was built in ad hoc sections from the 1920s onwards: much of it personally spearheaded by Parks Board stonemason James Cunningham over a 32-year period. From the 1970s, plans emerged to link these strips of promenade together and, in 1980, when the final stretch between Second Beach and Third Beach was paved, the full seawall circuit was officially opened. It's now the city's most popular outdoor destination.

- After shortcutting north through the center of the park past the Vancouver Aquarium, you'll start your seawall stroll at Lumberman's Arch. While the wooden archway here marks the region's logging industry, this waterfront clearing has a much older provenance. A giant First Nations midden was discovered here several years ago. Primarily comprised of seashells—the mound was up to 8 feet/2.4 metres deep in places—it indicated that a traditional Coast Salish community had once lived here, probably for more than a century. The shells were so numerous that many were later used in surfacing the park's main roads.

- Turn left along the seawall here and follow the route northwest. The promenade can be bustling in summer, but the crowds usually thin out the farther you head along the seawall, enabling nature to soak into your senses. You'll enjoy magnificent North

Shore mountain views on your right. On your left, the verdant temperate rainforest towers above you. Keep in mind, however, that much of the park was logged in the 1800s, and there's likely no authentic old-growth forest left here now. Keep your eyes peeled for marine birdlife as well as a giant tanker or two. You might also catch sight of one of the mammoth cruise ships slipping past en route to Alaska.

- One mile/1.6 kilometres from Lumberman's Arch, you'll see a bronze plaque almost buried in the grass on your right. Looking like a gravestone, it actually marks the spot where Stanley Park was declared open by then mayor David Oppenheimer. A year later, Lord Stanley arrived from Ottawa to officially recognize the park that had been named after him. The discreet plaque was installed in 1988, the park's centenary year. As you continue along the seawall, you'll also see the impressive visage of Vancouver's most famous bridge looming ahead of you.

- Re-attaching your neck after all that bridge craning, you'll round one of the seawall's narrowest corners here and find yourself at Prospect Point. There a little whitewashed lighthouse nestled on your left, although it's not quite as picturesque as its Brockton Point sister. The rock face rises steeply behind the lighthouse, with trees tenaciously hanging from the almost sheer wall. This is the area of Stanley Park that was most affected by the 2006 storm when an estimated 10,000 trees were blown down. If you take a floatplane ride over the park, you'll see how much this side of the forest has thinned out.

- Continue following the seawall west and within 1 mile/1.6 kilometres, you'll round a corner where the shoreline is dominated by a volcanic crag known as Siwash Rock. This tall outcropping looks like a rough-hewn bowling pin, but according to local First Nations myth, it is the transformed spirit of an unselfish man, preserved in this way to honor him. This stretch also displays a plaque dedicated to stonemason James Cunningham, who built the seawall, and whose ashes are buried in the wall itself.

- The wind will likely be whipping at your face here, coming in off the strait on your right, so turn your collar up and continue along the track to Third Beach for a welcome rest. This sandy expanse is an idyllic rustic treasure just a few minutes from the heart of the city. Popular with sunbathers, and a much-loved promontory for sunset watching, it's one of the park's best attractions. There's a concession stand and restrooms just above the beach.

## Back Story: Bridge to Nowhere

By the time you pass under it, you'll be almost overwhelmed by the scale of the Lions Gate Bridge. Closely resembling a green-painted version of San Francisco's much larger Golden Gate, this soaring steel span—officially named the First Narrows Bridge—was opened in 1938 and was a private project funded by the Guinness family. At the time, there seemed little reason to build it: there was already ferry service to the North Shore, and the bridge led to an underdeveloped area. But Guinness family members had bought large swathes of land across Burrard Inlet and were creating an upscale new housing development called the British Properties. While some locals argued the bridge would ruin the park—a large causeway had to be cut through the trees to service it—the 5,890-foot/1,823-metre crossing was officially opened by King George VI and Queen Elizabeth on their 1939 cross-Canada royal visit. Though the Guinness family later sold the bridge to the province, they funded the 1986 installation of lights that now give the span a festive nighttime glow.

- If you're really hungry, continue along the seawall to Ferguson Point and take the signposted side trail uphill to the left of the main seawall drag. It'll take you straight to the Teahouse. In a casual but elegant landmark building, the restaurant focuses on Pacific Northwest cuisine with fusion twists: think maple-glazed salmon or curried BC mussels with lemongrass. If it's warm, snag a table on the patio for panoramic views of English Bay. Keep in mind that there's another, even more celebrated, restaurant coming up.

- Head back down to the seawall and continue south. It won't be long before you hit the park's other main beach. A little more accessible (and crowded) than its Third Beach neighbor, Second Beach is a traditional gathering spot for families drawn to its picnic area and playground. If you don't fancy dipping in the briny water here, there's also a large waterfront heated pool that seems to attract almost every child in the city on balmy summer days. If it's too crowded, continue on your way: the seawall takes you around the seafront side of the swimming pool—look for Point Grey and Kitsilano across the water.

- Leave the seawall here, stroll east through the Second Beach parking lot and wander along Lagoon Dr. Within a couple of minutes you'll reach the Fish House in Stanley Park on your right. The park's best fine-dining restaurant, it's an ideal spot to reward your seawall exploration. Dedicated to delectably prepared regional seafood, it's also part of BC's Ocean Wise sustainable fishing initiative. This gable-roofed eatery is set in a lovely landscaped garden; it's like a large English cottage in the countryside. Built in 1930, this was originally the park's Sports Pavilion clubhouse and it now serves an ever-changing seasonal menu with highlights like warm salmon salad, cedar planked arctic char, and sticky chili sablefish.

- If you've had your fill, continue east along Lagoon Dr. Within a few minutes, you'll be at the park's main W. Georgia St. entrance.

# POINTS OF INTEREST

**Second Beach Swimming Pool** Stanley Park Dr., 604-257-8371

**The Teahouse** Ferguson Point, 604-669-3281

**Fish House in Stanley Park** 8901 Stanley Park Dr., 604-681-7275

# route summary

1. Start at Lumberman's Arch.
2. Turn left along the seawall.
3. Follow the seawall northwest to Prospect Point.
4. Follow the seawall southwest to Siwash Rock.
5. Follow the seawall south to Third Beach.
6. Follow the seawall south to Ferguson Point.
7. Follow the seawall southeast to Second Beach.
8. Cut through the Second Beach parking lot to the Fish House in Stanley Park.
9. Continue along Lagoon Dr. to the park's main W. Georgia St. entrance.

*Stanley Park seawall*

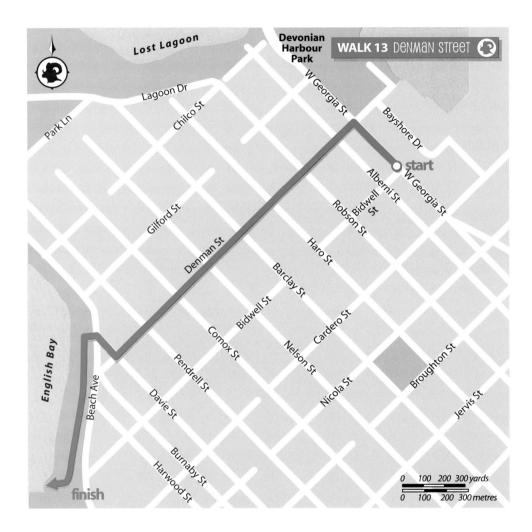

Lost Lagoon

Devonian
Harbour
Park

Lagoon Dr

Park Ln

Chilco St

W Georgia St

Bayshore Dr

start

W Georgia St

Alberni St

Bidwell St

Robson St

Gilford St

Haro St

Denman St

Barclay St

Comox St

Bidwell St

Cardero St

Nelson St

Pendrell St

English Bay

Beach Ave

Davie St

Nicola St

Broughton St

Jervis St

Burnaby St

Harwood St

finish

0   100   200  300 yards
0   100   200  300 metres

# 13 DENMAN STREET: ART, FOOD AND AN OCEAN STROLL

BOUNDARIES: **W. Georgia St., Denman St., English Bay**
DISTANCE: **½ mile/¾ kilometre**
DIFFICULTY: **Easy**
PARKING: **There's a parking lot at the north foot of Denman St., abutting Devonian Harbour Park There's also metered street parking on Alberni St. and the side streets radiating from Denman.**
PUBLIC TRANSIT: **Bus 5 runs along Robson and Denman Sts. Bus 6 runs along nearby Davie St.**

Colorful Denman St., one of the West End's main thoroughfares, must have more eateries than any other in the city. In fact, there are so many places to stuff your face on this bustling strip that locals need the proximity of Stanley Park to ensure they jog off their excess on a daily basis. But Denman is not just about noshing. The only Vancouver hockey team to win the Stanley Cup used to play at a stadium near its northern end; there's an evocative reminder of Expo '86 near its southern end; and the street leads straight into English Bay, one of the city's favorite beachside playgrounds. Having said all that: you'd be nuts not to eat something while you're here, so this walk is liberally sprinkled with first-hand foodie recommendations.

● **Start on the north side of W. Georgia St., just past the intersection with Bidwell St. Strolling west in the shadow of the Bayshore condo towers, keep an eye on the manicured landscaping and burbling water features on your right. The Japanese maples here produce a riot of scarlet foliage in the fall. Look out for a little walkway that disappears between them. Detour down this a few steps to find a hidden public artwork comprising a lifelike adult horse with a gangly foal peering at you from the bushes.**

● **Return to W. Georgia and continue west a few more steps. You'll soon come to Douglas Senft's *Leaf Stream* artwork, a series of large, overlapping bronze maple leaves enlivened by the gentle percolation of water along its slight incline—ironically, the real leaves that rain on this installation every fall tend to clog its natural flow. There are some benches clustered around the feature where you can sit and watch the W. Georgia St. traffic failing to move toward the often-clogged Stanley Park Causeway.**

● Maintaining a westerly amble, cross Denman St. and nip onto the paved southeast corner of Devonian Harbour Park. Surrounded by a crescent of flowery borders and verdant palm trees, you'll catch sight of an elderly lady seated on a park bench searching through her handbag. She looks a little stiff. And kind of shiny. Which is not surprising since she's made of cast bronze. This life-size public artwork is a popular tourist photo op. Illustrating the affection she triggers, a little posy of real flowers is often present in her cupped hands. Sports fans might also like to recall that the Denman Arena, home of the old Vancouver Millionaires hockey team, once occupied a site near here. The stadium burned down in 1936, leaving locals with fond memories of the city's one and only (so far) Stanley Cup win in 1915.

● Re-cross Denman St. and then cross south over W. Georgia St. Stroll past the bike rental outfits on the left side of Denman, then take the crosswalk at Alberni St. to Denman's right-hand sidewalk. Continue south on this side. This is the start of Denman's restaurant row, with almost every business here tempting your taste buds with lunch and dinner specials. In the next few seconds, you'll pass a romantic French bistro, a clamorous Mongolian barbecue joint and a couple of Japanese noodle eateries that attract crowds of chattering language students.

● Continue south along Denman, crossing the end of Robson St. The incline is a little steeper here but there are even more restaurants if you need a respite. If it's winter, consider some stick-to-the-ribs perogies and cabbage rolls at Ukrainian Village on your right or nip across the street for a good-value Montreal-style barbecue chicken meal at Rooster's Quarters. If you need to satisfy your sweet tooth, continue on to True Confections at the intersection with Haro St. There are usually a couple of dozen freshly made giant desserts winking at you in the display cabinet, such as hazelnut Belgian mousse gateaux, white-chocolate raspberry cheesecake, and deep-dish banana cream pie.

● Cross Haro St. and walk farther south on Denman past the West End Community Centre on your left. While this main West End drag is lined with shops and businesses and locals bustling between them, peer along the side streets and you'll see rows of mid-sized apartment buildings, many built during a burst of concrete tower construction in the 1950s. Not all the buildings here are from that era, though. On your right, before the Barclay St. intersection, is a large heritage-designated yellow and blue Art Deco building. Original home of the old art house Starlight Theatre, it was built in 1938 and now houses restaurants and shops.

● Pass the large palm tree at the corner of Barclay St.—stay on the right side of Denman if you want to avoid the lure of the Funorama candy shop calling to you from across the street—then pick up the pace. You've likely sensed the proximity of the sea not far ahead.

Before you strip down and run for the waves, though, check out the menu of Raincity Grill, on your right at the intersection with Morton Ave. This place pioneered the idea of the 100-mile diet, sourcing the best regional ingredients for its menu, long before it became fashionable among other area restaurants. Drop in and make a dinner reservation for later. Delectable dishes like Fraser Valley duck and Queen Charlotte halibut and a BC wine list that may be the best in the city are highlights. Alternatively, poke your head through the unlikely takeout window at the front of the restaurant where daily gourmet picnic specials like salmon sandwiches or fish and chips are offered for around $10. The beach is not far, so takeout is an ideal option.

● With the sea breeze licking at your face here, delay the pleasure by taking a sharp right west along Morton Ave. Crane your neck at the tall apartment towers on your right and you'll see that one of the top floor penthouses has a very large tree growing in its patio garden. You'll soon be standing outside one of the city's most character-filled old inns. The ivy-covered, brick-built Sylvia Hotel was constructed as an apartment block in 1912. Before the 1950s building boom, this handsome seven-story brownstone dominated the West End skyline. Its waterfront rooms look out over English Bay, but if you haven't booked a room, you can still enjoy the stunning view from the hotel's comfy lounge.

● You've been teased enough: it's now time to hit the water. Cross Beach Ave. and the seawall walkway and you'll come to the sandy crescent gently curving around English Bay. The panoramic views of the strait are among the best in the city and this beach is also one of the most popular: in summer, finding a patch of sand to call your own is a challenge. It's completely different off-season, when you might even have the beach all to yourself. Except on January 1st, that is, when hundreds of locals jump into the icy brine en masse during the annual Polar Bear Swim. It's been a tradition here since 1917.

● Pull up a log and enjoy the views here, or continue your southward walk along the sand. On your left is the boxy old English Bay Bathhouse, with its castellated Art Deco architectural flourishes. Built in 1932, it once housed the original Vancouver Aquarium, which moved to Stanley Park in the 1950s. Restored and added to the city's heritage list in 2004, the building now houses restroom and change facilities for swimmers.

● Continue past the bathhouse and within a couple of minutes you'll reach the end of the beach. Keep walking south onto the little grassy promontory that juts out like an elbow into the water. Lined with ocean-facing benches that are ideal for quiet maritime reflection—that's Kitsilano across the water—the main attraction here is the towering Inukshuk stone figure that dominates the park. Created for Expo '86, where it was displayed at the Northwest Territories Pavilion, this sculpture is based on a traditional Inuit navigational aid that now symbolizes hospitality.

## POINTS OF INTEREST

**Ukrainian Village** 815 Denman St., 604-687-7440

**Rooster's Quarters** 836 Denman St., 604-689-8023

**True Confections** 866 Denman St., 604-682-1292

**Raincity Grill** 1193 Denman St., 604-685-7337

**Sylvia Hotel** 1154 Gilford St., 604-681-9321

# route summary

1. Start on the north side of W. Georgia St., just past the Bidwell St. intersection.

2. Continue west on W. Georgia.

3. Cross to the west side of Denman St.

4. Return to the east side of Denman.

5. Cross over W. Georgia, staying on the left side of Denman.

6. Continue south on Denman until the intersection with Alberni St.

7. Take the crosswalk over to the right side of Denman.

8. Continue south on this side of Denman.

9. Cross to the left side of Denman at the Haro St. intersection.

10. Re-cross Denman.

11. Stay on the right side of Denman until Morton Ave.

12. Turn right along Morton.

13. Cross over Beach Ave. to the waterfront.

14. Continue south along the sand.

15. Follow the waterfront south until you reach the Inukshuk figure.

*Inukshuk figure in English Bay*

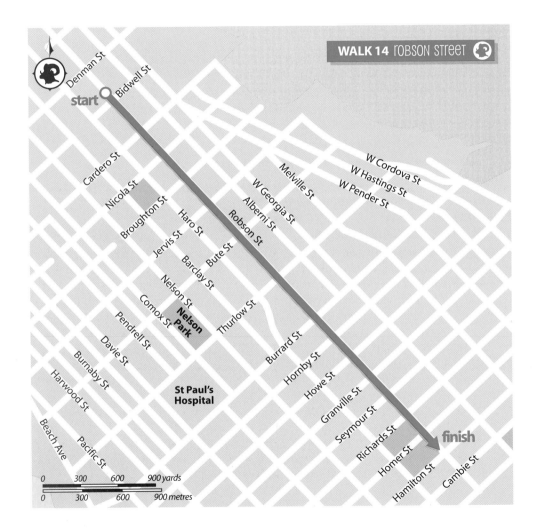

Denman St

start

Bidwell St

Cardero St

Nicola St

Broughton St

Haro St

Jervis St

Bute St

Robson St

Alberni St

W Georgia St

Melville St

W Cordova St

W Hastings St

W Pender St

Barclay St

Nelson St

Comox St

Pendrell St

Davie St

Burnaby St

Harwood St

Beach Ave

Pacific St

**Nelson Park**

Thurlow St

Burrard St

Hornby St

Howe St

Granville St

Seymour St

Richards St

Homer St

Hamilton St

Cambie St

**St Paul's Hospital**

finish

0    300    600    900 yards

0    300    600    900 metres

# 14 robson street: grand shopping thoroughfare

BOUNDARIES: **Denman St., Robson St., Hamilton St.**
DISTANCE: **1¼ miles/2 kilometres**
DIFFICULTY: **Easy**
PARKING: **There's a parkade at the Empire Landmark Hotel in the 1400 block of Robson St. There's also metered street parking on the side streets along Robson and on Alberni St., which runs parallel.**
PUBLIC TRANSIT: **Bus 5 runs along Robson.**

Jostling with the international tourists along Vancouver's favorite shopping promenade on a balmy summer's afternoon may not be everyone's idea of a great day out, but it's an echo of the fact that Robson St. has always been a cosmopolitan thoroughfare. Legions of German immigrants colonized this stretch in the 19th century, creating a teeming "Little Germany" of pastry cafés and grocery stores hawking schnitzel and sauerkraut. The area's continental feel—it was known as "Robsonstrasse" for many years—was cemented for decades by now-forgotten businesses like European News and Mozart Konditorei. As the German immigrants moved away or died out, many of the usual generic chain stores took their spots. But the street's original international élan was not lost forever: in recent years, the western end of Robson has been colonized by a host of colorful Asian shops and eateries. Expect to shop while you're strolling the area today, but beware—just because Robson occupies the priciest property square on Canada's Monopoly game board doesn't mean you have to act as if you've just passed "Go."

● You'll start on the left-hand side of Robson St. in the 1700 block, just past the intersection with Denman. This stretch is lined with little sushi, izakaya, and noodle cafés that reflect the neighborhood's surfeit of English language schools aimed at traveling international students. You'll see many of these youngsters hanging around the street corners between classes. Robo Sushi and Jang Mo Jib (its bibimbap dish is recommended) are justifiably popular.

● Continue east up the slight incline of Robson. Cross over to the right side at Bidwell St. and you'll soon come to Robson Street Public Market. Don't get too excited, it's not nearly as enticing as its sister markets at Granville Island and Lonsdale Quay. But if you're looking for a pizza slice or a Nanaimo bar treat (who isn't?), nip inside. The glass building echoes the shape of Victorian London's Crystal Palace.

- Continuing east on Robson, cross Cardero St. and then Nicola St. On your right is the concrete tower of the Empire Landmark Hotel. The property's highlight is its Cloud 9 revolving bar and restaurant on the 42nd floor. It's a quirky spot to head for a drink and you'll be looking down on almost every other building in the vicinity, including some rooftop gardens that most Vancouverites don't even know are there.

- Return to terra firma and continue east. Check out the Listel Hotel a few steps along on your right—it's self-proclaimed as Vancouver's artiest hotel. Head into the lobby and take the first turn to your left up the stairs. Here you'll find a little hidden gallery displaying an ever-changing selection of curated exhibits, often including sculptures, large canvases, or naturalistic photography. Follow the corridor into the hotel's adjoining O'Doul's Restaurant & Bar. This is a recommended weekend brunch spot but it's also worth coming back at night when the place is enlivened by free jazz shows.

- Leave O'Douls and continue east along Robson. Scratch your chin at the bizarre public artwork on the corner of Jervis St. It looks like a couple of coils from a giant orange Slinky. Continue on this side of Robson for a couple more minutes and drop into Minna-No-Konbiniya, a colorful Japanese convenience store. Every Pocky stick flavor you can imagine (from coconut chocolate to green tea) is here along with unfamiliar soft drinks just begging to be tried. Sample the unfortunately named Calpis and Pocari Sweat, or pick up a hot can of sweetened coffee.

- Stay on this side of the street and continue east across Bute St. This is the heart of Robson's chain store strip, including such luminaries as Aritzia, Guess, Esprit, and American Eagle. Expect to be pushing past crowds of teenagers here, enjoying mall shopping without the mall. You'll also catch a few buskers. If you're looking for lunch or dinner, the entrance to CinCin Ristorante—the easy-to-miss stairway through the terracotta-red archway on your right—is here. A popular spot for spotting celebs, the Tuscan-accented restaurant serves the best gourmet pizzas in town.

A couple of doors along, drop by Lululemon Athletica, the Vancouver-based international chain that made yoga wear a fashion for people who wouldn't know a lotus position from a hole in the wall. This is its flagship downtown store. When it opened in 2003, the owner dared customers to queue naked outside for a discount and dozens dutifully obliged. The offer is closed now, so try to keep your skivvies on when you stroll through the entrance.

● Continue on to the intersection with Thurlow St.—reputedly the only corner in Canada where two Starbucks outlets face each other—and cross over to the left side of Robson. After some casual window shopping among the shoe shops and clothing boutiques, drop into Rocky Mountain Chocolate Factory on your left. The chocolatiers can often be seen mixing their latest confections in a large copper bowl in the window. Even if you don't buy anything, you have to admire the artistry of their decorated candy apples and the sheer decadence of their brick-sized fudge slabs.

● Continue east on the same side, crossing over Burrard St. at the next intersection. Immediately ahead of you is the giant HMV store. The building—one of the city's best Modernist structures—was Vancouver's main public library from 1957 until 1995, and its offices now include the local newsroom of the *Globe and Mail*. Before you pass on, nip north along the Burrard St. face of the building. At its northwest corner, look up and you'll find an unusual abstract sculpture adorning the exterior. Called *Symbols of the Cruciform*, it's by Lionel Thomas.

● Return to Robson, turn left and continue east. Cross Hornby St. and on your left is the Vancouver Art Gallery. Pass by the stone stairway and turn left toward the gallery's main entrance. Before you go in, look up and catch the three unlikely boat models perched on the building's roof corners. The VAG is the city's leading downtown cultural attraction. There's usually at least one blockbuster show a year here. Check out the shop on the ground floor: it's full of tempting artsy trinkets and is a good place to pick-up your Museum of Modern Art Christmas cards. In summer, the patio of the mezzanine level Gallery Café is an excellent spot for lunch or coffee.

● From here, you can access the Pacific Centre shopping mall via the Sears department store across Howe St. or continue your leisurely eastward stroll along Robson. Within five minutes, you'll cross Homer St. and will be facing the soaring visage of the "new" Vancouver Public Library that replaced the one on Burrard. One of downtown's most distinctive landmarks, this curving, Coliseum-shaped structure was designed by Moshe Safdie. Despite appearing undeniably grand, it's a highly welcoming space. The library is often used as a movie set and was transformed into the headquarters of a cloning factory in the futuristic Arnold Schwarzenegger flick *The 6th Day* in 2000. There's a coffee shop near the entrance where you can rest your trek-weary feet.

## POINTS OF INTEREST

**Robo Sushi** 1709 Robson St., 604-684-3353

**Jang Mo Jib** 1715 Robson St., 604-687-0712

**Robson Street Public Market** 1610 Robson St., 604-682-2733

**Empire Landmark Hotel** 1400 St., 604-687-0511

**Listel Hotel** 1300 Robson St., 604-684-8461

**O'Doul's Restaurant & Bar** 1300 Robson St., 604-661-1400

**Minna-No-Konbiniya** 1238 Robson St., 604-682-3634

**CinCin Ristorante** 1154 Robson St., 604-688-7338

**Lululemon Athletica** 1148 Robson St., 604-681-3118

**HMV** 1160 Robson St., 604-685-9203

**Vancouver Art Gallery** 750 Hornby St., 604-688-2233

**Vancouver Public Library** 350 W. Georgia St., 604-331-3603

# route summary

1. Start in the 1700 block of Robson, just past the intersection with Denman St.

2. Head east on the left side of Robson.

3. Cross to the right side of Robson at Bidwell St.

4. Continue east on this side of Robson.

5. Cross to the left side of Robson at Thurlow St.

6. Continue east on this side of Robson to the intersection with Burrard St.

7. Cross east at this intersection and walk half a block north along Burrard.

8. Return to Robson and continue east.

9. Continue east on the left side of Robson until you reach the Vancouver Public Library, just past the intersection with Homer St.

*Vancouver Public Library*

start

Denman St
W Georgia St
Bidwell St
Cardero St
Nicola St
Haro St
Broughton St
Jervis St
Melville St
W Cordova St
W Hastings St
W Pender St
Alberni St
Robson St
Barclay St
Nelson St
Comox St
Bute St
Thurlow St
Pendrell St
Nelson Park
finish
Burrard St
Davie St
Hornby St
Howe St
W Georgia St
Burnaby St
St Paul's Hospital
Smithe St
Granville St
Seymour St
Richards St
Harwood St
Homer St
Hamilton St
Pacific St
Cambie St
Beach Ave

0    300    600    900 yards
0    300    600    900 metres

# 15 WeST eND: SaVING HISTOrY ONe HOUSe aT a TIMe

**BOUNDARIES:** **Bidwell St., Haro St., Thurlow St, Comox St.**
**DISTANCE:** **1 mile/1½ kilometres**
**DIFFICULTY:** **Easy**
**PARKING:** **There is a parking lot on Robson St., near the intersection with Bidwell. There is also metered street parking throughout the West End.**
**PUBLIC TRANSIT:** **Bus 5 runs along nearby Robson and Denman Sts. Bus 6 runs along nearby Davie St.**

Once a dense woodland abutting what later became Stanley Park, the West End was acquired in the 1860s by three Brits who hoped to establish a brick-making factory. Their overly ambitious plans came to naught and the three—known as "The Three Greenhorns" due to their commercial naivety—sold the claim at a loss to developers. When the Canadian Pacific Railway later established its Western terminus in Coal Harbour, on the area's north shore, the forested swathe suddenly became highly desirable. Within a few years, the West End was Vancouver's poshest neighborhood, lined with stone, and wood-built mansions. However, by the turn of the 19th century, so many people were living here it had lost its exclusive luster. The new Shaughnessy Heights development beckoned and the well-to-do packed up their monogrammed suitcases and decamped across town. The mansions they left behind were transformed into apartments or torn down—especially in the 1950s, when tower blocks made the West End reputedly North America's most densely populated neighborhood. It's still home to thousands of Vancouverites, including a large gay community. The old homes that survived the purge are now among the city's most expensive. Strolling here today, you'll find an Aladdin's cave of these magnificent clapboard buildings.

● You'll start on Bidwell St. in the short stretch between Nelson and Barclay Sts. On the east side of this tree-studded thoroughfare, you'll find three handsome heritage homes. This is your introduction to the area's collection of magnificent turn-of-the-19th-century houses, many now protected by preservation orders.

● Point yourself south and turn left onto Nelson. Head east for two blocks, checking out another nest of cozy-looking, gable-topped homes crowding the intersection with Cardero St. At the southwest corner of Nicola St., the next intersection, you'll come to the busy No. 6 Fire Hall that has jurisdiction over all this pretty kindling. Sensibly brick-built in 1907, this gabled, double-doored shed was one of the first in North America specifically designed for motorized fire trucks. You'll usually see two shiny vintage or newer models parked and ready out front. Refurbished in 1988, the fire hall is now also on the city's heritage list.

● Head north along Nicola and take the next right onto Barclay St. While it seems a no-brainer today to protect the West End's historic homes, the battle to achieve this level of preservation took place right here only a few years ago. The crumbling houses in this area were acquired by the Vancouver Parks Board in the 1960s and were slated to be cleared and replaced with a small urban park. History-minded locals created an ad hoc coalition of Heritage Canada, the Community Arts Council, and celebrated national historian Pierre Berton. A compromise was eventually reached: a smaller park was created and nine of the old houses were saved.

● Cross over to the other side of Barclay and stroll east. On your left will be the corner plot of the sky-blue, deep-verandahed Weeks House. It was built in 1896 for George Weeks who was the manager of the city's main Hudson's Bay department store.

Next door is the even more ornate mustard-yellow Barclay Manor, the oldest house on the block. Check out the stained glass windows and filigree woodwork on the gables. Built in 1890, this was originally the home of Charles Tetley, the city's chief accountant. This property has a long and intriguing history: it was transformed into a private hospital in 1908, before becoming a residence for Catholic working girls a few years later. In the 1920s, it changed its purpose again: like many of the West End's larger homes, it was converted into a rooming house under the name Barclay Manor. It's now a senior center.

● Next up, also on your left, is the little park that almost gobbled up the entire block. Now a popular neighborhood hangout, it's a great spot to perch on a park bench and reflect on the evocative perimeter of historic houses. On the east side of the grassy

## Back Story: roedde House rumble

Designed by Francis Rattenbury, the noted English architect who created many of BC's signature buildings, this green-painted treasure is the centerpiece of Barclay Heritage Square. Built in 1893 for the Roedde family of printers and bookbinders, the large Queen Anne–style mansion includes an ornate cupola and an array of deep bay windows. Uniquely among the area's antique houses, its interior is accessible for history buffs to check out. Opened as Vancouver's only house museum in 1984, the meticulously recreated, richly decorated period rooms include cozy bedrooms, a lavish parlor, and a utensil-forested kitchen. Staffed by volunteers, it's worth dropping by on summer Sundays when tours of the house include tea in the garden. At Christmas the interior is decorated in full Victorian finery.

square is Roedde House, the handsome architectural gem that inspired the preservation campaign.

- Continue east along Barclay and take the next turn left onto Broughton St. You'll pass three identical heritage homes on your left in the 800 block. These houses were built around the turn of the 19th century and one of them was owned by expat Scot Malcolm MacLean, Vancouver's first mayor. Although he never lived in the house, he's remembered for pioneering the re-building of the city after the 1886 fire. These homes look comfortably lived-in today and you can expect to see a languid cat or two sunning themselves on the deep porches here.

- Turn right at the next intersection onto Haro St. and stroll east. On either side of you are the 1950s concrete towers that replaced much of the West End's original housing stock. With immaculate gardens and kitsch names like Ocean Towers, Greatview Manor and the Caribbean, some of these Modernist-Futurist towers have in recent years gained their own following among architecture buffs.

- Continue east along Haro, crossing Jervis, and turn right into the paved park space that links two sections of Bute St. Stroll south and then take the next turn left onto

Barclay St., continuing east downhill on Barclay. Within a couple of minutes on your right—hidden behind a tall, deciduous hedge—you'll come to the 'O Canada' House. Now a sumptuous, antique-lined B&B, this clapboard 1897 Queen Anne–style home was built for bank president Ewing Buchan. The house's name commemorates Buchan's patriotism, which led him to compose English language lyrics to the tune that became "O Canada." One of several English versions, Buchan's was not chosen as the official version. Despite its provenance, the house was designated for demolition in 1995—an extensive renovation saved it and the project won a city heritage award two years later.

● Continue east along Barclay and turn right at the next intersection onto Thurlow St. Head south uphill here, passing the handsome Biltmore apartment building on your right, and then cross over Nelson St. You're now in Nelson Park, one of the West End's most popular grassy hangouts. Redeveloped in 2007, it's well-used by locals, some of whom garden in the small plots dotting its flanks. On Saturdays from May to early October, the park's southern edge is the home of the West End Farmers Market. You can expect to find aromatic BC chanterelles, sweet strawberries, and luscious Okanagan peaches and nectarines here, depending on the month.

● Whether there's a market or not, head to the park's southern side to conclude your visit. The immaculate heritage homes—they look like they've just been built—on this Comox St. stretch comprise the other area of old West End houses that were threatened by Vancouver Parks Board demolition a few years ago. The threat triggered a standoff when locals defended the need to retain affordable housing in the area, but it wasn't until 1999 that the city eventually agreed. The Mole Hill Community Housing Society opened its first fully renovated heritage homes, painted in historically authentic colors, on this strip in 2003. It now provides subsidized rental properties to singles, couples, and families.

# POINTS OF INTEREST

**Roedde House** 1415 Barclay St., 604-684-7040

**West End Farmers Market** Nelson Park, 1100 block of Comox St.

**'O Canada' House** 1114 Barclay St., 604-688-0555

# ROUTE SUMMARY

1. Start on Bidwell St., between Barclay and Nelson Sts.
2. Head south and turn left onto Nelson.
3. Continue east on Nelson for two blocks.
4. Turn left along Nicola St.
5. Turn right onto Barclay St.
6. Head east on Barclay.
7. Turn left along Broughton St.
8. Turn right onto Haro St.
9. Continue east on Haro for two blocks.
10. Turn right along Bute St.
11. Turn left onto Barclay St.
12. Continue east on Barclay.
13. Turn right along Thurlow St.
14. Continue south along Thurlow.
15. Turn right along Comox St.

*Barclay Manor*

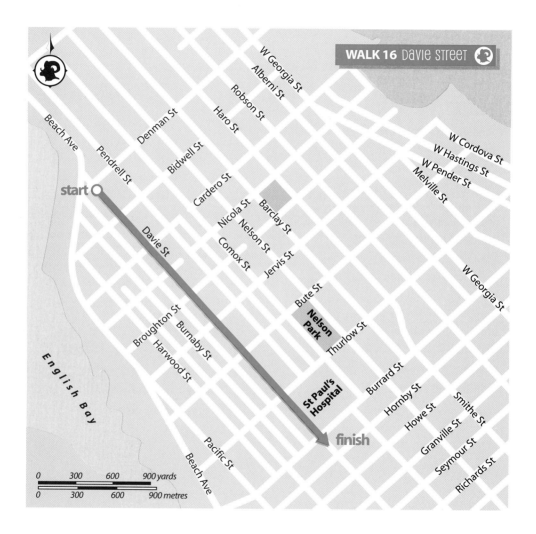

W Georgia St
Alberni St
Robson St
Haro St
Denman St
Bidwell St
Cardero St
Nicola St
Barclay St
Nelson St
Comox St
Jervis St

Beach Ave
Pendrell St
Davie St

start

W Cordova St
W Hastings St
W Pender St
Melville St

W Georgia St

Bute St

**Nelson Park**

Thurlow St

Broughton St
Burnaby St
Harwood St

Burrard St

Hornby St

Howe St

Smithe St

Granville St

Seymour St

Richards St

**St Paul's Hospital**

finish

**English Bay**

Pacific St
Beach Ave

0   300   600   900 yards
0   300   600   900 metres

# 16 Davie Street: The Gay Village

BOUNDARIES: **Denman St., Davie St., Burrard St.**
DISTANCE: **1 mile/1½ kilometres**
DIFFICULTY: **Easy**
PARKING: **There's a parking lot in the 1200 block of Davie St. There's also metered street parking on Davie and along its side streets.**
PUBLIC TRANSIT: **Bus 5 stops on nearby Denman St. Bus 6 runs the length of Davie St.**

One of the main commercial spines of the West End for the last few decades, the clamorous Davie St. thoroughfare was named after A.E.B. Davie, the province's eighth premier. Around the time of his premiership, the area was slowly becoming Vancouver's first exclusive neighborhood with palatial mansions for well-to-do families dotting the woodlands overlooking English Bay. When the rich moved on to other parts of the city and the working classes moved in to colonize the old streets, the Davie strip was soon lined with busy neighborhood shops and bustling mid-price restaurants, gradually transforming it into a local high street. The area developed a third identity in the 1970s, when Vancouver's gay community began calling this part of town home. Known as Davie Village, the street forms part of the route for the annual Pride Parade where every summer around 500,000 Vancouverites—gay and gay-friendly—join in the city's biggest Mardi Gras-style party event, complete with marching bands, more than 150 floats, and the Dykes on Bikes motorcade crew. Strolling the colorful Davie stretch today, you'll find plenty of browse-worthy shops and eateries along with several vivid reminders of the area's historic past.

● **You'll start at the intersection of Davie and Denman Sts. Turn your back on the English Bay waterfront and flex your calf muscles on the eastward uphill stroll along the right side of Davie. You'll pass cheap and cheerful restaurants and chatty neighborhood grocery stores serving residents of the dozens of older apartment buildings in the area. You'll also notice that many of the bus shelters and garbage cans are painted pink, while businesses and streetlamps sport rainbow-colored flags and decals: this shock of color announces your entry into Vancouver's gay village, one of the largest in North America.**

## Back story: The West's End's very own Palace

Built in 1900 for expat New Yorker and sugar refining baron Benjamin Rogers (he was known as the "Sugar King" and his products are still readily available in stores here), Gabriola Mansion was reputedly the most opulent in the city. Designed by Samuel Maclure, its textured, decorated exterior was built from sandstone cut from the Strait of Georgia island that bears its name. The home was an elaborate confection of leaded windows, a grand carriageway entrance, and a circular corner porch that overlooked lavishly landscaped gardens. When Rogers died in 1918, his widow moved to the swanky new Shaughnessy Heights neighborhood, following most of the other bluebloods who had abandoned the West End. Gabriola Mansion is a reminder that this area was once studded with palatial homes built for the well-to-do, the kind of men who grew extremely wealthy from forestry, coal, and commodity shipping. Many of their estates were unceremoniously cleared for the new apartment-building wave of the 1950s. Gabriola Mansion is one of the very few to remain. Designated as a heritage building in 1974, it has been restored and reinvented, most recently as a restaurant.

● Continuing east, take the first turn right onto Bidwell St. Tucked around the corner, you'll find one of the area's most unusual old buildings. Now occupied by a steakhouse and burlesque cabaret known as Maxine's Hideaway, this yellow-painted 1920s Spanish Revival mansion has a colorful past, which includes doing time as both a beauty school and a rather exotic rooming house. The building was even a brothel for a few years, complete with stories of secret tunnels running from some of the nearby mansions directly to the building's basement. Rumor has is that a ghost or two haunts the building.

● Cross to the left side of Davie here and continue east. Just before the intersection with Nicola St., you'll come to Gabriola Mansion, the West End's best-looking heritage pad and a reminiscent echo of the upper crust who originally made this Vancouver's most exclusive neighborhood.

- Continue east on Davie and you'll cross Nicola and Broughton Sts—the steepest part of the climb—before leveling off just before Jervis St. Cross over and turn right along Jervis for a quick peek at two of the area's best-looking old apartment buildings, both constructed before the concrete boom. Facing each other at the top of Jervis, these magnificent red-brick complexes—Blenheim Court and Jervis Lodge—recall heritage New York apartments.

- Return to Davie and maintain your eastward amble into the bustling heart of the Davie Village "gayborhood." You can expect to see plenty of same-sex couples strolling around holding hands here. If it's time for a pit stop, half a block past the Jervis intersection on your right you'll find Melriches Coffeehouse. Its elderly mismatched dark wood tables and chairs make it instantly cozy, especially on rainy days when you'll find a handful of java addicts hunkered in the corners.

  Interested trekkers should also consider nipping into next door's Little Sister's Book & Art Emporium. A long-established resource for the local gay, lesbian, bisexual, and transgendered community, this busy shop sells everything from classic gay literature to sex toys and even wedding gifts: after Canada legalized same-sex marriage in 2005, Vancouver quickly became one of the world's top gay-wedding destinations.

- Continue east along Davie, crossing Bute St. Among the many mid-priced restaurants lining this area, you'll soon come to Stepho's Greek Taverna. Without any advertising, this eatery has gained a massive word-of-mouth following over the years. It's worth noting that while the food—think souvlaki, kleftico, and hummus—is little more than traditional fare, the reason the regulars keep coming back is the heaping, great value portions. If you haven't eaten all day and you're prepared to brave a line-up that often stretches down the street, this is the place for you. Once seated, order the roast lamb—it's always melt-in-the-mouth soft.

- Once you've readjusted your straining belt, waddle east along the right side of Davie. Cross Thurlow St. and you'll soon come to Marquis Wine Cellars, one of the city's best boutique wine shops. The knowledgeable staff here are friendly and helpful and there's a real snob-free approach to assisting. They also stage regular wine tastings and wine education events.

You're now in the nightlife heart of the gay village. Opposite Marquis Wine Cellars, you'll see the Fountainhead Pub. It's the neighborhood's fave hangout and the patio is usually teeming with drinkers on balmy summer evenings, when anyone and everyone is likely to get wolf-whistled as they stroll past. A little farther on, on the opposite side of Davie, you'll also spot Celebrities, one of the area's most popular gay nightclubs.

● If you're not feeling particularly gay on your visit, continue east and cross Burrard St. Just past the intersection on your left—the entrance is tiny, so it's easy to miss— you'll see Bin 941. This narrow little nook is one of the city's best tapas hangouts and it's often full right up to its 2 a.m. closing. It's a great place to chat with friends over sharing-plates of crab cakes, beef satay, or saucy mussels. There's also a good wine selection as well as bottles of ultra-strong Quebec beer. The perfect place to conclude your Davie St. stroll, you'll likely make a few new friends here: since you'll be elbow-to-elbow with the surrounding tables, it's hard not to start chatting with everyone around you.

## POINTS OF INTEREST

**Maxine's Hideaway** 1215 Bidwell St., 604-689-8822

**Melriches Coffeehouse** 1244 Davie St., 604-689-5282

**Little Sister's Book & Art Emporium** 1238 Davie St., 604-669-1753

**Stepho's Greek Taverna** 1124 Davie St., 604-683-2555

**Marquis Wine Cellars** 1034 Davie St., 604-684-0445

**Fountainhead Pub** 1025 Davie St., 604-687-2222

**Celebrities Nightclub** 1022 Davie St., 604-681-6180

**Bin 941** 941 Davie St., 604-683-1246

# route summary

1. Start at the intersection of Denman and Davie Sts.
2. Head east up Davie, on the right-hand sidewalk.
3. Turn right along Bidwell St.
4. Return to Davie St.
5. Cross to the north side of Davie and continue east.
6. Cross to the right side of Davie at Jervis.
7. Stroll half a block south on Jervis.
8. Return to Davie and turn right.
9. Continue east on the right side of Davie.
10. Cross to the left side of Davie at the Burrard St. intersection.

*Gabriola Mansion*

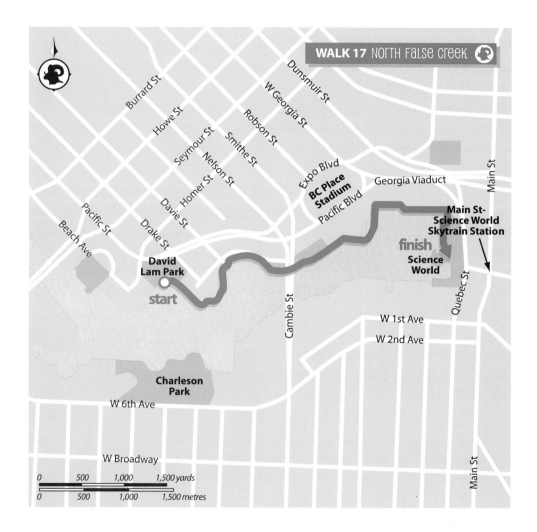

Burrard St

Howe St

W Georgia St

Dunsmuir St

Robson St

Seymour St

Smithe St

Nelson St

Homer St

Davie St

Expo Blvd

BC Place Stadium

Georgia Viaduct

Main St

Pacific St

Drake St

Pacific Blvd

Main St-
Science World
Skytrain Station

Beach Ave

David
Lam Park

finish

Science
World

start

Quebec St

Cambie St

W 1st Ave

W 2nd Ave

Charleson
Park

W 6th Ave

W Broadway

Main St

| 0 | 500 | 1,000 | 1,500 yards |
| 0 | 500 | 1,000 | 1,500 metres |

# 17 NORTH False Creek: Legacy of Expo '86

BOUNDARIES: **David Lam Park., Davie St., Marinaside Crescent, Quebec St.**
DISTANCE: **1¼ miles/2 kilometres**
DIFFICULTY: **Easy**
PARKING: **There's a parking lot on the 1300 block of Richards St., near the intersection with Drake St. It's a short walk south to David Lam Park.**
PUBLIC TRANSIT: **Buses C21 and C23 stop outside David Lam Park. Across the street from Science World is a SkyTrain station.**

Ask at the Tourist InfoCentre where the seawall is and they'll point you to Stanley Park, where you'll be jostling with camera-wielding tour groups and the kind of tottering cyclists that haven't been near a bike since the 1970s. Alternatively, consider a different but intriguing waterfront stretch that only Yaletown locals seem to know about. Originally one of Vancouver's grittiest areas, the north shore of False Creek was formerly an industrial ghetto of small factories and warehouses, clinging to the lifeline of the nearby Canadian Pacific Railway (CPR) freight terminal. With Depression-era decline killing off many of these businesses, the area sank into a grubby and ignominious shambles, becoming a no-go wasteland of squatter's hovels, rusting machinery, and abandoned shacks. But waterfront is waterfront, and False Creek received its long overdue re-launch when the giant Expo '86 world exposition took over the strip, replacing its seedy buildings with sparkling pavilions. Leaving a sanitized blank slate after the fair's conclusion, this post-Expo area eventually became a forest of condo towers complete with waterfront parks, public artworks, and a new seawall extension. Hit the trail with the Yaletowners to find out what makes the area tick—and to catch a few reminders of the past.

● You'll start at verdant David Lam Park, just off Pacific Blvd. Lining an elbow-shaped wedge of grassland at the neck of False Creek, this 10-acre/4-hectare space was named after a former BC Lieutenant Governor and was completed in stages between 1995 and 2003. The park slopes gently to the waterfront and is a popular spot for free open-air concerts during the annual Vancouver International Jazz Festival. Head straight to the waterfront, then follow the promenade east along with the local joggers and dog walkers.

- With the water on your right, follow the seawall for a few minutes to the edge of the park and you'll come to *Brush With Illumination,* an unusual public artwork by Buster Simpson that resides a few feet offshore. Resembling a giant Flash Gordon-like intergalactic ray gun, it's often topped with resting cormorants that treat it as a handy perch. It's worth keeping your eye on the water here, since aquatic birdlife often passes through this area. You'll likely also spot a few swift-moving kayakers and bobbling sailboats sliding past.

- Continuing along the seawall for a few more minutes, you'll come to Quayside Marina at the foot of Davie St. Those of us who don't own one of the shiny boats on display can pick up an Aquabus Ferry here and pootle off to several spots along both sides of False Creek. Onshore, the marina is semi-circled by shops and businesses. It used to be a hub of a different kind: the nearby Roundhouse Arts & Recreation Centre was a major CPR freight terminal for decades and goods were transferred here between boats, trains, and the surrounding warehouses. The only goods being moved around these days are macchiato orders at the Starbucks and yuppie grocery purchases at the chic Urban Fare supermarket. If you're looking for a nosh spot, Provence Marinaside here is one of those Vancouver restaurants that rarely get the kudos they deserve. Serving some of the best regionally sourced seafood in town, its highlight is the seafood platter, piled high with clams, lobster, mussels, scallops, and prawns.

- Once you've had your fishy fill, cross Marinaside Crescent back to the seawall. Almost directly in front of the restaurant, you'll see another public artwork, this one reflecting the area's once-dominant industries. Called *Lookout* and created by Chris Dikeakos and Noel Best, it's one of a three-part series—you'll spot the other two a little farther along. It's comprised of metal panels punched with images of shop tools, shoreline workers, and even a steam locomotive or two.

- The seawall takes a gentle southerly turn here alongside the boats, then curves back east: just keep following the path and you can't get lost. Looming ahead of you is the Cambie Bridge, but first you'll find one of the city's oddest public artworks, standing on the pebble-strewn shore to your right. Called *Time Top* and created by Jerry Pethick, it's a 1950s-style, tri-legged UFO, complete with a little glass-domed top. And just in case you're wondering what the imagined back story might be, there's a sci-fi comic strip embedded in the wall just in front to give you the lowdown.

## Back Story: Vancouver's Big Party

Coinciding with the city's centenary, Expo '86—the first time this author visited Canada—was a giant world exposition themed around transportation and communications (an early proposed name for the event was "Transpo '86."). With colorful pavilions from more than 50 countries, it was opened by the Prince and Princess of Wales, along with then-Prime Minister of Canada Brian Mulroney. The fair's highlights included a 650-foot/200-metre-long concrete highway sculpture bristling with full-size cars, bikes, and buses; a hall of priceless ancient Egyptian treasures; a gallery dedicated to Norwegian explorers; and a levitating magnetic train from Japan that visitors could ride. A huge success, the five-month fair attracted more than 22 million visitors. While there are few reminders of Expo on the site today, many of Vancouver's landmark buildings and infrastructure developments were built for the event, including Canada Place, Science World, and the SkyTrain system. Expo '86 is credited with putting the city on the world stage, but it also rehabilitated a lost area of the waterfront: without this event, the seawall promenade you're walking on would likely not be here today.

● Stay on the seawall and pass under the Cambie Bridge. The third and least picturesque of the three roads spans traversing False Creek, the first wooden version of this crossing was called the Connaught Bridge, although locals soon began calling it after the street it serviced. The bridge's second version was a steel span resembling the current Granville Bridge. It had a swing mechanism that opened for large boats to pass underneath. In 1915, this bridge, its deck inadvisably lined with creosoted wood, caught fire and a large section, complete with streetcar tracks, plunged into the water. After decades of precarious patch-ups, the present functional but aesthetically boring concrete span was opened in 1985 after a nine-month project that cost $50 million.

● Continuing east, you're now entering the heart of the old Expo '86 site, which transformed a 173-acre/70-hectare area that had long been a derelict wasteland. If you were at the event, close your eyes and try to remember the sights, sounds, and smells of that sunny summer all those years ago.

● With the water still on your right, continue along the seawall and you'll soon come to one of the area's biggest reminders of Expo '86. The Plaza of Nations was the fair's main open-air concert venue: Sheena Easton, the Beach Boys, and Johnny Cash all played here. While its glass canopy was removed in 2007 due to safety concerns, the site's original layout remains the same. The forest of poles here that once flew flags from around the world now displays the fluttering colors of Canada, BC and the busy Edgewater Casino that currently occupies the adjacent building. Sadly, the floating McDonald's restaurant that served Expo visitors here—dubbed the "McBarge"—was removed several years ago and now resides in derelict retirement in Burnaby.

● Follow the marked trail around the left side of the casino building and you'll soon be in the home stretch. Not the most picturesque section, the waterfront here is a little scrubby and in need of finishing but the trail is intact. On your left, you'll see General Motors Place stadium, the home of the Vancouver Canucks hockey team. If you have time, you can detour in here and visit the team shop or take a stadium tour.

● Alternatively, continue east along the shoreline, parallel with the SkyTrain line, and you'll pass a large open area that probably won't remain empty for too many more years. In the interim, when Cirque du Soleil comes to town, this is where they pitch their stripy tents.

● Dodge the surfeit of bikes sharing the trail with you here and round the corner right to one of Vancouver's most impressive landmarks. Science World—officially named Science World at Telus World of Science—is among Expo '86's best architectural legacies. Topped with a silver-mirrored geodesic dome sprinkled with 391 twinkling point lights at night, it was the fair's signature building and marked the entrance to the site. After a giant fund-raising campaign, the building was opened as Science World in 1988 and is now among the city's most popular family attractions. It's a good place to end your stroll: nip in and fill up at the White Spot restaurant, then catch a movie in the large-format Omnimax movie theatre. And if there aren't too many kids around, check out all the hands-on experiments on the second floor.

## POINTS OF INTEREST

**Provence Marinaside** 1177 Marinaside Crescent., 604-681-4144

**Edgewater Casino** 750 Pacific Blvd South., 604-687-3343

**General Motors Place** 800 Griffiths Way., 604-899-7400

**Science World** 1455 Quebec St., 604-443-7443

## ROUTE SUMMARY

1. Start at David Lam Park and stay on the seawall east.
2. Follow the seawall to Quayside Marina.
3. Pass under the Cambie Bridge.
4. Curve around the left side of Edgewater Casino.
5. Follow the seawall to Science World.

*Science World*

107

WALK 18 SOUTH FALSE CREEK

Burrard St
Howe St
W Georgia St
Robson St
Dunsmuir St
Seymour St
Smithe St
Nelson St
Davie St
Homer St
Expo Blvd
Georgia Viaduct
Main St
BC Place Stadium
Pacific Blvd
Main St-Science World Skytrain Station
Pacific St
Drake St
Science World
Beach Ave
start
David Lam Park
Quebec St
W 1st Ave
Cambie St
W 2nd Ave
finish
Charleson Park
W 6th Ave
Main St
W Broadway

0    500    1,000    1,500 yards
0    500    1,000    1,500 metres

# 18 SOUTH FALSE CREEK: OLYMPIAN STROLL

BOUNDARIES: **Quebec St., False Creek, Duranleau St., Granville Island**
DISTANCE: **1½ miles/2½ kilometres**
DIFFICULTY: **Easy**
PARKING: **There is a parking lot at Science World and an alternative lot at the southeast corner of Quebec St. and Terminal Ave.**
PUBLIC TRANSIT: **The Main Street-Science World SkyTrain station is just across the street from Science World. Bus 50 can pick you up at the end of your trek at Granville Island.**

While the seawall snaking along the north side of False Creek has been open for years, pedestrians have long gazed at the tumbledown wasteland on the creek's southeastern shore, hoping that one day the giant piles of muddy rubble and fenced-off no-go areas might one day be cleared for walkers. Successive administrations deemed the job too big—until an even bigger project came along. There are more than a few Vancouverites critical of the vast sums spent on the 2010 Olympic and Paralympic Winter Games, but consolation comes with a stroll along the newest stretch of seawall, kick-started by the construction of the Olympic Village near Science World. The village is the cornerstone of a new neighborhood and hopes are high that the Olympics will do for South False Creek what Expo '86 did for North False Creek. But even if you don't live here, this final stretch of a seawall trail that now runs uninterrupted from Coal Harbour to Kitsilano is arguably the best, complete with planned natural features, street furniture doubling as public art, and a snazzy pedestrian bridge that looks like it came from a sci-fi movie. It's all a far cry from the area's gritty past, when sawmills, foundries, boat builders, and even a slaughterhouse lined this industrialized waterfront.

● **Facing the entrance to Science World, at the point where North False Creek becomes South False Creek, turn to your left into the small, grass-fringed Creekside Park and check out a couple of unexpected artworks. While the cedar tree stumps here might look like the last vestiges of three dead trees, they have carvings hidden inside like cloaked-figures. Created by a young artists group called Collective Echoes, they reflect the ancient First Nations food gatherers that once called this area home— there's also a concrete ribbon of aquatic life showing that fish was a big part of the food chain here.**

- Hit the seawall west along the south side of the inlet. On your right is the floating Aquabus Ferry terminal, where you can climb onboard a little boat and make straight for Granville Island, bypassing all these walking shenanigans. False Creek is the heart of Vancouver's mini-ferry system and while the service had a slow start in the early 1980s—grubby industry and derelict wasteland ruled the area in those days—Expo '86 made the idea of bobbing across the water in a rainbow-colored, bathtub-sized vessel suddenly popular. Two companies now ply the waters here, crisscrossing the creek and serving tourists and commuters alike.

- If you're saving your sea legs for another day, continue west along the seawall and on your left you'll see the towers of the 2010 Olympic Village. Home to around 3,000 athletes for the duration of the games, this giant new waterfront development is the site of a sparkling new Vancouver neighborhood that, post-Games, will contain around 5,000 condos. It's one of the city's biggest-ever housing developments.

- Continue along the front of the Olympic Village and you'll come to arguably the best stretch of seawall walkway the city has yet produced. The steel framed, Douglas fir deck of the boardwalk here is flanked by detailed flourishes that make slowing down a very good idea. Giant granite block from Jervis Inlet on the Sunshine Coast are interspersed with Mexican feather grass, while platforms poking out into the water on piles are topped with metal swivel chairs, white-painted steel loungers, and oversized nautical cleats that serve as seating. Stop and drink in the views of BC Place Stadium, Science World, and the Plaza of Nations across the glassy water, watching passing boats and birdlife.

- Continue west—passing a couple of solar powered compactor garbage cans—and within a few minutes you'll be crossing the shiny, 131-foot/40-metre-long pedestrian bridge that tapers on each end like a large canoe. The deck has been designed as a grid to allow aquatic life in the water to still benefit from sunlight. Nature is a big part of this seawall stretch: hundreds of trees have been planted here and, although the Mexican grass is not indigenous, almost everything else is.

- Follow the waterfront trail for a few more minutes and you'll find an even bigger commitment to nature. Shimmering in the water on your right, Habitat Island, created from rock, sand, and gravel and topped with trees, shrubs, and flowers, is designed to eventually become a favored sanctuary for passing cormorants, blue herons, and peregrine falcons. The fringes of the island have also been set with snags and shady nooks to encourage marine visitors like crabs and starfish. Once established over the next few years, the enclave will welcome pedestrians and will be accessible via a rocky walkway that will disappear beneath the water at high tide.

● Sauntering west, you'll pass under the Cambie Bridge—the messy City Works Yard here is one of the last remnants of the area's grubby past and is scheduled to become a park in future years—and emerge at Stamps Landing. An area of seawall first established in the 1970s, it's very different from the swanky new promenade you've just passed through. But with its crazy paving, low-rise condos, and brown-hued buildings, this stretch has a cool, retro feel that reflects the era it was created in. It's also a well-established, middle-class community of more than 6,000 people. There's a mini-ferry terminal here if your legs are telling you to bail out.

Ahead of you, perched over the water on piles, is Monk McQueens. One of the city's most popular older restaurants, it's a seafood-lovers utopia where delectably prepared regional favorites like wild salmon and Queen Charlotte halibut are joined by quirky alternatives like lobster corndogs and oyster BLT sandwiches. Weekend brunch is popular here and the large, sunset-loving patio is a highly sought after spot on balmy summer evenings.

● Continue your westward walk around Monks and you'll come to the superbly named Leg-in-Boot Square, the heart of this waterfront community. Originally an area where supplies were hauled ashore for a long-forgotten False Creek logging operation, this crescent-shaped stretch is named after a mysterious severed leg that rolled up onshore here in the 1800s. Now surrounded by a small clutch of shops and businesses, this is a good spot to stop and compare the low-density housing here—where nothing is more than a few stories high—with the 20-story glass towers on the opposite False Creek shore.

● You'll soon pass the bottom of Ferry Row and come alongside Charleson Park on your left. Well-used by playground-loving kids, local dog-walkers, and esurient picnickers, this elbow-shaped, tree-lined park is perhaps ironically named after Donald Brims Charleson, a logger responsible for clearing the entire area of its lucrative forest more than a century ago. Behind the park, you'll see the busy neighborhood of Fairview Slopes rising in steps from the water. One of the city's oldest districts, it's home to streets of old-style wooden houses built when the city was rapidly expanding in the early 1900s. It's also the location of Vancouver's Art Deco City Hall.

● As you follow the seawall past the end of the park, Spruce Harbour Marina is on your right. The trail forks here, but follow the concrete boardwalk over the water for a closer look at the boats. While it may look like any other marina, many of these vessels are occupied year-round. Planned in the 1970s as a live-aboard aquatic community in the heart of the city—"pure" houseboats are not allowed, unless they move under their own power—slips here are highly sought-after and there's a waiting list of more than five years. The vessels are hooked up directly to the sewage system and there's a central building with laundry, kitchen, showers, and a sauna.

● Passing on, you'll soon see the buildings crowding the eastern tip of Granville Island ahead of you. Follow the seawall alongside the little inlet at the back of the island. This sheltered area is called Alder Bay and was originally used by the Squamish and Musqueam First Nations as a clever fish trap: the fish entered the enclosed area at high tide but were prevented from leaving at low tide. It's now a handy spot for first-time kayakers since its calm, protected waters are usually as smooth as glass.

● Continue west alongside the curve of the bay and you can cross to Granville Island on the little wooden bridge. Before you launch yourself on the island's many attractions, check out the handsome, near-hidden totem pole on your left. Carved by 800 people and erected in 1999, it's 56 feet/17 metres tall and has a time capsule hidden in its base that's not to be opened until 2099. From here, you can drop into one of the island's many restaurants or coffee shops for an after-walk respite.

## POINTS OF INTEREST

**Science World** 1455 Quebec St, 604-443-7443

**Aquabus Ferries** 1333 Johnson St, 604-689-5858

**Monk McQueens** 601 Stamps Landing, 604-877-1351

**Spruce Harbour Marina** 1015 Ironwork Passage, 604-733-3512

## ROUTE SUMMARY

1. Start at Science World and head west along the south side of False Creek.
2. Following the seawall, pass the Olympic Village on your left.
3. Pass under Cambie Bridge.
4. Pass around the left-hand side of Monk McQueens.
5. Pass alongside Charleson Park to your left.
6. Pass alongside Spruce Harbour Marina.
7. Walk alongside the eastern tip of Granville Island and
   follow the seawall onto the island.

*Seawall and Charleson Park*

W 2nd Ave

start

E 3rd Ave

E 2nd Ave

E 1st Ave

Manitoba St

Ontario St

Quebec St

E 4th Ave

E 5th Ave

Main St

Scotia St

E 6th Ave

E 7th Ave

Brunswick St

E 8th Ave

**Guelph Park**

E Broadway

Kingsway

0    100    200    300 yards

0    100    200    300 metres

E 10th Ave

finish

# 19 OLD MOUNT PLEASANT: VANCOUVER'S FIRST SUBURB

BOUNDARIES: **Ontario St., 2nd Ave., Main St., E. 10th Ave.**
DISTANCE: **¾ mile/1¼ kilometres**
DIFFICULTY: **Easy**
PARKING: **There's metered street parking on Ontario St. and on the nearby side streets around Main.**
PUBLIC TRANSIT: **Bus 3 runs along Main St. Buses 9 and 99 B-Line stop at the nearby Main and Broadway intersection. The SkyTrain stops at Main Street-Science World, a short walk north of E. 2nd Ave.**

Old Mount Pleasant, located on the southeast rise above False Creek, first emerged in the 1880s, when industry began unfurling itself around the edges of the inland waterfront. Soon, a series of breweries—taking advantage of a nearby stream—colonized the area and, by 1890, the first streetcars from downtown Vancouver began trundling up the incline of what was then called Westminster Ave. As industry increased, workers' housing crowded the slope's lower area, with middle-class homes for managers located in the upper. By the early 1900s, the large community was regarded as a separate entity to Vancouver. The suburb's bustling town center was situated at the intersection of three major roads, each lined with landmark commercial buildings. These three roads were renamed around 1910: their grand new monikers—Main St., Kingsway, and Broadway—reflected Mount Pleasant's established importance. But when the Great Depression swept through and industry declined around the region, the area began a slow decline. In recent years, Vancouver's hipsters, looking for less expensive living, have claimed the neighborhood as their character-filled new home. Strolling the streets today, you'll find plenty of striking reminders of the past, along with some of the city's best indie coffee shops, art galleries, and one-of-a-kind bars and restaurants.

● **You'll start with a late breakfast at one of Vancouver's few authentic old-school diners, in a city that used to be full of them. The Argo Cafe, just off E. 2nd Ave. about half a block south along Ontario St., is fronted by a jaunty painted exterior** that suggests you're about to enter a youth club. Instead, you'll find a friendly eatery with vinyl booths, a warm welcome, and the kind of heaping, home-cooked nosh that gives bacon and eggs a good name. Reflecting the area's changing demographic, your fellow grease monkeys include manual laborers from the nearby labyrinth of little factories, and office drones from the tech and publishing businesses increasingly colonizing the area.

● After brekky, turn right when you leave the cafe. Stroll north along Ontario and turn right at the next corner onto E. 2nd Ave. Head east and check out the magnificent hulking old building on the other side of the street. Completed by Dominion Construction in 1918 for the Columbia Block and Tool Company and later known as the Opsal Steel building, this huge complex of antique timber-built sheds is one of the last reminders of the heavy industry that used to crowd this area. The building's exterior has remained surprisingly intact, despite being abandoned for decades and being controversially removed from the city's heritage list in 2002. With the nearby Olympic Village development transforming the area into a new residential neighborhood, plans are afoot to preserve Opsal as part of a new condo development.

● Continue east for a couple of minutes along E. 2nd, then turn right along Main St. and head uphill. Crane your neck like an owl and check out the view behind you—the North Shore mountains are especially noticeable from here and you might be able to pick out the lights of Grouse Mountain. Continue uphill to E. 6th Ave. and over to the other side of Main at the nearest crossing. The handsome brown brick building on this corner was recently offered for sale for $2.5 million. If it's not too early for a drink, save your money for the bar occupying its southeast corner. The Whip looks like a traditional English pub from the outside, but inside it's an art-lined neighborhood hangout specializing in sociable dining and great beer: drop by on Sunday afternoons when they crack open a guest keg of local ale.

● Return to Main St., re-cross to the other side of the road, and continue your southern uphill stroll. On your right, at the intersection with E. 7th Ave., you'll come to Foundation, the first indication that you've now entered hipsterville. Peer through its condensation-covered windows or, if you're feeling cool enough, duck inside and take one of the mismatched retro tables. A popular beer and grub hangout for student-types, the food here is vegetarian-friendly and the ale is usually of the quality regional-brew variety.

- Back outside, you'll notice that the road forks, with Main continuing south and Kingsway branching southeastward. Stay on the right side of Main and continue south. This is the heart of old Mount Pleasant, so you'll start to notice a smattering of elderly stone buildings around you. There's also an ornate public clock in the middle of the road here. Trams used to trundle to and from downtown on either side of this timepiece.

- Just beside the clock, take the crosswalk over to the left side of Main and nip into the cafe at the flatiron-style tip of this shopping row. You can't sneeze around this area without hitting an independent coffee shop and Gene, a multi-windowed nook of whitewashed walls and chunky cedar benches, is arguably the best. Expect to see Dostoyevsky-reading singletons and young parents whose toddlers already dress cooler than you hogging the seats. The coffee here is richly satisfying and the home-baked cookies and cakes will fortify you as you hunker in a corner.

- Continue south along this side of Main—the hill has leveled off here, so the climb is over—and a few doors along from Gene you'll come to Pulp Fiction. It's one of the best used bookstores in the city and, as well as the stand of eclectic bargain books outside, its interior is stacked to the rafters with browsable and highly tempting tomes.

- Amble a little farther south to the bustling intersection with E. Broadway and turn left. One block in, you'll come to the JEM Gallery ("JEM" stands for "just east of Main"). Showcasing Western Canada's most eclectic art—often of the kitsch, lowbrow, or outsider variety—the JEM is an unassuming storefront gallery where the regularly changing exhibitions can range from local veteran Jim Cummins' latest painted surfboards to Calgarian Lisa Brawn's cleverly ironic pop-culture woodcuts. Drop by on an opening night to meet some of Vancouver's more colorful artsy characters and save time for the back room, with its tempting array of locally created prints, jewelry, and curios priced to go. If it's closed on your visit, check out the colorful mural on the side of the building. Centered on a clattering old streetcar, it recalls old-time Mount Pleasant.

● Return west on E. Broadway to Main St. and cross over to the other side of Main. Occupying the northwest corner, the Lee Building, named after original owner H.O. Lee, is one of the area's best-known heritage structures. Completed in 1912 as one of the city's first skyscrapers, this brown-brick apartment building has an old-school, New York élan. Still residential with shops flanking its bottom, it was infamous in recent years for the mammoth billboard sign that sat atop its roof. Billboards like this were banned by the city in the 1970s but this one was installed in 1998, triggering a lengthy legal battle. The building's owners argued it brought in much-needed revenue that helped preserve the building. After almost 10 years, including an appeal to the Supreme Court of Canada, the city bylaw was finally enforced.

● Continuing south on Main, cross E. Broadway and check out some of the stores lining the area on your right. Make a note of Slickity Jim's here: its oddball, memorabilia-lined interior has helped make it one of the area's favorite breakfast spots, especially on weekends. A little farther along, you'll come to Motherland Clothing where the neighborhood's bright young things pick up their American Apparel T-shirts, revolutionary-sloganed tops, and cute-and-interesting silkscreen-print dresses. Many of the designers featured on the racks here are Canadian and the prices are surprisingly good.

● If it's looking like time to wind down for the day, cross to the other side of Main and enter the Cascade Room. Its electric-blue exterior sign recalls 1950s Vegas, but this intimate hangout is a knowing reinvention of mid-century cocktail bars. Perch at the front and watch the clamorous street scene unfold or decamp to a darkened back table amidst the faux flock wallpaper to sip on Singapore Slings and Hemingway Daiquiris. There's also a fresh list of seasonal specials and a small but well-chosen selection of microbrew beers (R&B's Red Devil Ale is best). Make note of the sobering etched-glass maxim near the entrance on your way out: "Keep calm and carry on."

# POINTS OF INTEREST

**Argo Café** 1836 Ontario St., 604-876-3620

**The Whip** 209 E. 6th Ave., 604-874-4687

**Foundation** 2301 Main St., 604-708-0881

**Gene Café** 2404 Main St., 604-568-5501

**Pulp Fiction** 2422 Main St., 604-876-4311

**JEM Gallery** 225 E. Broadway, 604-879-5366

**Slickity Jim's** 2513 Main St., 604-873-6760

**Motherland Clothing** 2539 Main St., 604-876-3426

**Cascade Room** 2616 Main St., 604-709-8650

# ROUTE SUMMARY

1. Start on Ontario St., just south of the intersection with E. 2nd Ave.
2. Head north on Ontario and turn right along E. 2nd Ave.
3. Stroll east along E. 2nd, then turn right along Main St.
4. Cross over at E. 6th Ave. and stroll half a block east along E. 6th.
5. Return to Main.
6. Re-cross to the west side of Main and continue south uphill.
7. Cross over to the other side of Main behind the public clock.
8. Turn left along E. Broadway for half a block.
9. Return west on E. Broadway and cross to the west side of Main.
10. Stay on this side of Main and continue south.
11. Cross to the east side of Main.

*Argo Cafe*

Parker St

NapierSt

William St

**Grandview Park**

Charles St

Kitchener St

**Victoria Park**

Grant St

Odlum Dr

McLean Dr

Woodland Dr

Cotton Dr

Commercial Dr

Salsbury Dr

Grant St

Graveley St

E 1st Ave

E 2nd Ave

E 3rd Ave

McLean Dr

E 4th Ave

Victoria Dr

Semlin Dr

Lakewood Dr

N Grandview Hwy

E 5th Ave

**start**

**finish**

**McSpadden Park**

0    100   200   300 yards

0    100   200   300 metres

# 20 Commercial Drive: Vancouver's Tasty Bohemian Promenade

**BOUNDARIES:** **E. 5th Ave., Commercial Dr., Grandview Park, Parker St.**
**DISTANCE:** **¾ mile/1¼ kilometres**
**DIFFICULTY:** **Easy**
**PARKING:** **There is metered street parking on Commercial Dr.**
**PUBLIC TRANSIT:** **The Broadway-Commercial Dr. SkyTrain station is a short walk from Commercial's main shopping area. Bus 20 also stops at many points on Commercial.**

Strolling "the Drive," Vancouver's colorful, counterculture strip, it's easy to think that the bohemians have always been here. But while the stretch is now all about independent shops, laid-back bars, one-of-a-kind restaurants, and quirky coffee shops, Commercial has a long and storied history. Originally part of the main transportation link between New Westminster and Vancouver, a streetcar service trundled right down the middle of the street here from the 1890s, triggering development of the grubby no-mans-land on either side. Without the line (which ran until 1954), you wouldn't be sipping your soy macchiato here today. But while plans to develop the strip into a chichi Shaughnessy-like enclave were sidelined by WWI, Commercial thrived as an area of light industry, busy neighborhood shops, and clapboard houses built for working families. Generations of immigrants have called the area home, including a wave of Italian expats who transformed the area into "Little Italy" and whose excellent family-run coffee shops still rule the Drive's java selection. Wait for a sunny day, plan a leisurely stroll, and dip into Vancouver's best eclectic promenade. And make sure you bring your appetite—there are plenty of indulgences along the way.

● Slip into the Drive's counterculture groove at Cafe Deux Soleils (named after its older sibling up the street, Cafe du Soleil). Colonizing a space that was formerly part of a crumbling old gas station, this grunge-tastic neighborhood hangout is an ideal spot to rub shoulders with the friendly, serially tattooed locals. The center of Vancouver's thriving live poetry scene, there are regular slam contests and open mike nights here, as well as live music. If you mosey in during the day, you can grab a free-trade coffee or tuck into a hearty vegetarian meal. The place is usually hopping for weekend brunch (the ginger teriyaki tofu scramble is recommended).

● Continue north along Commercial on the same side of the street. Look out for the steaming mugs of coffee stenciled into the concrete sidewalks. You'll also catch a whiff or two of illicit substances scenting the air. Just before the E. 4th Ave. intersection, you'll come to the Bibliophile Book Shop on your right. One of the city's best used book nooks, the selection here is eclectic with a surprisingly good array of new-ish and vintage Canadian fiction stacked along the narrow aisles. In recent years, the shop has also started hawking an odd assortment of folk art, which explains the random elephant trunk carvings and twirling wooden ducks crowding any space where books don't fit.

● Cross E. 4th Ave. and nip into the Prado Cafe on your right. Commercial is the destination of choice for coffee-lovers planning a java crawl and this is the first serious contender if you're strolling north. But unlike the old Italian joints farther up, the Prado has an austere, whitewashed interior that attracts the kind of laptop-hugging hipsters who prefer nothing to detract from their free wi-fi. The artistry here, though, is all in the coffee: expect the foam of your excellent latte to be decoratively etched.

● Once you're fully wired, continue north a couple of doors to encounter the Barefoot Contessa, a popular clothing store for in-the-know fashionistas. Originally only on Main St. (the old location is still open), this satellite store opened in 2008, just around the corner from the owner's house. There are plenty of cute but demure tops, hats, and dresses collected from Canadian and international designers, plus a wall of sparkling baubles if you need to brighten up your life. If you're a visiting fella, ask for advice from the friendly staff and they'll help you choose something impressive for your gal.

● If you're still in a shopping mood, cross over to the other side of Commercial and just before the E. 2nd Ave. intersection, you'll come to Wonderbucks Trading Company. As you will have noticed along the side streets, there are lots of small apartment buildings and old homes where floors are rented out to individual tenants. At some point, almost everyone living in this area drops into this store to find something for their home. Priding itself on cut-price chic, it's a challenge to leave without something in your bag.

● Elvis-shaped salt and pepper shakers in hand, continue north on this side of Commercial, crossing over E. 2nd Ave. You're now in the original heart of "Little Italy." On your left is La Grotta Del Formaggio. When you step inside, the heady aroma of matured cheese hits you like a particularly inviting wet sock. Peruse the lip-smacking deli selection on one side of the narrow store (if you want a picnic in the nearby park, get a made-to-order grilled panini) then check out the wall of marzipan, olive oil, and cream crackers lining the other. Recalling the Sistine Chapel, the ceiling is painted with a cloud-strewn sky. You can catch another elaborate painted ceiling at next door's kitsch Cafe Calabria, one of the Drive's best Italian java spots.

- Continue north on Commercial, then cross over E. 1st Ave., Graveley St., and Grant St. At the Grant intersection, on your left, you'll come to The Charlatan. The Drive isn't just about coffee and this unpretentious neighborhood bar is a great place to catch a hockey game, lounge on the willow-shaded side patio, or just sample some of the drafts in the gleaming taps dominating the rounded bar—try Alberta's Big Rock Traditional Ale. The food is of the pub grub variety with heaping nacho plates a favorite.

- Continue north from here and staying on the left of the street you'll soon be at Grandview Park, Commercial's alfresco neighborhood hub. Its name comes from its magnificent mountain views, but you'll have a hard time looking up from your people-watching: on a sunny day there'll be doting dads and kids, neo-hippies, and maybe a band on the bandstand, or at least some buskers.

- Cross to the other side of Commercial here and consider nipping into Havana for a quick drink. Fronted by the Drive's best patio, this popular Cuban-themed dining and watering hole has a couple of unusual features that have endeared it to its artsy neighbors. The back room doubles as a gallery and theatre space where avant-garde shows are staged, while the walls of the main room are lined with junk shop prints and graffiti messages carved into the tobacco-colored paintwork. If you're looking for a drink suggestion, the mojitos are dangerously addictive.

- If you're craving a final tipple or two, cross back to the other side of Commercial. On the corner of William St., you'll come to Stellas Tap & Tapas Bar. This bright and chatty spot has an astonishing roster of Belgian beer that true connoisseurs will appreciate. Before you make your selection, ask to see the "fresh sheet" of ever-changing drafts. Once you've exhausted the menu you can move onto the bottled varieties: try the citrussy Belge if you want something relatively light; dark beer fans will prefer the rich X.O., made with cognac.

- If you've abstained, skip across to the other side of Commercial at this point. If it's time to line your stomach or soak up that over-indulgence, duck into the Reef. This kaleidoscopically decorated Caribbean restaurant offers smile-triggering dishes like Bajan fried chicken with yam fries and hot Jamaican curries that will blow away any possibility of a Belgian beer hangover. And while the fruity cocktail menu (try the Dark & Stormy) is highly tempting, each one of them can be prepared sans alcohol if you've decided you'll never drink again.

- With your Commercial Dr. amble drawing to a close, there's just time for one more flavorful treat. A couple of doors past the Reef on the same side, Dutch Girl Chocolates is a real hidden treasure. This little creaky-floored shop is artfully draped with an Aladdin's cave of treats, many made in the kitchen you'll glimpse in the back. Pick up some milk, white, or dark chocolate models of cars or tennis racquets, peruse the old-fashioned jars of licorice sweeties, or create a selection box of handmade truffles and bonbons from the cabinet in the front.

# POINTS OF INTEREST

**Cafe Deux Soleils** 2096 Commercial Dr., 604-254-1195

**Bibliophile Book Shop** 2010 Commercial Dr., 604-254-5520

**Prado Cafe** 1938 Commercial Dr., 604-255-5537

**Barefoot Contessa** 1928 Commercial Dr., 604-255-9035

**Wonderbucks Trading Company** 1803 Commercial Dr., 604-253-0510

**La Grotta Del Formaggio** 1791 Commercial Dr., 604-255-3911

**Cafe Calabria** 1745 Commercial Dr., 604-253-7017

**The Charlatan** 1446 Commercial Dr., 604-253-2777

**Havana** 1212 Commercial Dr., 604-253-9119

**Stellas Tap & Tapas Bar** 1191 Commercial Dr., 604-254-2437

**The Reef** 1018 Commercial Dr., 604-568-5375

**Dutch Girl Chocolates** 1002 Commercial Dr., 604-251-3221

# ROUTE SUMMARY

1. Start on Commercial Dr. just past the intersection with E. 5th Ave.
2. Continue north on Commercial on the right-hand side of the street.
3. Cross to the left-hand side just before E. 2nd Ave.
4. Continue on this side of Commercial to Grandview Park.
5. Cross over to the right-hand side of Commercial.
6. Cross back at William St.
7. Re-cross to the right-hand side after half a block.

*Cafe Calabria*

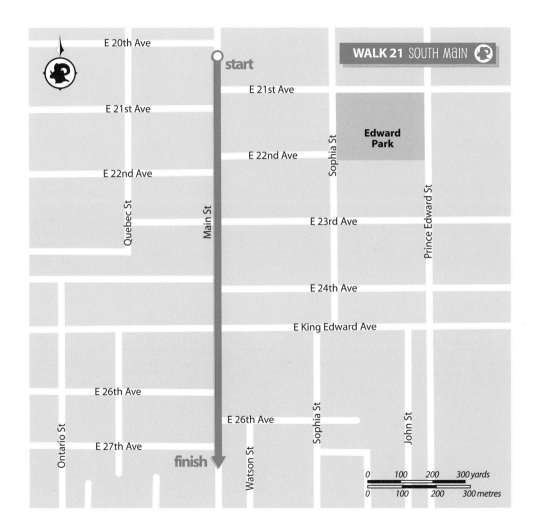

E 20th Ave

start

E 21st Ave

E 21st Ave

Sophia St

**Edward Park**

E 22nd Ave

E 22nd Ave

Quebec St

Main St

E 23rd Ave

Prince Edward St

E 24th Ave

E King Edward Ave

E 26th Ave

E 26th Ave

Sophia St

John St

Ontario St

E 27th Ave

finish

Watson St

0    100    200    300 yards

0    100    200    300 metres

# 21 SOUTH Main: UrBan HiPSTer STroLL

BOUNDARIES: **E. 20th Ave., Main St., E. 27th Ave.**
DISTANCE: **½ mile/¾ kilometre**
DIFFICULTY: **Easy**
PARKING: **There's parking on the side streets near the start of this walk.**
PUBLIC TRANSIT: **Bus 3 runs along the length of Main St.**

The city's old working class residential heartland, this area had some crumbling, idle stretches for much of the last century. But although the neighborhood still has its dodgy pockets, it's been largely reclaimed in recent years by the city's young artsy set—those who couldn't find anywhere else to live in Vancouver for the amount of rent they could afford. The positive influence of this influx is especially prevalent in the shop-lined strip of Main St. now called South Main (or SoMa if you want to believe the marketers). Especially from the southward strip stretching past the intersection with E. 20th Ave., it's teeming with Vancouver's best independent stores. Echoing Commercial Dr. with its indie vibe, South Main is an intriguing spot to spend an afternoon. Bring your credit cards and an empty backpack to fully enjoy the experience. And remember it's not just about shopping: this strip has plenty of cozy coffee stops, distinctive one-of-a-kind restaurants, and quirky bar and live music hangouts to keep strollers occupied.

● You'll start on the east side of Main St., just past the intersection with E. 20th Ave. Stroll south and on your left is Smoking Lily, one of the originators of the South Main indie renaissance. While student-girl tops printed with microscopes and purses adorned with periodic tables are the backbone of the collection here, the tiny shop has branched out in recent years with whimsical men's tractor-print T-shirts, sea-horse luggage tags, and a natty array of silk tea cozies adorned with Warhol-like images of Louis Riel and Pierre Trudeau.

● Continue south on Main to the E. 21st Ave. intersection. Take the crosswalk here to the right side of Main and you'll be almost in front of Lazy Susan's. You'll spend most of your time here spotting irresistible trinkets for people you know. That might mean Scrabble tile earrings, old ties transformed into coin purses, or vintage reproduction greetings cards from the 1950s for your favorite ironic birthday buddy. Like most stores in this area, Lazy Susan's is a small, owner-operated shop and its staff is ever-ready to chat and offer suggestions if you're having trouble choosing between an art print T-shirt or a brooch shaped like a palm tree.

● Continue south on the right side of Main and keep your eyes on the sidewalk where you'll spot mannequins, coffee mugs, and open scissors artfully stenciled into the concrete. A couple of doors up from Lazy Susan's, nip into Twigg & Hottie on your right. Named after owners Glencora Twigg and Christine Hotton, this is one of the strip's most beloved clothing destinations for women. Despite its small scale, this wood-floored nook showcases the distinctive garments of dozens of Canadian designers: it's the place to come if you want to be wearing something that nobody else has. In recent years, the store has focused on sustainable designers and has introduced artful jewelry and accessories.

● If you're thinking this area is only about women's clothing, continue on this side of Main for a couple more steps and you'll come to the blue-painted, double-fronted Eugene Choo shop. There's plenty for the ladies to peruse here, but guys—especially those who can pull off geek chic—also get a look in with slick hoodies, tailored suits, and handmade shoes.

● If you need a respite from all that feverish shopping, continue south to the next inter-section. On the corner here, head into Liberty Bakery. This tiny neighborhood favorite offers an array of the kind of treats that look and taste like they were handmade by a team of expert grandmothers, led by Liberty Gustafson. Peruse the displays of fluffy lemon cakes, rich banana slices, jaunty gingerbread men, and little birds' nest short-bread cookies topped with strawberry jam. You can also grab a sandwich here—the grilled paninis and homemade soups are recommended. Tuck into your feast at a farmhouse-style table inside or, if it's sunny, find an outdoor seat and watch the Main St. bustle.

● Now that you're re-fueled, cross over to the other side of Main here. The triple-fronted store crowding your view requires more than a couple of minutes' perusing. Front & Company includes a giant but carefully chosen consignment department with thou-sands of vintage and gently used items. In addition, Front has adjoining mini stores hawking artsy homewares and kitsch gifts like peace sign ice trays, dinosaur-shaped nightlights, and razorless shaving razors.

- Cross Main again and continue south. Check out the side streets radiating on either side of you here: you'll notice lots of older, gabled wooden homes that are not quite historic enough to be heritage listed. You'll also notice that the stores on Main—not all of them trendy, and many of them old mom-and-pop operations—are almost exclusively one story. This area will likely be one of Vancouver's hottest developer districts in years to come, so consider buying here while you still can.

- Continue on this side of Main and cross over E. 23rd Ave. On the corner is the ugly, windowless Tudor-style Army, Navy, and Air Force Veterans building. Just past it is Crave. One of Main's most popular local hangouts (especially its backyard patio), this laid-back restaurant-bar is a great spot to come back to at the end of the day, when the dinner selection covers all the right comfort food bases—try the braised lamb shank and mashed potatoes or sun-dried tomato and basil meatloaf. The ambiance is equally comfy, with candlelit tables and good-value beer pitchers.

- Cross back to the left side of Main. Opposite Crave is one of the street's most unusual shops. The Regional Assembly of Text is a pilgrimage spot for stationery nuts, complete with a back wall of filing cabinets and a counter accented with vintage typewriters. Founded by art school grads, salivating literati flock here to stock up on Little Otsu journals, handmade pencil boxes, and American Apparel T-shirts printed with everything from disembodied dolls heads to blueprints for 1940s prefabs. Check out the tiny under-stairs reading room and consider dropping by for the free monthly letter-writing club where you can sip tea, gobble cookies, and hammer away on the typewriters.

- Continue south on the left side of Main, dropping into Lucky's Comics if you need a chuckle, until you reach E. King Edward Ave. At this intersection, cross to the right side of the street. Along this stretch, the Main St. family businesses, Chinese restaurants, and cheap neighborhood grocery stores remain dominant. Glance at the handsome black and white 1910 Walden Building on your left and continue south for two more blocks.

● Just past E. 27th Ave., you'll come to Red Cat Records on your right. Dive deeply into Vancouver's flourishing indie music scene at this High Fidelity-style record store. It's run by two members of local alt-country-rock band the Buttless Chaps. Singer Dave Gowans and guitarist Lasse Lutick are usually on-hand to offer tips about must-see area acts like Destroyer, Black Mountain, and Fond of Tigers and you can listen to their recommendations at the in-store turntables and MP3 players—then buy tickets for gigs at cool venues like Biltmore Cabaret and the Railway Club.

● With your stroll now drawing to a close, head across to the other side of Main one more time and toast your day out with a beer or three at The Main. A chatty bar hang-out even before this area was cool, there's often a singer-songwriter or two on the evening roster.

## POINTS OF INTEREST

**Smoking Lily** 3634 Main St., 604-873-5459

**Lazy Susan's** 3647 Main St., 604-873-9722

**Twigg & Hottie** 3671 Main St., 604-879-8595

**Eugene Choo** 3683 Main St., 604-873-8874

**Front & Company** 3772 Main St., 604-879-8431

**Crave** 3941 Main St., 604-872-3663

**Regional Assembly of Text** 3934 Main St., 604-877-2247

**Lucky's Comics** 3972 Main St., 604-875-9858

**Red Cat Records** 4307 Main St., 604-708-9422

**The Main** 4210 Main St., 604-709-8555

# route summary

1. Start on the east side of Main St., just past the E. 20th Ave. intersection.
2. Stroll south on this side of Main and cross to the other side at E. 21st Ave.
3. Continue on this side of Main to Liberty Bakery, then cross to the left side.
4. After visiting Front & Company, cross back to the right side of Main.
5. Continue south on the right side of Main until just past the E. 23rd Ave. intersection.
6. Re-cross to the left side of Main.
7. Continue south on this side of Main, then cross over to the right side at E. King Edward Ave.
8. Continue along the right side of Main until just past E. 27th Ave.
9. After Red Cat Records, cross back to the left side of Main.

*Wall mural on a South Main side street*

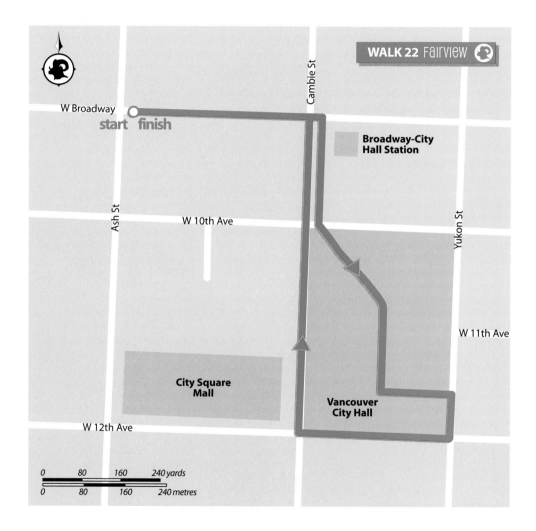

W Broadway

start  finish

Broadway-City
Hall Station

Cambie St

Ash St

W 10th Ave

Yukon St

W 11th Ave

City Square
Mall

Vancouver
City Hall

W 12th Ave

0        80        160      240 yards
0        80        160      240 metres

# 22 Fairview: Broadway to City Hall and Beyond

BOUNDARIES: **Ash St., W. Broadway, Yukon St., W. 12th Ave.**

DISTANCE: **½ mile/¾ kilometre**

DIFFICULTY: **Easy**

PARKING: **There's a parkade at City Square Mall on Cambie St., just across from City Hall and metered street parking on W. 10th Ave.**

PUBLIC TRANSIT: **Canada Line trains stop at the Broadway-City Hall Station. Buses 9 and 99 B-Line stop nearby on W. Broadway, while 15 stops along Cambie St. just across from City Hall.**

When the Canadian Pacific Railway's Lauchlan Hamilton came over to survey this forested slope in the 1880s, he looked back down at the fledgling Vancouver and its mountain backdrop and coined the name "Fairview." A few years later, the first Cambie Bridge was built across False Creek and a streetcar service began trundling up the Fairview slope, opening the new neighborhood for a surfeit of housing and development. Some of the wooden homes from this era still survive. While marine industries began crowding the shoreline below, upper Fairview soon housed the Vancouver General Hospital and the first incarnation of the University of British Columbia. But it's the handsome Art Deco City Hall that now dominates—although the first question visitors often ask is why it isn't located in the city center. The answer is to do with timing: the building was constructed just after the amalgamation of Vancouver, South Vancouver and Point Grey and Fairview was considered central to all three. This is an ideal walk if you want to combine some picturesque history with the busy shops and eateries of bustling Broadway.

● Like any task, it's always best to start with the reward so begin your stroll with a frothy latte and a bulging oatmeal cookie at Elysian Coffee on the corner of Ash St. and W. Broadway. Perch on a stool at the front window to watch one of the city's busiest workaday thoroughfares. Immediately opposite is the Cactus Club Café, which used to be a chain of humdrum eateries until top-end local chef Rob Feenie (the first Canadian to win TV's Iron Chef America challenge) departed his famed Lumière restaurant to take over the Cactus menu. The outlets are now arguably the best spots in Vancouver to dine high-end for a mid-range price. Consider coming back for lunch or dinner.

- Once the java kicks in, head east along W. Broadway. On the street's right-hand side, you'll pass a string of small, family-owned Asian eateries serving everything from Japanese and Chinese to Thai and Indian dishes. Pho Kim Penh Xe Lua, complete with its well-worn, hole-in-the-wall décor, is recommended if you're looking for a great Cambodian and Vietnamese spot. It's often teeming with chattering locals hunched over comforting bowls of steaming pho soup.

- The next intersection—W. Broadway and Cambie St.—is one of the city's busiest crossroads. But less than 150 years ago it was densely forested and occupied by a First Nations community, until the bridge, streetcar line, and workers' housing began crowding the slope. The latter-day version of the streetcar is right under your feet. The new subterranean Canada Line runs right up Cambie here from downtown and its construction—a disruptive "cut and cover" approach, rather than the less obtrusive but pricier tunnel burrowing method—was a major headache for area retailers, many of whom were forced to close as the noisy two-year project frightened shoppers away. Cross over to the intersection's southeast corner where the line's Broadway-City Hall station is located.

- Check out the sterling northward vista then head south up the incline of Cambie St. on the left-hand side. It was named after CPR surveyor Henry John Cambie who plotted Western Canada's first transcontinental rail line through the treacherous Fraser Canyon to Burrard Inlet. After crossing W. 10th Ave., you'll come to the corner of a small, sloped park space. Head up the steps and follow the pathway diagonally through its leafy center.

- On your right, and depending on the season, you might spot the large white blooms of a dogwood tree, BC's official flower. The tree was planted by Prince Charles and Princess Diana in 1986, kicking off the dual revelries for Vancouver's centenary and the opening of Expo '86.

- A few steps farther along, at the crossroads of the walkway, you'll come to a large boulder almost entirely covered with a wordy inscription. Part of the city's unusual Portrait V2K millennium project, locals were asked for their memories of Vancouver. From the hundreds submitted, 230 stories, along with photos, were made into plaques and 10 others were engraved on large stones to be placed in appropriate

## BacK STORY: MCGeer'S PaLace

Gerry McGeer was the colorful, sometimes controversial mayor who spearheaded the development of the ostentatious, spare-no-expense City Hall at a time when the Great Depression had caused unprecedented belt-tightening across the region. In fact, hundreds were living in shantytowns throughout the city. McGeer defended the project—which saw the building completed in just over 12 months—as a make-work plan for the idled construction industry. But the mayor was not a big sympathizer with the economically challenged working (or more often non-working) classes. Believing that Bolshevism was taking hold among the city's unemployed in the 1930s, he empowered the Vancouver Police Department to crack down on protests with impunity. And when hundreds of disgruntled jobless locals congregated in Victory Square in 1935, he turned up and read them the Riot Act. A few weeks later, the police and around 1,000 protestors fought a three-hour street battle on the East Vancouver waterfront with clubs, rocks, and tear gas, resulting in dozens of injuries to both sides. Rumors at the time claimed the police had machine guns ready to fire on the protestors. This event became known as the Battle of Ballantyne Pier and is among the most famous in Vancouver labor history.

locations around the city. This boulder contains the recollections of 95-year-old Ida Trudgeon who once lived in a house on this very site.

- The walkway forks just past the rock. Instead of heading into the depressing-looking 1960s concrete block on your left, stroll south uphill to the grand stairway ahead of you. Plod up the 29 steps and you'll be greeted at the top by a handsome statue of Captain George Vancouver, the man who gave the city its name. He appears to be pointing at the ugly East Wing building you've just passed.

The East Wing really isn't that bad, but it suffers next to the magnificent Art Deco structure looming behind Captain Van—especially when you consider the same architectural firm designed both. Detour around the statue and check it out. Built for Vancouver's half-century in 1936 for a then-considerable $1 million, the tiered, wedding cake exterior of City Hall is one of the West Coast's best Deco structures.

Check the wave-patterned banding snaking around its upper edges and the red neon clock topping its central tower. Above the entrance, granite panels depict the city crest, featuring two men holding an axe and a fishing net to reflect regional resource industries. You'll also spot the official city motto: "By sea and land we prosper," later amended to "By sea, land, and air we prosper."

- Push through the golden-doored entrance and you'll find a compact but sumptuous marble-lined lobby that's changed little since its inception. Spend time here perusing interior flourishes like the mirrored ceiling, streamlined signs, elongated cylindrical lanterns, and shiny, embossed elevator doors. Duck inside one of the elevators to peruse their impressive inlaid wood design. While City Hall was accorded heritage status in 1976, these elevator interiors were given their own protection order a few years later.

- Once you've circled a few times—the reception desk staff is used to gawkers—exit the lobby on the building's south side. Turn left along the walkway and you'll come to a stately bust of Gerry McGeer.

- Head east over the grass here and leave the City Hall precinct. You're now on Yukon St., which houses a magnificent string of heritage mansions (apart from two repro-duction imposters right ahead of you). Cross over Yukon and stroll uphill south on the left side of this street. One of the most impressive structures is Baxter House, the one with the BC flag in the garden. Check out its unusual snaggle-brick ground floor exterior. This Queen Anne-style residence was built in 1913 for Vancouver mayor T.S. Baxter and although its exterior retains many period flourishes, inside is a nest of 10 modern suites: like many large Vancouver heritage homes, it was transformed into an apartment complex.

- Continue south up Yukon and cross over W. 12th Ave. Head west on this street. Dominating the corner is the enormous Morin House, built in 1909 by the same archi-tects who created Gastown's flatiron Hotel Europe. Its extraordinary corner turret echoes the frontage of Shaughnessy's Canuck Place children's hospice. Spend a few minutes perusing the deep verandah, wood-sided exterior, and leaded windows and note the towering monkey puzzle tree in the garden. This house is also now an apart-ment complex.

● Amble slightly downhill along W. 12th, checking out the string of heritage houses on your left. Cross over Cambie St. and nip into FigMint for an end-of-walk rest. The loungey restaurant bar of the Plaza 500 Hotel, this is a good spot for a tasting plate snack and a beer—they have the excellent Crannog Back Hand of God stout here. Once you're fully sated, head north downhill on Cambie and within minutes you'll be back on W. Broadway.

## POINTS OF INTEREST

**Elysian Coffee** 590 W. Broadway, 604-874-5909

**Cactus Club Café** 575 W. Broadway, 604-714-6000

**Pho Kim Penh Xe Lua** 500 W. Broadway, 604-877-1120

**City Hall** 453 W. 12th Ave., 604-873-7011

**FigMint** 500 W. 12th Ave, 604-875-3312

## ROUTE SUMMARY

1. Start at W. Broadway and Ash St.
2. Turn right onto Cambie St.
3. Cross to other side of Cambie, cross W. 10th Ave. and enter park space.
4. Follow walkway through park and make for City Hall.
5. Enter City Hall and exit through south side of the lobby.
6. Turn left onto City Hall walkway.
7. Cross over to Yukon St.
8. Walk south on Yukon.
9. Cross over to south side of W. 12th Ave.
10. Follow W. 12th westward.
11. Cross over Cambie St. and stroll north back to W. Broadway.

*Morin House*

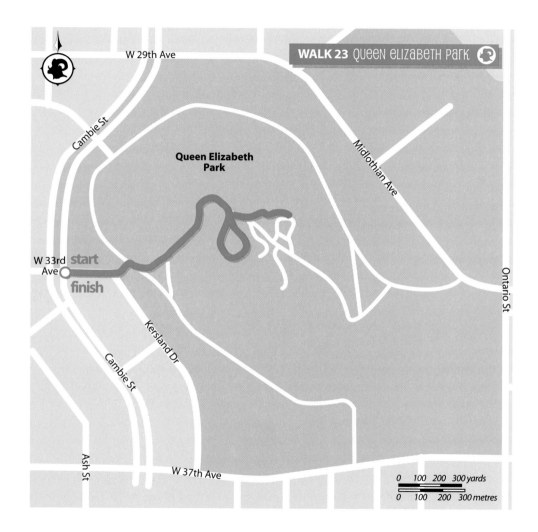

W 29th Ave

Cambie St

Queen Elizabeth
Park

Midlothian Ave

W 33rd
Ave

start

finish

Ontario St

Kersland Dr

Cambie St

Ash St

W 37th Ave

0   100   200   300 yards
0   100   200   300 metres

# 23 Queen Elizabeth Park: Quarry Makeovers and City Vistas

BOUNDARIES: **Cambie St., W. 33rd Ave.,**
DISTANCE: **¼ mile/½ kilometre**
DIFFICULTY: **Easy**
PARKING: **There's a parking lot just inside the entrance to Queen Elizabeth Park on W. 33rd Ave., plus an additional lot close to the Bloedel Conservatory entrance.**
PUBLIC TRANSIT: **The 15 bus stops at the W. 33rd Ave. entrance.**

Like Victoria's legendary Butchart Gardens, Queen Elizabeth Park wouldn't be here at all if it wasn't for heavy industry. Both sites were originally quarries, busily servicing the colonial era's penchant for monumental stone architecture and rock-foundation roadways. But while Jennie Butchart set about beautifying her quarried-out land in the early 1900s, the hilltop in Vancouver—known locally as Little Mountain—was left as a cratered scar where kids built camps and hid from their parents. The days of this ad hoc playground were numbered though, when the Canadian Pacific Railway sold it to the city in 1928 for $100,000. The Great Depression put paid to any grand plans and it wasn't until 1940 that the name Queen Elizabeth Park was created, honoring the 1939 royal visit of King George VI and Queen Elizabeth. WWII created another hiccup in the development plans and it was several years after the war before the area was properly laid out and landscaped. Very different to Stanley Park, the highlights of a stroll here today are the immaculate garden areas occupying the old quarry craters, the breathtaking hilltop vistas over the unfolding cityscape and the jungly, bubble-covered conservatory.

● **Start your walk at the intersection of Cambie St. and W. 33rd Ave., the park's main entrance. Follow the avenue east into the park and stroll up the slight incline on the left-hand sidewalk. The traffic clamor from Cambie soon dissolves away as the grassy slopes and leafy woodland take over. While much of the foliage around you, including healthy holly and rhododendron varieties, is decades old, it's all been** planted by human hand, unlike in Stanley Park, where the dense, temperate rainforest is comparatively wild.

- Pass Kersland Dr. on your right and continue on W. 33rd to the next intersection. Ignore the large sign pointing toward Bloedel Floral Conservatory and cross east to the other side of the intersection. There's a narrow walkway curving up the hill here: follow it. Within a few steps on your left is a magnificent fir tree fronted by an intriguing plaque remembering "the freedom fighters who died in Hungary in 1956." The memorial marks the Hungarian Revolution, a small resistance movement in Budapest against Soviet occupation that quickly escalated into a nationwide uprising and a swift overthrow of the Stalinist government. Within a few weeks, the Soviet army re-invaded and took back the country, crushing opposition and forcing 200,000 to flee across the border. Canada stepped up and accepted 37,000 Hungarian refugees, with the largest contingent arriving in BC. This plaque was dedicated in 1989 by the descendants of those original immigrants.

- Continue east along the uphill path and after a few more steps, you'll come to a fork. Take the path that leads you across the humpbacked wooden bridge to your left. Halfway across, you'll have a dramatic view over the Large Quarry Garden fanning out beneath you. This highly ornamental landscaped plot, complete with manicured lawns, coiffured flower borders, and a waterfall tumbling down the granite from beneath the bridge, was one of the country's first civic arboretums when it opened in 1949. The original goal was to plant as many native Canadian trees as possible for the leisurely enjoyment of locals. In later years, exotic, non-indigenous species have also been added to the mix. If you want a closer look, a nearby walkway can take you down into the heart of the garden.

- Continue to the end of the bridge and on your immediate right is a large boulder that's grandly named the Centuries Rock. Underneath it is a time capsule from 1954 that's stuffed with items and documents chosen to reflect the era they were buried in. Presumably that means hula hoops, early rock and roll records, and a few White Spot hamburgers. If you can't budge the rock out the way to find out, wait until 2054 when the copper capsule is due, with quite a drum roll, to be opened.

- Continue uphill along the path ahead of you. The dome of the conservatory is on your right, but before you duck in to see what it contains, stroll east to the crest of the hill. This is one of the most panoramic of Vancouver views. Check out the crop of downtown landmarks to your left and the distant towers of Burnaby ahead of you, all framed by a dramatic backdrop of encircling mountains—often trailed with mist or topped with laser-white snow caps.

- Once you've breathed a few deep ones, turn right and walk to the Bloedel Floral Conservatory entrance a few steps away. The park's green-thumb highlight, this opaque, triodetic dome was one of the biggest in the world when it opened in 1969, following a large donation from the Bloedel forestry family. Occupying the park's highest point, the dome comprises 1,490 convex triangular panels and is illuminated like a nicely parked spaceship at night. But it's the lush hothouse interior of plant and birdlife, divided into three main habitats, that draws most visitors. Expect your glasses to steam up as you step inside the balmy tropical zone, where exotic highlights include Malaysian fig trees, Brazilian jelly palms, and Central American trumpet trees. You can also expect to spot Technicolor parrots, macaws, and other exotic feathered critters—including Charlie, a gregarious Indonesian cockatoo who likes to chat.

- After exiting the conservatory, turn to your right and head up the short flight of steps. The expansive concrete plaza here is dominated by a ring of covered wooden benches arranged around a large central fountain built in 2007. The newest addition to the park, this area is popular with wedding parties: you can expect to pass several photo-shooting wedding groups here on most summer days. But even if you're not getting hitched, this a good spot to catch the synchronized water show from the fountain's 70 wooshing jets. There are restrooms nearby.

Circle the fountain and check out the large Henry Moore bronze sculpture perched on its western edge. Called *Knife Edge–Two Piece*, it was also donated by the Bloedels when they wrote the check for the conservatory. This is one of four identical bronze pieces cast by Moore in the mid-1960s. One of the others is on display at Kew Gardens in London.

- Head back down the steps from whence you came and turn right. Ahead of you will be a handsome red-painted clock looking like a cherry lollypop on a stick. Bear to the left and you'll come to another of the park's great hilltop views. Spread beneath you here is the Small Quarry Garden, sometimes called the North Quarry Garden. Created later than its sibling, this one was built in 1961 on the city's 75th anniversary. In contrast to its colorful partner, this garden is a little more subtle: look out for some delicate Japanese influences. For a closer look, there's a walkway that can take you into the heart of the botanical action. Otherwise, stay on the cliff and drink in the city and mountain vistas—just like the three life-size bronze figures taking a couple of snapshots here. Entitled *Photo Session*, it's by J. Seward Johnson.

- You've seen the park's main highlights now, so reward yourself by following your stomach growls to the restaurant on your right-hand side. A table at Seasons in the Park offers some of the best views in the city. While you fill up on the downtown cityscape and the twinkling ski lift lights of distant Grouse Mountain—you might even spot a bald eagle or two swooping past—you can tuck into a side dish or two of Pacific Northwest favorites like miso-marinated black cod or the highly recommended crab and shrimp-stuffed mushrooms. It's something Boris Yeltsin and Bill Clinton might have enjoyed together when they dined here during their 1993 summit. Or maybe it was on the menu at Sarah McLachlan's wedding reception a few years later.

- Once you're totally stuffed, take it easy with a gentle, downhill stroll back the way you came. If you didn't check out the quarry gardens at ground level the first time you passed through, now's the time. Otherwise, head back out along W. 33rd Ave. where, if you're transiting, you can pick up the 15 bus to downtown.

## POINTS OF INTEREST

**Bloedel Floral Conservatory** Queen Elizabeth Park, 604-257-8584

**Seasons in the Park** Queen Elizabeth Park, 604-874-8008

## ROUTE SUMMARY

1.  Start at the park entrance at Cambie St. and W. 33rd Ave.
2.  Follow W. 33rd Ave. east into the park.
3.  Pass Kersland Dr. and cross over the next intersection.
4.  Follow the path uphill east toward Bloedel Floral Conservatory.
5.  Follow a left-hand route around the edge of the conservatory.
6.  Enter the conservatory.
7.  Exit the conservatory, turn right and head up the steps.
8.  Circle the fountain and return down the same steps.
9.  Turn right then follow the path past the left side of the clock.
10.  Check out the view over the Small Quarry Garden.
11.  Visit Seasons in the Park restaurant on your right.
12.  Retrace your steps and exit the park via W. 33rd Ave.

*Landmark clock and Bloedel Floral Conservatory*

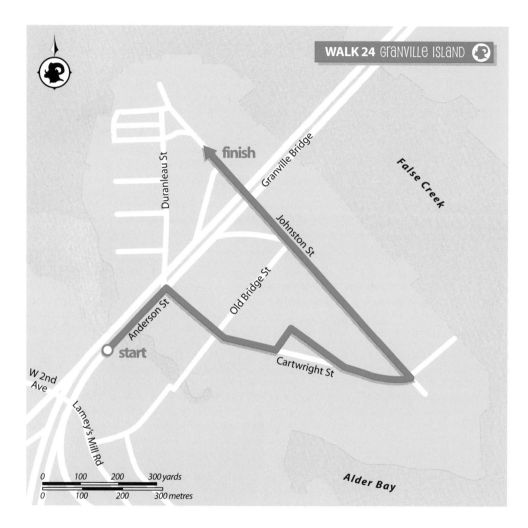

finish

start

Duranleau St

Granville Bridge

False Creek

Johnston St

Old Bridge St

Anderson St

Cartwright St

W 2nd Ave

Lamey's Mill Rd

Alder Bay

| 0 | 100 | 200 | 300 yards |
| 0 | 100 | 200 | 300 metres |

# 24 Granville Island: a crafty Stroll

BOUNDARIES: **W. 2nd Ave., Cartwright St., Johnston St., Duranleau St.**
DISTANCE: **½ mile/¾ kilometre**
DIFFICULTY: **Easy**
PARKING: **There are parking lots around the island, including those near the Public Market on Durenleau St. and on both sides of Old Bridge Street near Railspur Alley.**
PUBLIC TRANSIT: **Bus 50 stops at Anderson St. and W. 2nd Ave., near Granville Island's main entrance.**

Vancouver's favorite lazy afternoon hangout, clamorous Granville Island was originally a gritty harborside industrial district. But the 38-acre False Creek neighborhood wouldn't be here at all if it wasn't for an early 20th-century project to top up sandbanks under the old Granville Bridge. One million cubic yards of landfill and $342,000 later, the new "island"— actually a peninsula attached to the "mainland" by road and rail—welcomed its first tenants in 1915. A thriving community of cement, rivet, and chain manufacturers soon developed, while nicknames like Mud Island and Industrial Island were eventually superceded by a more appealing moniker reflecting the looming bridge, rebuilt as a steel girder span in 1954. By then, the island's economic fortunes, first dented by the Great Depression, had declined and it was little more than a shady enclave of squatters and half-empty sheds. The 1970s saw a surprising second incarnation, this time as a center for performance, artisan studios, and quirky shops of the non-chain variety. Strolling the labyrinthine streets today, it's this combination of cultural bustle framed by reminders of past industry that generates the area's distinctive flavor.

● You'll start on the boardwalk under the retro-look neon sign, straddling the bridge stanchions at the island's Anderson St. entrance. With brightly painted buildings and camera-toting tourists ahead, it's hard to believe this was originally one of Vancouver's toughest areas, with dozens of small industries colonizing a shadowy maze of greasy workshops. In the Depression-era 1930s, when many of these micro-businesses failed, the island became home to hundreds of desperate families in a ragged shantytown called Bennettville, named ironically after the prime minister of the time. There was also a second entrance to the island nearby: a rickety wooden stairway snaking down from the overhead bridge directly into this makeshift residential area. It was dismantled in WWII to prevent sabotage from any enemy agents who might be lurking about.

- Continue north under the bridge into the heart of the island and, if it's raining, duck into the Umbrella Shop on your right. Founded in 1935, this legendary, family-run business still makes and repairs umbrellas with ancient sewing machines across town at its Broadway headquarters. Alternatively, the cavernous Kids Market next door is a Technicolor smorgasbord of kites, soft toys, and Japanese action figures.

- Turning right onto Cartwright St. at the next corner, you'll spot train tracks still embedded in the road, evidence of an internal rail system once used for moving goods around the island. On your left, check out the Mission-style façade of Granville Island Brewing. Vancouver's first microbrewery when it opened in 1984 and now the region's biggest independent beer maker, production has mostly shifted to a larger out-of-town facility. You can still take a sudsy tour of the small-batch production room, culminating in the beam-ceilinged Taproom, where you'll be treated to samples of Cypress Lager, English Bay Pale Ale, and the recommended Kitsilano Maple Cream Ale.

- Weaving along Cartwright St., you'll enter the island's performing arts core. The Waterfront Theatre on your right and the Carousel Theatre on your left—as well as the Arts Club Theatre's Granville Island Stage near the Public Market—are testaments to the deep greasepaint undercurrent here. The area houses more than a dozen theatrical venues and is the home of September's giant 10-day Vancouver International Fringe Festival. If you're here during the event, expect to be regularly accosted by crazy clowns, chatty drag queens, and penny-farthing-riding eccentrics promoting their shows.

  But art is not just about performance on Granville Island and many of the former industrial sheds now turn out swirly blown glass, filigree silver jewelry, or hand-hewn musical instruments. Just past the Waterfront Theatre, the Crafthouse Gallery, run by the Crafts Association of BC, showcases high-end, locally produced paintings, intricate stained glass, and elegant driftwood carvings. Across the street is the Gallery of BC Ceramics, a cornucopia of rustic teapots, pottery wall hangings, and achingly appealing glazed mugs.

- Duck along the little pathway beside this gallery and you'll hit the somewhat hidden Railspur Alley. Lined with a dozen small stores and galleries (plus an attendant old rail line) consider dropping in for coffee at Agro Cafe, where you can hang out with paint-stained artists and an attendant clutch of dedicated hipsters. Incongruously, a couple of doors away is Vancouver's only artisan sake maker.

- Follow the train tracks east and you'll soon re-join Cartwright St. You'll pass a little boat-building operation on your left, as well as the Federation of Canadian Artists Gallery, before the Granville Island Hotel looms ahead of you. A boutique sleepover with waterfront views, non-guests can also partake of the restaurant and brewpub here: the patio is one of the best in the city for a long chat on a summer evening. You're at the eastern tip of the island now, so it's probably best to stop walking unless you want to get your feet wet.

- Turn back west along Johnston St., the island's parallel artery, and take a quick right-hand detour under the yellow dock crane—another reminder of the area's industrial heritage. It's accompanied by an odd assortment of rusting maritime ephemera, including a painted buoy that resembles a giant, discarded Christmas ornament. Step onto the waterfront boardwalk here and take in the view. Across shimmering False Creek, you'll see the forest of shiny condominium towers that inspired local lad Douglas Coupland to name his observational book on Vancouver *City of Glass*. Look down, though, and you'll encounter a different way of living. The houseboats clinging to the island's north bank here are of the high-end variety. Complete with Modernist designs, expansive patios, and flower-lined rooftop gardens, these may be some of Vancouver's most desirable residences.

- Doubling back to Johnston St. and continuing west, you'll start running into a younger demographic. The student slackers hanging out on the sidewalks here are evidence that you've stumbled onto the campus of Emily Carr University. Named after BC's most famous painter—you can see her rich, nature-themed canvases at the Vancouver Art Gallery downtown—this revered institution trains the next generation of artists in a variety of genres. Duck into the university's Charles H. Scott Gallery on your right for a glimpse of student and graduate artwork. There's also an annual portfolio show every May where piquant photography, challenging multimedia, and predictably odd installations occupy several additional rooms.

- By this stage, you might have concluded that the island has turned its back on the industry that founded it. But a few steps past the university, you'll come across the gray silos and towering grit pyramids of Ocean Construction Supplies. The area's oldest tenant, the still-working cement-maker started here in 1917 and now cranks out enough product to build a 10-story tower block every week. The company hosts regular open days for curious visitors and has transformed some of its churning trucks into unusual advertising for Granville Island—look out for the giant strawberry truck trundling around town.

- Continuing your westward weave along Johnston St., you'll soon spot an open-air First Nations carving shed on your right, fashioned into the shape of a traditional longhouse. Fronted by a handsome pair of Coast Salish "houseposts"—check out the copper-painted eyes on the swimming salmon—expert totem pole carvers can often be seen here working the wood in front of mesmerized visitors watching the animals emerge in cedar before them.

- If your westward route has suddenly become more congested, you've reached the area's star attraction. On your right, Granville Island Public Market is the main reason many locals and visitors come here. A cornucopia of tempting produce—highlights are local seasonal cherries, apples, and blueberries—as well as a supporting cast of delectable deli treats, the market is a foodie paradise. Follow your nose as you weave around the stalls and you'll find an international food court where the likes of battered oysters, butter chicken, and salmon wraps are on offer. Guided culinary tours of the market are also offered.

  Hungry or not, the market is the ideal place to conclude your Granville Island trawl. Step outside to the waterfront here—where buskers and fish and seagulls share the patio—for sigh-inducing views of the nearby Art Deco Burrard Bridge and the craggy Coastal Mountains peeking at you from tree-studded North Vancouver. Consider heading into the sunset from here on one of the tiny Tonka toy ferries that ply the waters between here and downtown, or stroll back via Duranleau St. to your original departure point.

# POINTS OF INTEREST

**Umbrella Shop** 1550 Anderson St., 604-697-0919

**Kids Market** 1496 Cartwright St., 604-689-8447

**Granville Island Brewing** 1441 Cartwright St., 604-687-2739

**Waterfront Theatre** 1412 Cartwright St., 604-685-3005

**Carousel Theatre** 1411 Cartwright St., 604-669-3410

**Arts Club Theatre Company Granville Island Stage** 1585 Johnson St., 604-687-1644

**Crafthouse Gallery** 1386 Cartwright St., 604-687-6511

**Gallery of BC Ceramics** 1359 Cartwright St., 604-669-3606

**Agro Cafe** 1363 Railspur Alley, 604-669-0724

**Federation of Canadian Artists Gallery** 1241 Cartwright St., 604-681-8534

**Granville Island Hotel** 1253 Johnston St., 604-683-7373

**Emily Carr University** 1399 Johnston St., 604-844-3800

**Ocean Construction Supplies** Johnston St., 604-261-2211

**Granville Island Public Market** 1689 Johnston St., 604-666-6477

*Mini-ferry parked at Granville Island*

## route summary

1. Start at the island entrance and head north on Anderson St.
2. Turn right onto Cartwright St.
3. Turn left at the Gallery of BC Ceramics to Railspur Alley.
4. Head east on Railspur Alley and re-join Cartwright St.
5. Turn left at the end of Cartwright St. and head west along Johnston St.
6. Continue along Johnston St. to Granville Island Public Market.
7. Return to the island entrance via Duranleau St. and Anderson St.

*Taproom at Granville Island Brewing*

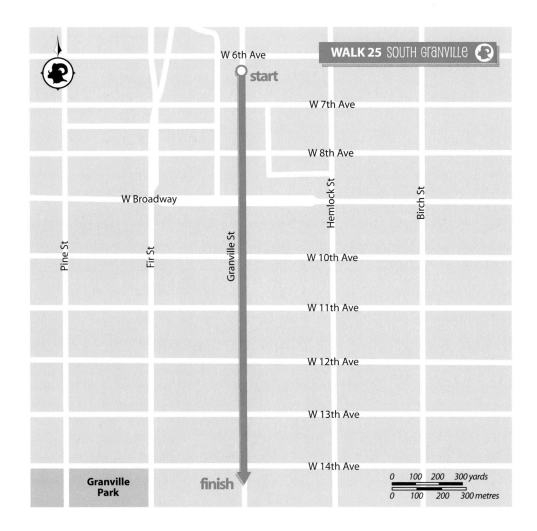

W 6th Ave

start

W 7th Ave

W 8th Ave

Hemlock St

Birch St

W Broadway

Pine St

Fir St

Granville St

W 10th Ave

W 11th Ave

W 12th Ave

W 13th Ave

W 14th Ave

Granville
Park

finish

0    100   200   300 yards

0    100   200   300 metres

# 25 SOUTH GranVILLE: arTSY SHOPPING Promenade

**BOUNDARIES: W. 6th Ave., Granville St. W. 15th Ave.**
**DISTANCE: ½ mile/¾ kilometre**
**DIFFICULTY: Moderate**
**PARKING: There's a parkade at the Seymour Medical Centre, half a block west of Granville on W. 7th Ave, and another on the east side of the 2600 block of Granville. There's also metered street parking on most Granville side streets.**
**PUBLIC TRANSIT: Buses 4, 7, 10, 16, 17, and 50 run from downtown and stop on the south side of Granville Bridge,**

Enthusiastically marketed in recent years as "South Granville Rise"—a name that cleverly spins the steep uphill stroll starting just past the south end of Granville Bridge in a positive light—this area is popular with the kind of shoppers who prefer alfresco storefront promenades to hermetically sealed mega-malls. Bring your credit cards and you'll have a great time strolling the galleries, boutiques, and restaurants—just remember you'll have to carry anything you don't eat. But first, a little name-based context: George Leveson-Gower, Earl of Granville, who was Queen Victoria's Colonial Secretary, graciously lent his moniker to the fledgling Gastown-area settlement in 1870. Unfortunately (or fortunately) the colony became a province a year later. The little settlement expanded, and "Vancouver" was adopted as the city's new name in 1886, leaving the noble lord to content himself with a mere street name. Luckily, he would have fitted right in on this side of the bridge; while Granville St.'s north-of-the-bridge stretch has a long and sometimes seedy history as Vancouver's main entertainment strip, South Granville has always been more sedate—perhaps due to the sobering proximity of upper-class Shaughnessy Heights rising over its southern shoulder.

● **Begin your leisurely amble with a walk-fueling breakfast at the cozy Paul's Place Omelettery, on the right-hand side of Granville St., just past the intersection with W. 6th Ave. This under-the-radar eatery has a loyal following among a growing number of locals—many from the shiny new condo buildings across the street. Classic breakfasts are on offer as well as burgers and sandwiches if it's closer to lunchtime. Carnivores should tuck into the Da Vinci omelet, made with wild game and chorizo sausage.**

● Head south uphill on Granville. Scratch your chin in a musing, intellectual manner at Heffel Fine Art Auction House just before the W. 7th Ave. intersection. This bright gallery space—colonizing a brick-built 1912 bank building—often displays a grand selection of Canadian artworks. If you're lucky, you'll find an E.J. Hughes or two. This revered but eminently humble Vancouver Island artist painted iconic, stylized BC landscapes and his work has leapt in value since his 2007 death. Before you move on, head outside to the gallery's southern exterior for a reminder of another famed BC painter. The unexpected bronze artwork here depicts a jaunty Emily Carr with her animal chums, including a pet monkey.

● Continue south up Granville's right side—don't worry, the steep climb will soon be over—and check out the string of galleries past W. 8th Ave. Recommended stops are the contemporary-focused Equinox Gallery, which sometimes displays Fred Herzog's brilliant nostalgic photographs of 1950s Vancouver; the Douglas Reynolds Gallery, where contemporary and historic First Nations works, ranging from carvings to lithographs, are elegantly exhibited; and the Monte Clark Gallery, renowned for its eye-popping array of challenging works by modern artists from Canada and beyond.

● If you've scratched enough of your artistic itches, keep going south on Granville to the next intersection. One of Vancouver's busiest crossroads, Granville and Broadway is lined with shops on all four corners. You may want to peruse Oscar's Art Books and the other bookstores nearby, or just cross to the southeast corner and check out the area's most intriguing building. Completed in 1929, the sandy-colored Dick Building was constructed by the team who also built City Hall. Similarly ornate, this narrow brick edifice combines Art Deco flourishes with Gothic-style arches and dozens of panels packed with a regimented flower pattern. The building's main corner also features a lovely old neon sign.

● Cross back to the right side of Granville and continue south into the area's shopper-hugging heartland. On your right is the white-painted façade of Vancouver's only Restoration Hardware outlet. Across the street is the Pottery Barn and farther up is Williams-Sonoma. There are also women's clothing stores like DKNY, Bellisima, and Ashia Mode. Cross over W. 10th and W. 11th to a purple-fronted corner shop offering far more affordable treats. Family-run Purdy's Chocolates opened its first shop, on Robson St., in 1907. Many of the finger-licking recipes developed then are still used today, despite the company now operating 50 stores across the country. As Western Canada's largest chocolate maker, production has since shifted to a state-of-the-art facility on Kingsway. Drop in here and try in vain to resist the pecan-packed Sweet Georgia Browns or the truffle-filled chocolate hedgehogs.

- Cross Granville and stroll half a block east along W. 11th. You'll quickly come to one of the city's favorite dine-out spots, although one of its chosen ingredients might have you rushing back to Purdy's. Operated by husband-and-wife team Meeru and Vikram Vij, Vij's has taken an adventurous fusion approach to East Indian cuisine since its 1994 opening. But while dishes like marinated mango sablefish and cream-curried lamb popsicles are firm favorites, the restaurant recently experimented with dried, high-protein locusts on its menu. Before you picture munching on crunchy insect legs, the idea is to crush the locusts into a fine flour for chapatti flatbreads. Don't worry: a non-bug alternative is always available.

- Returning to Granville, turn left and within a few seconds you'll be standing under the canopy of the historic Stanley Theatre. Opened in 1931 as a live venue and movie house, this beloved 1,200-seat theatre has an exterior that's an unusual mélange of Art Deco and Moorish. Closed in 1991 and threatened with demolition, the venue was instead painstakingly restored and eventually taken over by the Arts Club Theatre Company. It now hosts a regular season of productions, with musicals especially popular. A time capsule containing photos of the current streetscape was recently buried outside the theatre and is scheduled to be pried open in 2107.

- Tap dance farther south along Granville to the end of the 2700 block. On the corner, you can exercise your shopping muscles again at Bacci's. This little store combines artsy women's clothing on one side and a room full of hard-to-resist trinkets piled high on antique wooden tables on the other. Check out the large bull's-eye painted on the store's exterior; it marks the spot where a car smacked into the side of the building (sans injuries) a few years ago.

- Cross back to the right side of Granville. Looming over you is one of the street's most impressive landmarks. Designed by William Todd, the Georgian revival Douglas Lodge opened as a bank in 1912 but later became an office and apartment complex. Its handsome red-brick exterior was restored in 1980 and the seven-story block is now the strip's most sought-after apartment address. Crane high and you'll see the foliage of a rooftop garden spilling over the top. The building has a colorful celebrity past: Emily Carr once gave painting lessons here and past residents include Ted Danson, John Candy, and Sarah McLachlan.

● Wind up your walk by continuing south, crossing W. 12th and W. 13th and then re-crossing to Granville's left side. Just past the intersection with W. 14th Ave. is Meinhardt Fine Foods. One of the city's favorite luxury nosh stores, this large deli and grocery store is a fun browse even if you're not planning to buy anything. Check out the high-stacked shelves of ultra-fine olive oil and imported breakfast cereals and keep an eye on the clientele: immaculately dressed ladies of a certain age and income who clearly buy all their groceries at the highest prices and quality around.

## POINTS OF INTEREST

**Paul's Place Omelettery** 2211 Granville St., 604-737-2857

**Heffel Fine Art Auction House** 2247 Granville St., 604-732-6505

**Equinox Gallery** 2321 Granville St., 604-736-2405

**Douglas Reynold Gallery** 2335 Granville St., 604-731-9292

**Monte Clark Gallery** 2339 Granville St., 604-730-5000

**Purdy's Chocolates** 2705 Granville St., 604-732-7003

**Vij's** 1480 W. 11th Ave., 604-736-6664

**Stanley Theatre** 2750 Granville St., 604-687-1644

**Bacci's** 2790 Granville St., 604-733-4933

**Meinhardt Fine Foods** 3002 Granville St., 604-732-4405

# route summary

1. Start on the west side of Granville St., just south of the W. 6th Ave. intersection.
2. Head uphill south on this side of Granville until Broadway.
3. Cross over to the other side of Granville at Broadway.
4. Cross over Broadway.
5. Cross back to the right side of Granville across the south side of Broadway.
6. Continue south on the right side of Granville.
7. Cross over Granville at W. 11th Ave.
8. Continue half a block east along W. 11th.
9. Return to Granville and turn left.
10. At Granville's 2700 block, cross back to right side of the street.
11. Continue on the right side of Granville to W. 14th Ave.
12. Cross back to the left side of Granville.

*Douglas Lodge*

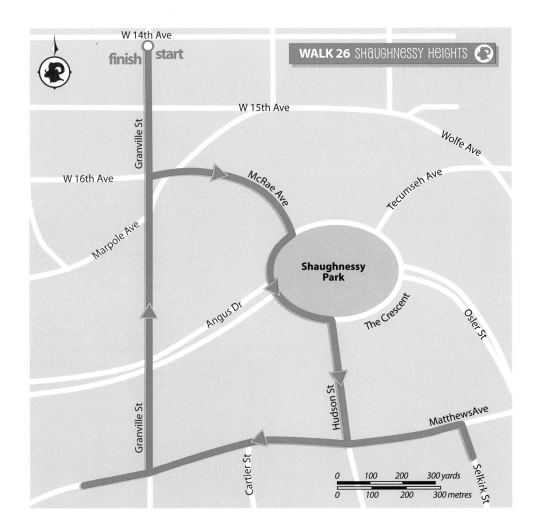

W 14th Ave

finish start

WALK 26 SHAUGHNESSY HEIGHTS

W 15th Ave

Granville St

Wolfe Ave

W 16th Ave

McRae Ave

Tecumseh Ave

Marpole Ave

Shaughnessy Park

Angus Dr

The Crescent

Osler St

Granville St

Hudson St

MatthewsAve

Cartier St

Selkirk St

| 0 | 100 | 200 | 300 yards |
| 0 | 100 | 200 | 300 metres |

# 26 SHAUGHNESSY HEIGHTS: VANCOUVER'S GRAND OLD DAME

**BOUNDARIES:** **W. 14th Ave., The Crescent, Selkirk St., Matthews Ave.**
**DISTANCE:** ¾ **mile/1¼ kilometres**
**DIFFICULTY:** **Easy**
**PARKING:** **Metered street parking on nearby Granville St. There's also a parkade half a block west along W. 16th Ave., just past the intersection with Granville St.**
**PUBLIC TRANSIT:** **The 10 bus stops just before W. 14th on Granville St.**

If you're a lottery winner looking for a new home, strolling Shaughnessy Heights' leafy avenues is a handy house-hunting walk and an eye-opening glimpse of how the other half lives. But this sumptuous heritage district wasn't always thus. After 19th-century logging, the area was left bald and barren with little hope for development: deemed too far from downtown, nobody in their right mind wanted to live out here. But this remoteness was interpreted as exclusivity when the Canadian Pacific Railway began eyeing sites for a new super-rich neighborhood. Company president Sir Thomas Shaughnessy lent his name to the fledgling utopia for fat cats and hundreds of workers arrived in 1909 to lay out the streets and infrastructure. The local glitterati—huddled in drafty old mansions in the West End at the time—wanted a change and had the money to pay for it. Within five years, 250 palatial new homes had been built and occupied, signaling Vancouver's entry into a new age of opulence. Many of these homes are still occupied by the city's oldest families, and walking the area today is like wandering a museum of architectural styles from revivalist Tudor and Georgian to colonial Dutch and Spanish.

● Start on the left-hand side of Granville St. just past the intersection with W. 14th Ave. Adjoining the popular Meinhardt Fine Foods outlet, there's a little café called Picnic where you can grab a bench seat at the giant communal table. It's a good spot to fuel up—the breakfast muffins are recommended—and it's worth tucking a few cookies into your backpack here to keep you going on the walk ahead.

● Continue south on Granville, up the incline, and cross over the intersection with W. 16th Ave. After crossing Marpole Ave., McRae Ave. is immediately on your left. Turn onto it

## Back Story: Shaugnessy's Favorite Pad

The almost palace-like, 30-room McRae Mansion—fronted by ivy-covered Neoclassical columns and encircled by a large landscaped garden strewn with sculptures—was completed in 1911. It first served as the residence of General Alexander Duncan McRae, whose fortune came from vast forestry and cannery operations. From its hilltop promontory, the home originally enjoyed stunning views across much of the low-rise city, although the family probably spent less time perusing the vistas and more time swanning around their teahouse, tennis courts, swimming pool, and wine cellar, which had its own secret entrance. The decadent parties held here, especially the 1920s New Year costumed balls, were the talk of the town. In the 1940s, after years of economic austerity, the home was donated to the government, becoming a convalescence home for war veterans. Several soldiers who died here at the time are said to haunt the property. The home is now run by the University Women's Club of Vancouver, whose regular social events include the popular Christmas at Hycroft open house, when rooms are richly decorated with Yuletide élan and seasonal crafts and baking are sold for charity.

and climb this steep but short street. You'll soon come to the stately McRae Mansion on your left. Known as Hycroft, this is one of the jewels of Shaughnessy Heights.

● Follow McRae Ave. and within a couple of minutes you'll come to the leafy heart of Shaughnessy Heights. Encircling the tree-studded, oval-shaped Shaughnessy Park—it's not much bigger than a large traffic roundabout—the Crescent is the road from which many of the neighborhood's poshest streets radiate. Peer down the wide, oak-tree-lined Osler Ave. and Angus Dr., in particular, and you'll see many of the city's largest heritage mansions. There's a tranquil, romanticized olde-England feel to this area. It's worth walking through the park: many of the trees were planted decades ago and there are several dozen carefully chosen varieties.

On the western outer edge of the park space, at the point where McRae joins the Crescent, check out the handsome mansion designed by Samuel Maclure, whose homes flavor the neighborhood like bottles of fine wine. Built in 1912, a few years after England's William Morris had spearheaded the Arts and Crafts movement as a synthesis of historic and modern esthetics, this large home looks both cozy and elegant. It was built for Walter Nichol, who founded the still-operating *Province* daily newspaper in 1890 and was BC lieutenant-governor from 1920 to 1926. Subsequently the home was owned for many decades by the Bentley family who themselves founded Canfor, the country's biggest softwood lumber export company. The last Bentley to live at the eight-fireplace property, which is reputed to have changed little since it was built, died in 2004. The property was later sold for $7 million.

● Follow the curve of the Crescent counterclockwise and cross over the end of Angus Dr. On the corner, you'll come to the Frederick Kelly House, designed for wholesale grocer Kelly by architects Townley and Matheson—the team that later created the Art Deco city hall. A departure from most of its determinedly English-style neighbors, this mansion looks more like an upscale barn conversion. Its picturesque 1920s wrap-over roof is a Dutch Colonial Revival style that is rarely found in the city.

● Continue counterclockwise around the Crescent and your next notable mansion is the stunningly ostentatious MacDonald House, a white-painted Neoclassical revival that looks like a transplant from colonial Virginia. Completed in 1913, it was built for high-ranking CPR official George MacDonald. Known among local glitterati as the Hollies, the home was sold just a few years later to Robert Mann, an executive at the rival Canadian National Railway. Later converted to apartments, in recent years it was changed back to its original single-family set-up, reflecting a drive among Shaughnessy locals to see the area's homes retained as private dwellings.

● After circling the Crescent a few times, stroll south along Hudson St., then take the next turn left onto Matthews Ave. At the next intersection, turn right onto Selkirk St. A minute or two in, on your right, you'll spot Rosemary, the grand home at 3689 Selkirk. One of Shaughnessy's largest estates, this verdant Tudoresque hulk was built in 1915 for lawyer and distillery owner A.E. Tulk who named the home after his only daughter. After WWII, it became a Catholic convent named after Our Lady of the Cenacle. In recent years, it's been returned to its original private residence status.

- Retrace your steps along Selkirk and turn left onto Matthews Ave. Continue west along this thoroughfare for five minutes or so, carefully crossing over Granville St until you reach the 1600 block of Matthews. On your left is arguably the area's most magnificent confection. Now the home of the Canuck Place children's hospice, this bright-painted clapboard mansion was built for William Lamont Tait in 1911. A Scottish immigrant (he named the home Glen Brae), he added the building's dominant twin turrets to remind him of Highland castles, but locals nicknamed it "Mae West." Tait and his wife died a few years after moving in and the house was later the Canadian headquarters for the Ku Klux Klan before becoming a daycare and then a private hospital. In 1995, the building became a picturesque and now much-loved children's hospice.

- Turn back along Matthews Ave. and make a left onto Granville. On your left-hand side, you'll come to 3589 Granville, one of the neighborhood's best Craftsman-style properties. Built in 1912 and renovated in 2008, the home makes good use of local quarried stone on its base and tops this with its handsome clapboard-clad upper floors, a curved glass turret, and a multi-gabled roof, complete with overhanging eaves. Its most colorful historic residents were the John Westaway Society. This band of religious philosophers lived and mused on the property for almost two decades from the 1960s onwards. The organization, still operating in Agassiz, BC, is opposed to medicine and worldly possessions and promotes vegetarianism.

- Glance across to the other side of Granville as you amble downhill. You might walk by without seeing a large building, the main office of the Consulate-General of the People's Republic of China. Obscured by trees, it could go unnoticed unless there's one of the ongoing protests by Falun Gong or Tibet supporters taking place outside its gates.

- Continue north on Granville and check out the magnificent Shaughnessy mansion now on your left. Brenchley House, a palatial black and white striped Tudor revival masterpiece designed by Maclure was built in 1912. Instantly identifiable as an English-style home, its steeply gabled roof, leaded windows, and "magpie" exterior includes a base of heavy stone that give it a distinctive West Coast twist. Built for Arthur Brenchley, a wholesale grocer, it's still a family dwelling and has been sympathetically restored in recent years. If you have a spare few million dollars on you, consider making an offer or amble downhill, back to Meinhardt's café for a rewarding slice of cake.

# POINTS OF INTEREST

**Picnic** 3010 Granville St., 604-732-4405

**McRae Mansion/Hycroft House** 1439 McRae Ave.

**Shaughnessy Park** The Crescent

**Nichol House** 1402 The Crescent

**Frederick Kelly House** 1393 The Crescent

**MacDonald House** 1388 The Crescent

**Rosemary** 3689 Selkirk St.

**Canuck Place** 1690 Matthews Ave.

**Consulate-General of the People's Republic of China** 3380 Granville St.

**Brenchley House** 3351 Granville St.

# ROUTE SUMMARY

1. Head south from the corner of Granville St. and W. 14th Ave.
2. Cross W. 16th Ave. and Marpole St. and turn left onto McRae Ave.
3. Head to the end of McRae.
4. Circle Shaughnessy Park on the Crescent.
5. Head south on Hudson St.
6. Turn left on Matthews Ave.
7. Turn right on Selkirk Rd.
8. Double-back to Matthews, follow it west, crossing over Granville St.
9. Continue on Matthews to 1600 block.
10. Return along Matthews and turn left onto Granville.
11. Follow Granville back to tour starting point.

*Canuck Place*

English Bay

Beach Ave

Vanier
Park

finish

Ogden Ave

Museum
of Vancouver

Burrard Bridge

Cypress St

Chestnut St

Burrard St

Cornwall Ave

Creekside Dr

Burrard St

W 1st Ave

Granville Bridge

Granville
Island

start

Fir St

W 2nd Ave

0   100   200   300 yards

0   100   200   300 metres

# 27 Vanier Park: FISH-FLavored Museum Stroll

BOUNDARIES: **Anderson St, W. 1st Ave., Creekside Dr, Ogden Ave.**
DISTANCE: **1¼ miles/2 kilometres**
DIFFICULTY: **Easy**
PARKING: **There is pay parking throughout Granville Island as well as individual parking lots at the Museum of Vancouver and the Vancouver Maritime Museum in Vanier Park.**
PUBLIC TRANSIT: **The 50 bus stops at Anderson St. and W. 2nd Ave., a minute or so from the seawall walk near the entrance to Granville Island and the start of this stroll.**

Many people come to Vanier Park with an outdoor activity in mind. The 30-acre/15.3-hectare elbow of waterfront at the southern entrance to False Creek is characterized by rolling grass banks, making it a blank slate for whatever visitors feel like doing. Among the well-to-do locals of nearby Kitsilano, this often includes jogging, dog-walking, or kite-flying. But the park is also home to three museums and is the temporary residence of two of the city's most beloved annual festivals. The land now occupied by the park also has a long, mostly forgotten history: it was once part of the 72-acre/29-hectare Kitsilano Reserve, created for the Squamish First Nation in 1870, and it included houses, orchards, a cemetery, and a large community longhouse, all nestled among old-growth forest. Eyeing the area for logging and industrial development, the provincial government later coerced these residents into selling it, and almost all vestiges of this First Nations heritage have been lost. In recent years, the Government of Canada has accepted the dubious nature of land sales like this and it recently compensated the Squamish people to the tune of $92 million, covering this and other lost reserves.

●   You'll start on Anderson St., facing the entrance to Granville Island. Instead of heading onto the island, though, turn left along the seawall, following the walkway as it snakes around the boat-packed waterfront. Just before the foot of W. 1st, turn your attention to a small plaque on the concrete lip of the shoreline. It marks the spot where, in 1971, a fledgling local activist group called the Don't Make a Wave Committee launched its "first action," setting sail to Alaska on board the chartered *Phyllis Cormack* to protest U.S. nuclear testing. While the boat was turned back by the U.S. navy and never reached its destination, the activists were inspired to continue making waves, and the following year changed their name to Greenpeace.

- Almost opposite the plaque on your left, you'll spot a seafood shack that has the kind of commitment to locally sourced, sustainable ingredients that would please any passing greenie. Go Fish is a true locals' favorite and along with its popular fish and chips, it serves an array of slightly more gourmet fare that would easily be at home in far pricier seafood joints. The scallop burger and fish tacones are recommended, but check the ever-changing specials board for whatever is new that day. The long line-ups can be a pain here and if you can't snag one of the limited number of alfresco seats, pack your nosh for a picnic in the nearby park.

- Continue park-bound along the seawall and you'll soon come to where Go Fish sources much of its fresh product. The Federal Fisheries Wharf is home to a small armada of commercial boats, part of the region's West Coast fishing fleet. While the fleet has shrunk markedly in recent years, due mainly to the collapse of fishing stocks, some of the fishers here still sell their fresh catch right off the back of the boats. Expect to see signs for fresh prawns and salmon.

- Follow the seawall west into the wharf's parking lot and then take a sharp left up the ramped entrance. At the top of the ramp, turn right and head up the concrete steps into Creekside Park. Follow the walkway around the elevated little park, taking time to drink in the panorama of idling fishing boats. You'll notice that the commercial boats are almost outnumbered by the pleasure boats crowding the left-hand side of the wharf. After a couple of minutes, the walkway drops you back down to ground level. At the crossroads, follow the sign to your right that says "Vanier Park."

- As you round the corner along the seawall trail, you'll find—almost hidden in the bushes on your left—a large, colorful totem pole. Its arms outstretched, it's a Squamish Nation welcome marker. Carved as a grandfather figure, it signifies the territory of the area's original inhabitants. Created by master carver Darren Yelton, the pole has a twin located at Ambleside Beach in West Vancouver. As you continue your stroll, it's worth reflecting on the First Nations who once called this place home: a 4,000 square foot/372 square metre longhouse sat directly in the area you're now walking on.

- As you round the corner, immediately before Burrard Bridge, check out the tiny park space on your right. Called Cultural Harmony Grove, it recognizes Vancouverites who have contributed to the city's intercultural unity. Their names are etched on little plaques affixed to rocks in the middle of the park. In their honor, the area is also a fledgling arboretum of prized plant life with little arbutus, monkey puzzle, and Japanese maple trees growing in the shadow of the bridge.

● Before you pass under the towering span, take some time to check out its architecture. Built to link downtown with the communities of Kitsilano and Point Grey, it's arguably the city's most beautiful crossing. Packed with Art Deco flourishes, the jutting boat prows and glowing, torch-like lamps at either end are especially handsome. A Royal Canadian Air Force seaplane was flown under the deck during its festive 1932 opening ceremony. The bridge was built at a time when traffic flows were much lighter, and city planners have struggled in recent years to come up with a scheme that increases its capacity without destroying its status as an architectural treasure.

● Stroll under the bridge here and continue west along the trail. Burrard Civic Marina is on your immediate right and the grassy knolls of Vanier Park are straight ahead of you. Bear to the right and follow the waterfront trail around the park perimeter. Usually fairly tranquil, this area is packed with crowds at choice times of the year. This is the home of the Vancouver International Children's Festival, a multi-day springtime extravaganza of kid-friendly shows, displays, and, of course, face painting. But it's the annual Bard on the Beach Shakespeare festival, staged in circus-like big tops, that draws the cultured locals. Spearheaded by energetic actor-director-entrepreneur Christopher Gaze, a professional troupe performs up to four plays here from May to September. A signature Vancouver moment is to catch a show accompanied by a mountain sunset winking at you through the open back of the stage.

● Continue west along the seaside stroll, blinking at the picture-perfect vistas of the West End, Stanley Park, and the tree-bristled peaks across the water on your right. It's an imposing, nature-dominated view that would have made plenty of jaws drop among the first Europeans to arrive here in the late 1700s. On your left is a Modernist public artwork recalling those first visitors. A monument dedicated to the 1792 arrival of Captain George Vancouver, *Gate to the Northwest Passage*, is a large, curve-bottomed steel square that looks like a giant window. If you stand behind it, you can frame a perfect view of the mountains.

● Maintaining your seawall stroll, follow the trail as it curves left toward the Vancouver Maritime Museum, a dramatic A-frame building rising like an arrow into the sky. It was constructed to house the famed RCMP ship *St. Roch*, the first vessel to sail in both directions through the Northwest Passage, a feat achieved between 1940 and 1944. When it later sailed from Vancouver to Halifax via the Panama Canal, it also became the first ship to circumnavigate North America. Take some time to peruse the boat— there's usually a free tour available to fill you in on the details—then lap up some of the attendant maritime ephemera documenting the region's salty seafaring past. It's also worth checking out the motley flotilla of boats moored in the water outside. These include the *Ben Franklin*, a NASA research submarine used for a record-breaking 30-day dive in 1969. It bears more than a passing resemblance to a certain Beatles-inspired vessel.

● Leave the waterfront and follow the signposted, tree-lined walkway from the Maritime Museum parking lot to a nearby building that's one of the most impressive in the city. Shared by the Museum of Vancouver and the H.R. MacMillan Space Centre, this UFO-shaped structure was gifted by a wealthy forestry family and opened in 1969. But while it has a pleasing sci-fi look, all is not as it seems. Recalling the area's original inhabitants, the sloped roof of the building was designed to echo the conical hats traditionally worn by the Coast Salish First Nation. Also check out the stainless steel crab sculpture fronting the building. Looking ready to snip at passing visitors, it reflects the Coast Salish belief that crabs are guardians of the nearby harbor. Under the sculpture, there's a time capsule due to be opened on July 1st 2067, Canada's 200th birthday.

● Give yourself some time to duck into the two attractions here. On the left-hand side of the building, the Space Centre is lined with kid-friendly, hands-on exhibits including flight simulators and showy physics experiments. On the right, you can indulge in some local nostalgia at the Museum of Vancouver, or you may want to make plans to return in the evening for a planetarium show. Once you've had your fill, head back to your car or stroll south, via Chestnut St., to Cornwall St. where bus 22 will take you back downtown.

## POINTS OF INTEREST

**Go Fish** 1504 W. 1st Ave., 604-730-5040

**Federal Fisheries Wharf** near the foot of Pennyfarthing Dr.

**Creekside Park** corner of Pennyfarthing Dr. and Creekside Dr.

**Cultural Harmony Grove** under east side of Burrard Bridge

**Burrard Civic Marina** 1655 Whyte Ave., 604-733-5833

**Vancouver Maritime Museum** 1905 Ogden Ave., 604-257-8300

**H.R. MacMillan Space Centre** 1100 Chestnut St., 604-738-7827

**Museum of Vancouver** 1100 Chestnut St., 604-736-4431

## route summary

1. Start before the Granville Island entrance on Anderson St.
2. Turn left onto the seawall.
3. Follow the seawall to the bottom of W. 1st Ave.
4. Continue on the seawall, turning left up the ramp in the Government Wharf parking lot.
5. Turn right into Creekside Park.
6. Follow the walkway sign right to Vanier Park.
7. Walk under Burrard Bridge.
8. Bear right for the seawall walk in Vanier Park.
9. Follow the seawall to the Vancouver Maritime Museum.
10. Follow the signposted walkway to the H.R. Macmillan Space Centre and Museum of Vancouver.

*The seawall trail in Vanier Park*

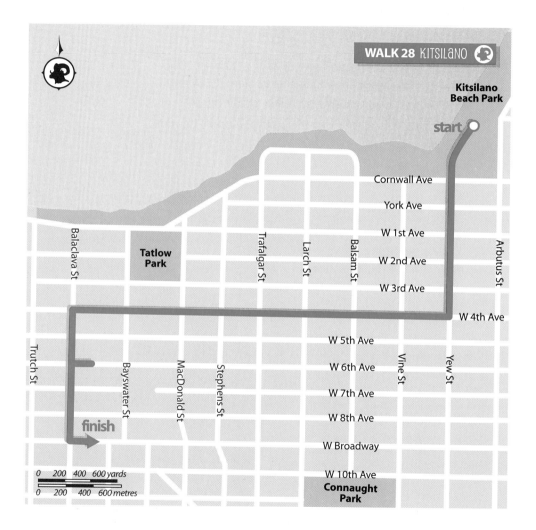

Kitsilano
Beach Park

start

Cornwall Ave

York Ave

W 1st Ave

W 2nd Ave

W 3rd Ave

W 4th Ave

W 5th Ave

W 6th Ave

W 7th Ave

W 8th Ave

W Broadway

W 10th Ave

Balaclava St

Tatlow
Park

Trafalgar St

Larch St

Balsam St

Arbutus St

Trutch St

Bayswater St

MacDonald St

Stephens St

Vine St

Yew St

finish

Connaught
Park

0   200   400   600 yards
0   200   400   600 metres

# 28 KITSILANO: HIPPY UTOPIA TO YUPPIE IDYLL

BOUNDARIES: **Kitsilano Beach Park, Yew St., Balaclava St., W. Broadway**
DISTANCE: **1½ miles/2½ kilometres**
DIFFICULTY: **Moderate**
PARKING: **There's paid parking at Kitsilano Beach Park. There's also metered street parking around Kitsilano.**
PUBLIC TRANSIT: **Buses 2 and 22 stop on Cornwall St. near Kitsilano Beach Park. Buses 9, 17, and 99 B-Line can pick you up along Broadway.**

While Kitsilano's name comes from Chief Khatsahalano, a long-ago First Nations leader, you'll find few reminders today that the Squamish and Musqueam people once called this area home. Among the first European colonists to move in was Sam Greer, an Irish settler who claimed the area in the late 1800s. At the time, Kitsilano Beach was known as Greer's Beach, and not just by him. Naturally, it wasn't long before the ubiquitous Canadian Pacific Railway muscled in on the action, evicting Greer and transforming the area into a commuter suburb and summer destination—a streetcar line soon ran along W. 4th Ave. and linked to the beach. By 1905, the stretch had been re-christened Kitsilano. A leafy enclave of mostly modest wooden homes for the next few decades, by the 1960s Kits was popular among students and hippies, who often shared houses here. During this period, a clutch of passionate area residents formed the Don't Make a Wave Committee to protest U.S. nuclear testing. A year later, they re-named it Greenpeace. Forty years on and the Kitsilano hippies have grown up and become rich: the clapboard houses they once spaced out in are now million-dollar heritage homes. When you stroll the immaculate, leafy streets today, you'll find landscaped gardens and yuppie-flavored shops and cafés: the counter-culture capital of Vancouver has become an alluring middle-class utopia.

● **Slap on the sunscreen and start your stroll at Kitsilano Beach Park. The sand is usually studded with drowsy sunbathers in summer and the rest of the year its trails are crisscrossed by wind-whipped joggers wearing Lululemon yoga gear. Alongside this rustic neighborhood hangout, the incongruously swanky Watermark eatery right in the center of the action ruffled some feathers when it opened in 2006. It's since become a popular haunt and is a good spot for brunch. If you can't snag a patio** table, spend some time on a beachfront log here drinking in one of Vancouver's best marine panoramas: sailboats dotting the glassy-calm water backed by the uninterrupted crags of the North Shore mountains.

- With your back to the restaurant patio, turn left onto the park's main walkway and follow it south as it curves around the waterfront. After a couple of minutes, you'll see Starbucks through the trees ahead of you. Follow the pathway toward the corporate coffee joint. At the edge of the park, cross over Cornwall St. and stroll past the side of Starbucks up Yew St. This southbound climb is quite steep, so be prepared for a calf-stretching hike. If you need a breather halfway up, check into Café Zen two blocks up on your right. With its cozy ambiance and red-check tablecloths, it's a friendly nook for a snack or light lunch.

- Continue up Yew for three more blocks (the climb levels off at W. 3rd Ave.), then turn right along W. 4th Ave. Kitsilano's commercial backbone, this hopping stretch of more than 300 stores and eateries is better than any mall in the city. If you want to add some extra strolling to this walk, head east along the street and check out popular lures like Zulu Records, Highend Organics, and Coast Mountain Sports. Otherwise, continue westward and within a couple of storefronts you'll come to Gravity Pope on your right. Reflecting the area's surfeit of well-off hipsters, this unisex store includes ultra-cool footwear and designer clothing for the pale and interesting set.

- Shopping bags in hand, continue west from here, rubbing shoulders with your fellow retail therapy practitioners. On either side of W. 4th, expect to be lured in by Vivid, Urban Rack, and American Apparel or elevate your mind by calling in at Duthie Books on your right-hand side

- Continue west on the right side of W. 4th among the single-story shops and, after Balsam St., you'll notice a string of boxy, two-level old apartment buildings on either side of you. Mostly well-maintained, some of these have heritage flourishes from bygone eras, including Art Deco plasterwork and streamlined, Art Moderne doorways. You're also strolling downhill now.

- Still ambling west on W. 4th, cross over to the left side just after Trafalgar St. Within a minute or so, you'll be in front of one of the few restaurant reminders of Kitsilano's

## Back Story: rise and fall of vancouver's Homegrown Book chain

While the unassuming, mid-sized Duthie Books seems to be just another local indie store, serving its regular clientele with a well-chosen array of new and classic titles, the history of this shop reads more like a thriller. The Duthie name once adorned a 10-outlet Vancouver chain that dominated the local literary scene. The first store, cleverly located on Robson St. near the public library of the time, was opened by Bill Duthie in 1957. Over the next few years, further outlets cracked open their spines on Seymour St., Hastings St. and W. 10th Ave. With the company soon becoming the largest bookstore chain in Western Canada, it was renowned for encouraging and promoting emerging Canadian writers. But when big box bookstores and their heavy discounting ways rolled into the city in the 1990s, Duthie's—by this time run by Bill's daughter—suffered a body blow from which it never recovered. After narrowly avoiding bankruptcy in 1998, the company launched a stock liquidation sale that can best be described as a feeding frenzy, with giddy customers carrying armfuls of books home for just a few dollars. This 4th Ave. store is now the only Duthie's in town.

hippy past. The Naam, with its long-standing 24-hour opening policy, lures locals as well as traveling tofu huggers with its wood-floored interior, plant-strewn patio, and cozy array of mismatched, almost antique furniture. Serially voted Vancouver's best vegetarian eatery, the menu is an eccentric array of influences, from Mexican to Japanese. There's also live music every night, often of the folksy singer-songwriter variety.

● Continue on this side of W. 4th for two more blocks. After Bayswater St., you'll be flanked by two mid-1990s condo developments that echo historic architectural movements. On your right is the Delano, a sandy-colored strip of low-rise Deco-style buildings, complete with curved corners and stylized friezes depicting Vancouver scenes—look for piston-legged cyclists, the Lions Gate Bridge, and some large lightening-forked clouds. Immediately opposite, the gabled Santa Barbara building recalls romantic, Moorish-themed Hollywood architecture of the 1930s, especially with its terra-cotta color scheme and palm tree-lined courtyards.

- Put in a bid for one of these condos then turn left along Balaclava St. at the next intersection. Strolling south into the residential heart of old Kitsilano, you'll be surrounded on either side by magnificent Craftsman homes from the early 19th century. Many of these shingle-sided houses still have their original wooden verandahs and leaded glass windows. Among the cheapest housing in the city in the 1960s, a large number are now heritage-protected and very expensive.

- Spend some time soaking up the tree-lined streetscape as you continue south on Balaclava. Then turn left along W. 6th Ave. A couple of houses in on your right, check out the garden that's like an alfresco art installation. Encircled by heavy chains doubling as a fence, rusty machine parts are fashioned into abstract sculptures, disembodied chrome fenders transformed into patio benches and, the highlight, the back end of a pink-painted 1950s car half-submerged in the earth. Angled like an arrow, it looks like it's been fired into the ground from a UFO.

- Retrace your steps along W. 6th and turn left back onto Balaclava. Continue south and, within a few minutes, turn left onto W. Broadway. This is the other main Kitsilano shopping and dining drag.

- Continue east along W. Broadway and, a few shops in on your left, you'll soon come to Vancouver's best travel bookstore. The Travel Bug is lined with maps, guidebooks, and literary exposition covering just about any place you might consider visiting. But aside from its bewildering array of titles, it also stocks a handy array of accessories. There are also regular readings and presentations here from visiting travel experts, often the kind of disheveled, cargo-panted authors who've just come back from kayaking down the Amazon armed only with a pocketknife.

- While your own travels might not be quite as exotic, you've still managed a hefty hike on this walk. Reward yourself by continuing a few doors farther along and ducking into Calhoun's Bakery Café on your left. With the rustic feel of a log cabin—the giant Canadiana paintings on the walls add to the pioneer élan—this chatty neighborhood hangout is great for a coffee pit stop or a hearty meal of the soup, sandwich, or pot pie variety. After you've filled your belly, head back outside. Carry on perusing the shops in this area or hop on a bus toward home.

## POINTS OF INTEREST

**Watermark** 1305 Arbutus St., 604-738-5487

**Café Zen** 1631 Yew St., 604-731-4018

**Gravity Pope** 2205 W. 4th Ave., 604-731-7673

**Duthie Books** 2239 W. 4th Ave., 604-732-5344

**The Naam** 2724 W. 4th Ave., 604-738-7151

**Travel Bug** 3065 W. Broadway, 604-737-1122

**Calhoun's Bakery Café** 3035 W. Broadway, 604-737-7062

*Delano Condominium building*

# route summary

1. Start in Kitsilano Beach Park, with the patio of Watermark behind you.

2. Turn left along the beachfront trail, with the water to your right.

3. Continue south along the trail.

4. When you see Starbucks through the trees, head toward it.

5. Cross over Cornwall Ave.

6. Head south uphill on Yew St.

7. Continue south for five blocks.

8. Turn right along W. 4th Ave.

9. Continue west along W. 4th. staying on the right-hand side of the street.

10. Cross to the left side of W. 4th at Trafalgar St.

11. Continue west on the left side of W. 4th.

12. Turn left along Balaclava St.

13. Turn left along W. 6th Ave. and walk for half a block.

14. Return west along W. 6th. and turn left onto Balaclava.

15. Continue south along Balaclava.

16. Turn left onto W. Broadway.

17. Continue east along W. Broadway for one block.

*Kitsilano Beach*

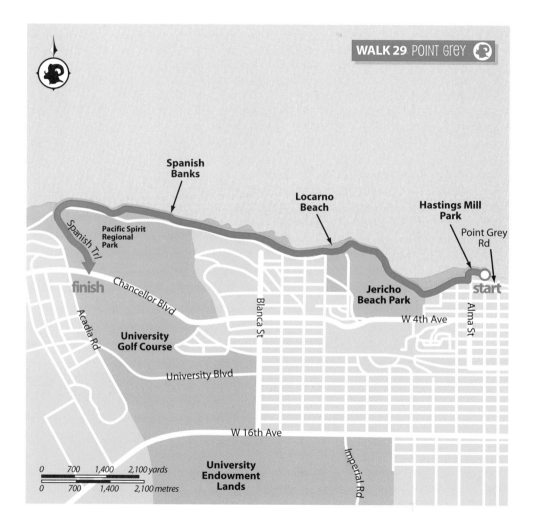

Spanish
Banks

Locarno
Beach

Hastings Mill
Park

Point Grey
Rd

Spanish Trl

Pacific Spirit
Regional
Park

finish

Chancellor Blvd

Jericho
Beach Park

start

Acadia Rd

W 4th Ave

Alma St

University
Golf Course

Blanca St

University Blvd

W 16th Ave

Imperial Rd

University
Endowment
Lands

| 0 | 700 | 1,400 | 2,100 yards |
| 0 | 700 | 1,400 | 2,100 metres |

# 29 POINT Grey: NeIGHBOrHOOD BeaCHCOMBING

BOUNDARIES: **Dunbar St., Burrard Inlet, Salish Trail, Chancellor Blvd.**
DISTANCE: **2¾ miles/4½ kilometres**
DIFFICULTY: **Moderate**
PARKING: **There's paid parking at Jericho Beach Park.**
PUBLIC TRANSIT: **Buses 4 and 44 run along W. 4th Ave.; alight around the intersection with Alma St. and stroll four blocks north to the waterfront.**

The spot where Vancouver's colonial history began, Point Grey is where the region's original Spanish and British explorers first stepped ashore looking, no doubt, for a handy Tim Hortons outlet. They weren't in luck then and they wouldn't be in luck now: this is where some of Western Canada's richest residents live and it's an area that's far too posh for Timbits. In fact, Point Grey marks a further step in the long quest among local bluebloods to find an area to call their own: they left the West End when it became too crowded, moved from Shaughnessy Heights when their drafty old mansions became too big; and eventually ended up here in newer homes that swapped palace-like grandeur for a slender peninsula of exclusivity. Strolling the area today, you'll see many of these magazine-perfect homes and the pristine SUVs their owners use to drive to the nearby shops. Luckily, you don't have to be rich to enjoy one of the main reasons they moved here. Point Grey is blessed with a lovely, highly accessible and virtually unspoiled coastline walking route that is one of Vancouver's finest natural gems. For the book's longest stroll, you'll need to be in good calf-busting fettle to fully partake of it. Pick a sunny day, hit the trail, and you won't regret it for a minute.

● With a not-too-heavy picnic stashed in your daypack, you'll start at the northern, waterfront tip of Dunbar St., just off Point Grey Rd. There's a tiny, two-bench grassy knoll here offering a sterling view over the shoreline. To your right is downtown Vancouver's compact forest of glass towers and ahead of you is the shimmering Burrard Inlet, framed by the tree-furred slopes of the North Shore mountains. Immediately below you is one of the finest untouched coastal nooks in the city (there's a steep-stepped walkway nearby if you fancy a water-level view). It's a haven for passing marine birdlife and you might see some grebes, blue herons, and even bald eagles.

● From here, turn left and follow the concrete path that hugs the cliff top. After a minute or two, you'll come to a short road called Cameron St. Follow it west to the end and ahead, across Alma St., you'll see the oldest surviving building in Vancouver. Constructed in 1865, Old Hastings Mill Store was originally located near Gastown, just far enough away from the main settlement to survive the 1886 fire that wiped out most of the township. In fact, the building was used as a makeshift morgue on the fateful day. Originally a general store, then a post office, and later a library, this large, shed-like structure was moved here by barge in 1930. It's now a museum (open on weekends only) and is worth nipping into to peruse the eclectic array of exhibits, including pioneer-era photos and clothing, a treasure trove of First Nations artifacts, and the 1930s table and chair from the mayor's office.

● The museum is situated in a small slice of grassy parkland. Stroll north along the park's eastern edge to the waterfront and then wander along the northern side, keeping your eye on the coastline to your right. The marina splayed out below you is lined with shiny pleasure boats, indicating the well-to-do neighborhood you're now wandering through. Check out the figurehead thrusting out to sea on the large white building just past the park's western edge.

● Head south up this western flank, away from the water, and turn right onto Point Grey Rd. On your immediate right is the building you've just been staring at. Occupying a magnificent shoreline promontory, the Royal Vancouver Yacht Club was founded in 1903, when it operated a floating clubhouse in Coal Harbour. With little moorage space and an expanding membership, the club moved here in 1927, expanding its second clubhouse into a swish, members-only complex in the 1970s. A hangout for Point Grey nautical types, the club hosts regattas and races throughout the year.

● Continuing west along Point Grey Rd., it's hard not to notice that you're in the most privileged of Vancouver neighborhoods. Expect new luxury cars, elegantly dressed locals, and handsome homes. As if on cue, you'll soon come to the stately, Tudoresque façade of Brock House on your right. Built in 1913 for mining industry executive Philip Gilman, it was designed by Samuel Maclure, creator of many of the mansions lining the leafy avenues of Shaughnessy. In fact, it looks like a direct transplant from that old-time chichi neighborhood. In 1922, Gilman sold the house to Reginald Brock, dean of UBC. He renamed it "Brockholm" and it's been known as Brock House locally ever since. Later serving as an RCMP divisional headquarters, it was handed over to the city in 1974. The fully renovated structure now houses a seniors' activity center as well as an atmospheric restaurant serving dinner and Sunday brunch.

- Continue west along Point Grey Rd. and cross onto the grass to your right when you see the sign for Jericho Beach Park. Just in front of the restrooms and the small café (a good spot to cool down with an ice cream), you'll come to the sandy, log-studded beach with its tree-lined park perimeter. One of the city's favorite outdoor stretches, Jericho is especially popular on languid summer evenings when a little sandy snoozing and some beachy barbecuing are de rigueur.

- After you've played around in the sand, follow the gravel walkway that runs parallel to the beach and keep going west. After a few minutes, you'll come to a large and incongruous-looking rectangular wharf hanging over the water on piles, complete with a rusting green railing perimeter. Built in the 1930s and called the Jericho Marginal Wharf, this concrete construction was originally a waterfront promenade and a Royal Canadian Air Force floatplane dock. The wharf has not been repaired for many years and plans are afoot to demolish most of it, leaving a small corner as a nostalgic reminder.

- You've almost certainly noticed a surfeit of kayakers and canoeists bobbing alongside you here. As you continue west along the shoreline trail, you'll come to the reason why: the Jericho Sailing Centre. On your left will be a string of boat rental operations followed by the two-story main building. Open to the public, this is a good spot to grab lunch—the second floor Galley Patio & Grill serves good pub grub (the wild salmon burger is recommended). Try for a patio table so you can watch the boats come in. If you're here in the evening, there are also great sunset views.

- The sand-covered trail in front of the sailing center finally gives up and dissolves into the beach here, so consider removing your shoes and socks to get the full effect. Continue west and on your right you'll soon come to a long wooden jetty fronted by three oversized boat cleats. Head onto the jetty for a blast of sea air. You'll be accompanied by a few seagulls perched on the railings, their beady eyes trained on the fishing rods of nearby anglers. Check out the sterling sea-to-sky vista here: much of it hasn't changed since those explorers arrived more than two centuries ago.

● Return to dry land and follow the trail as it curves south, then west again, along the coastline. You're now on Locarno Beach, one of the area's quieter sandy stretches, backed by a stand of tall fir trees. Its name is thought to derive from the Swiss town where a peace treaty was signed in 1925, four years before this area became a public park. If it feels like you've done enough walking for one day, this is an ideal spot to end: sit against a tree, pull out your picnic and take a restorative nap before heading up to W. 4th Ave. and taking a bus back to downtown.

● If you're feeling energetic, continue west on the trail past Locarno Beach. After a scenic amble, with the rustic waterfront to your right and the rich homes of Point Grey rising in steps on your left, you'll arrive at Spanish Banks. In 1792, British Captain George Vancouver met his Spanish counterpart Dionisio Galiano on the shore of what is now called English Bay. Both were exploring the Pacific Northwest and they shared navigational information during their meeting. Vancouver later named this area Spanish Banks in tribute to his seafaring buddies. While the British subsequently took regional control, the early presence of the Spanish is still recalled along the coastline with local islands sporting names like Galiano, Saturna, and Texada.

● Despite the Vancouver name sticking to this area, it's worth remembering that the Spanish got here first. Continuing west along the jogger-packed, park-lined beachfront, the dense forest of the Pacific Spirit Regional Park is now looming on your left. You'll eventually come to an odd-looking stylized anchor fashioned from concrete. This marks the bicentennial of Spain's regional explorations. The accompanying plaque notes that Captain Jose Maria Narvaez was the first explorer to poke his ship around here in 1791, several months before Captain Van turned up. Narvaez called the area now occupied by Spanish Banks Islas de Langara.

● Now at the end of your trek, perch on a waterfront log here and unpack your picnic-with-a-view. Make sure you finish everything: you'll need added energy to climb the steep Salish Trail located across N.W. Marine Dr. It will take you into the heart of the UBC campus for a bus back to town.

# POINTS OF INTEREST

**Old Hastings Mill Store Museum** 1575 Alma Rd., 604-734-1212

**Brock House Restaurant** 3875 Point Grey Rd., 604-224-3317

**Jericho Sailing Centre** 1300 Discovery St., 604-224-4177

**Galley Patio & Grill** 1300 Discovery St., 604-222-1331

# ROUTE SUMMARY

1. Start at the northern, waterfront tip of Dunbar St.
2. Turn left along the seafront pathway
3. Continue west onto Cameron St.
4. Cross Alma St. to the Old Hastings Store Mill Museum.
5. Stroll north along the park's edge to the waterfront.
6. Follow the park's northern waterfront flank westward.
7. Turn south up the park's western edge.
8. Turn right along Point Grey Rd.
9. Continue west on Point Grey Rd. and enter Jericho Beach Park.
10. Follow the beach trail west through Jericho Beach Park.
11. Follow the shoreline trail west to Jericho Sailing Centre.
12. Continue west along the beachline.
13. Follow the shoreline trail south and then west through Locarno Beach.
14. Continue west along the water to Spanish Banks.
15. Cross south over N.W. Marine Dr.
16. Follow the marked Salish Trail into Pacific Spirit Regional Park and the UBC campus.

*View of downtown Vancouver from the end of Dunbar St.*

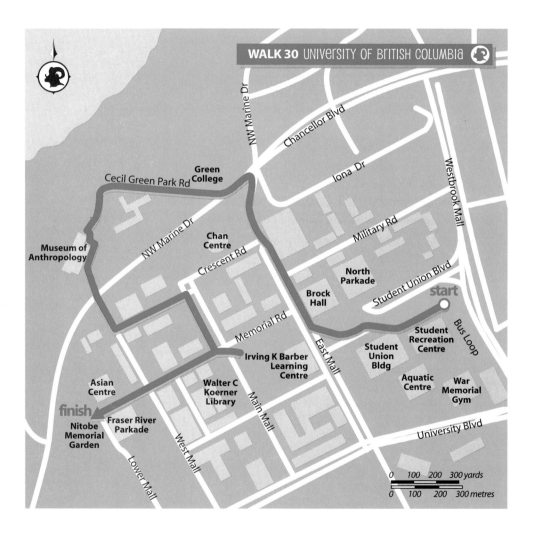

NW Marine Dr

Chancellor Blvd

Iona Dr

Cecil Green Park Rd

Green College

Museum of Anthropology

NW Marine Dr

Chan Centre

Crescent Rd

Military Rd

Westbrook Mall

North Parkade

Student Union Blvd

**start**

Brock Hall

Memorial Rd

East Mall

Bus Loop

Irving K Barber Learning Centre

Student Union Bldg

Student Recreation Centre

Asian Centre

Walter C Koerner Library

Main Mall

Aquatic Centre

War Memorial Gym

**finish**

Nitobe Memorial Garden

Fraser River Parkade

West Mall

University Blvd

Lower Mall

| 0 | 100 | 200 | 300 yards |
| 0 | 100 | 200 | 300 metres |

# 30 UBC: artworks and undergrads

BOUNDARIES: **Westbrook Mall, Cecil Green park Rd., Lower Mall, Memorial Rd.**
DISTANCE: **½ mile/¾ kilometre**
DIFFICULTY: **Easy**
PARKING: **North Parkade is just off Student Union Blvd., accessed via Gate 2 from Westbrook Mall. There are additional parking lots near the Chan Centre, Museum of Anthropology and the Asian Centre.**
PUBLIC TRANSIT: **Buses 4, 9, 17, 44, and the 99 B-Line stop at the University Bus Loop.**

Western Canada's largest university campus might feel intimidating if you haven't been there before; with a student population of 45,000, it feels more like a small city than a school. But once you get over the fact you'll never look as cool as the undergrad hipsters strolling around as if they own the place, there's a surprisingly diverse array of attractions to keep you occupied for an afternoon. Of course, the biggest problem is finding your way around. A detailed map is essential here if you want to navigate the dense labyrinth of the main University Town area with any degree of confidence. Once you've got your bearings, you'll need a little context: officially begun a century ago, construction of the new university campus was halted by WWI, reducing the fledgling school to temporary digs near the current site of Vancouver City Hall. By 1922, this site was seriously overcrowded and students marched from downtown to Point Grey, demanding the completion of their new university. The provincial government finally released some funding and three years later classes started at the shiny Point Grey campus.

● **Don those old undergraduate round spectacles and that oversized roll-neck sweater and relive your student days by starting at the University Bus Loop with the book-carrying locals. If you've arrived on campus by transit (preferably via the 99 B-Line express service), this is where you'll alight. If you're driving, there are several parking lots nearby.**

● **Look for the red-brick and steel Student Recreation Centre on the loop's western edge, then stroll along its right-hand flank. You're now in the heart of studentville, the concrete walkways and tree-lined avenues where BC's finest minds are honed. Just past the end of the Rec Centre, you'll come to the Student Union Building on your left. Nip up the steps and duck inside. You'll discover that student union buildings** don't change much. The dowdy, brown-tiled 1970s interior here is home to a straggle of shops and is the main fuel-up spot for starving students, hence the permanent toasted sandwich aroma. This is a good place to grab a coffee and a muffin while flicking through a copy of the *Ubyssey* (get it?) student newspaper.

● Re-emerge from the SUB and continue in your original direction. Just ahead of you is East Mall. Turn right along this street and stroll north. Within a few steps, you'll come to Brock Hall on your right and a colorful totem pole standing sentinel. If the pole looks a little new, that's because it was only carved in 2004. The original *Victory Through Honour* pole was created in the 1940s by Ellen Neel and was presented to the university by the Musqueam First Nation who originally occupied this land. At the time, Chief William Scow granted UBC the right to use the thunderbird symbol at the top of the pole to represent its sports teams. The weathered pole was restored and moved to the SUB exterior in 1973 but in 2001 it was severely damaged by vandals. A replica pole was carved and this was dedicated and returned to the original location in 2004.

● Continue on the right-hand side of East Mall and at the adjacent Brock Hall Annex follow the three steps down into the little courtyard. On one of the walls here is a large Modernist mural called *Untitled (Symbols for Education).* Commissioned by the graduating class of 1958, it's a coded, stylized map representing every UBC faculty and department of the time. Each is represented by symbols and colors rendered in intricate mosaic panels: try to identify the music, engineering, and home economics departments.

● Return to East Mall and continue in your original direction, crossing Walter Gage Rd. and passing the Faculty of Law on your right. When you reach Crescent Rd., cross over to the other side of East Mall. On your left will be the Chan Centre for the Performing Arts, a dramatic elliptical cylinder rising skywards. The university's pre-eminent concert venue, it opened in 1997 and has gained an increasing reputation for its excellent acoustics and roster of mostly classical performance; it's one of those rare university venues with a reputation beyond the campus. Check what's on while you're here; this is the new home of the former CBC Radio Orchestra, now re-named the National Broadcast Orchestra after being unceremoniously dumped by our public service TV and radio provider.

- Return to East Mall and follow its downhill curve to the right. At the next intersection, cross over to the other side of N.W. Marine Dr. Follow this road for a few steps west. Cecil Green Park Rd. will appear ahead of you, forking off to the right. Head along this road. You'll likely feel a blast of sea air here: the waterfront is just through the trees on your right. Follow Cecil Green Park Rd. all the way to the end and you'll come to the back of the Museum of Anthropology. Follow the signs to the entrance. Recently expanded, this is arguably Vancouver's best museum. Plan to spend some time perusing the treasure trove of First Nations artifacts here, including the totem poles dramatically displayed against a panoramic ocean vista. The building is an artwork in itself. Designed by Arthur Erickson, it echoes traditional post and beam structures.

- From the museum's front car park, cross over N.W. Marine Dr. and head south down West Mall. When you get to the next intersection, turn left along Crescent Rd. Stay on the left-hand side of Crescent for half a block, then take the flights of concrete steps on your left. At the top, you'll come to a fountain surrounded by a ring of slender ladies rendered in bronze. The work, entitled *Transcendence*, was created by Jack Harman who's also responsible for the popular bronze depiction of sprinter Harry Jerome in Stanley Park.

- Continue uphill on Crescent Rd. The Frederic Wood Theatre—check to see what's on, since the productions staged here by UBC's drama department are often excellent—is on your right. At the top of the incline, take in the oceanfront vista from the viewing area on your left. Then make a sharp right onto Main Mall. On your immediate right here is a large billboard with a picture of Baghdad and the slogan: *Because there was and there wasn't a city of Baghdad.* A 1991 artwork created in response to the first Gulf War, it remains a vibrant, contemporary commentary on world affairs.

- Continue south along Main Mall and within a few steps you'll come to what looks like a woodpile of chopped logs on your right. On closer inspection, the logs are made from concrete and are an art installation by Myfanwy Macleod. They signal that you're now at the entrance to the free-entry Morris and Helen Belkin Art Gallery. One of UBC's hidden gems, this excellent exhibition space is dedicated to contemporary art. Along with its permanent collection of more than 2,000 works, it hosts regularly changing and sometimes quite challenging visiting exhibitions.

- Returning to Main Mall, continue south. When you come to the roundabout, head right through the walkway in its center. This path points you to a large, strange-looking glass pavilion right ahead of you. Inside is a full-sized, antique black carriage, sans horses. Created by Rodney Graham, one of Vancouver's most revered contemporary artists, this work is entitled *Millennial Time Machine*. But it's not just for looks. A lens in the carriage focuses on a nearby tree, which is then projected, using pinhole camera technology, onto the inside of the carriage. To check out the image for yourself, you'll have to ask at the front desk of the Belkin Gallery and they'll escort you into the otherwise locked pavilion.

- Cross back over the roundabout and duck down Memorial Rd. Half a block along, on your left, is the Old Auditorium, or "the Old Odd" as it used to be commonly known. Built in 1925 as one of the campus's original buildings, this European-style opera house was UBC's primary performance space for decades, but suffered a slow decline throughout the 1960s, culminating in the collapse of its ornate plasterwork ceiling in 1970. A long overdue renovation was launched in 2008, aiming to bring the theatre back to its former glory and make it an equal partner with the state-of-the-art Chan Centre.

- Continue on the downhill incline of Memorial Rd. and cross over West Mall. On your right, you'll see the UBC Asian Centre, announced by the presence of a symbolic, Chinese-style rock garden on the corner. These five large boulders were imported from China and are inscribed with Confucian philosophies.

- Maintain your downhill Memorial Rd. stroll and end your UBC discovery tour with a final Asian flourish. Just ahead of you across Lower Mall, is a traditional Japanese-style wall topped by trees. Turn right along this wall and follow the cobbled walkway to the entrance of the Nitobe Memorial Garden. This tranquil spot is lined with verdant vegetation and carefully landscaped nooks, each reflecting deep facets of ancient philosophy. Consider partaking of a traditional tea ceremony here on summer Sundays. After your serenity fix, head back the way you came on Memorial and follow it right to the end. It intersects with East Mall right in front of Brock House, where you can retrace your steps back to the Bus Loop.

## POINTS OF INTEREST

**Student Union Building** 6138 Student Union Blvd.

**Chan Centre for the Performing Arts** 6265 Crescent Rd., 604-822-9197

**Museum of Anthropology** 6393 N.W. Marine Dr., 604-822-3825

**Frederic Wood Theatre** 6354 Crescent Rd., 604-822-2678

**Morris and Helen Belkin Art Gallery** 1825 Main Mall, 604-822-2759

**Old Auditorium** 6344 Memorial Rd.

**Nitobe Memorial Garden** 6804 S.W. Marine Dr., 604-822-6038

## ROUTE SUMMARY

1. Start at the Bus Loop.
2. Head west, past the Student Recreation Centre, to the SUB.
3. Turn right onto East Mall and continue to the end.
4. Cross N.W. Marine Dr. and head west.
5. Turn right along Cecil Green Park Rd.
6. After the Museum of Anthropology, head south along West Mall.
7. Turn left onto Crescent Rd.
8. Turn right onto Main Mall.
9. Turn right onto Memorial Rd.

Victory Through Honour *totem pole*

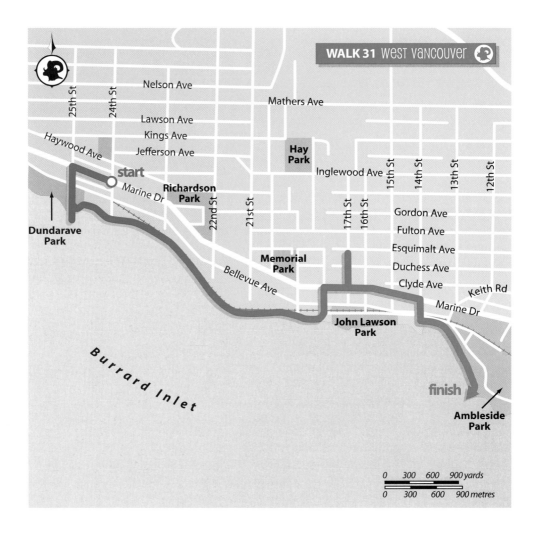

25th St

24th St

Nelson Ave

Mathers Ave

Lawson Ave

Kings Ave

Jefferson Ave

Haywood Ave

start

Marine Dr

Richardson Park

Hay Park

Inglewood Ave

15th St

14th St

13th St

12th St

22nd St

21st St

17th St

16th St

Gordon Ave

Fulton Ave

Dundarave Park

Memorial Park

Esquimalt Ave

Duchess Ave

Clyde Ave

Keith Rd

Bellevue Ave

Marine Dr

John Lawson Park

Burrard Inlet

finish

Ambleside Park

| 0 | 300 | 600 | 900 yards |
| 0 | 300 | 600 | 900 metres |

# 31 West Vancouver: Dundarave Village to Ambleside Park

**BOUNDARIES:** **25th St., Centennial Seawalk, Esquimalt Ave., Ambleside Park.**
**DISTANCE:** **1¾ miles/3 kilometres**
**DIFFICULTY:** **Moderate**
**PARKING:** **There's street parking on and just off Marine Dr. around the intersection with 24th St.**
**PUBLIC TRANSIT:** **Bus 250 runs from downtown Vancouver along Marine Dr. to Dundarave Village; to return, pick it up on Marine Dr. near Ambleside Park.**

Long regarded by those who've never actually been here as nothing more than a posh neighborhood of multi-million-dollar cliffside homes, West Vancouver is more accurately characterized as a string of cozy communities lining a picturesque waterfront. Of course, the chichi mansions do exist, but they perch imperiously on the mountainsides and largely keep themselves to themselves. For in-the-know visitors, the Dundarave, Hollyburn, and Ambleside areas are the main West Van draws: you'll find dozens of quirky little shops—many of the village-store variety—and you'll have plenty of opportunities to hit the Burrard Inlet waterfront for some sigh-inducing ocean and rustic beach vistas. Behind the idyllic élan, there's also plenty of history: West Vancouver was settled and shaped by pioneer families like the Lawsons and the McNaughtons; the century-old railway branch line from North Vancouver is still here (now trundling Whistler Mountaineer passengers); and the Coast Salish First Nations who originally called this area home are represented by a dramatic carving perched on the waterfront in Ambleside Park.

● Hop off the bus or park your car on Marine Dr. around the intersection with 24th St. The heart of West Van's Dundarave Village (named by pioneers after a Scottish castle), this short strip of shops and neighborhood cafés is an echo of the kind of homey, self-contained communities that used to stud the Lower Mainland. Strolling westward on Marine, you'll find busy little butcher, barber, and antique shops as well as the inviting Red Lion pub. The strip almost has the feel of a museum, but don't be fooled: drop into Delaney's coffee shop on the left side of the street and you'll find lively locals exchanging neighborhood gossip over a few opened copies of the *North Shore News*. If it's early in the day, consider a dark roast coffee and a warm breakfast cookie to fuel you up for the walk ahead.

- Once the caffeine is flowing through your veins, head back outside and continue westward on the same side of the tree-lined street. You'll pass a handful of small galleries—the Sun Spirit Gallery at 2444 is recommended for a kaleidoscopic array of First Nations art. If your tastes are less highbrow, cross to the other side of Marine and nip into Frankies Candy Bar, a decidedly cool sweets boutique with loose confections like skittles, jelly babies, and cola bottles. You can also pick up essential items like a marshmallow gun or a mini bubble gum factory.

- Continue west on Marine until the next intersection, then cross southwards down 25th St. On your left, check out the expansive wall mural by artist Jim McKenzie that colorfully depicts Burrard Inlet during the meeting of the first British and Spanish explorers. Now forested with homes and businesses, the area was then a natural wilderness of tree-lined islands punctuated by occasional beachfront First Nations settlements.

- Maintain your downhill seawards amble, crossing Bellevue Ave. and the single strand of railway tracks—they're still in use, so make sure you look both ways first. Ahead of you will be an incongruous clutch of three hardy palm trees. Just to the left is The Beach House, one of West Van's best restaurants. Make a mental note to come back here for lunch or dinner one day. The menu focuses on delectable West Coast fare and is especially recommended for its clever spins on seafood delicacies (try the honey-and-soy-glazed pan-roasted sablefish). It's not just about the nosh here, though: the restaurant offers panoramic views across the inlet, so try your hardest to bag a window seat.

- If you're not salivating too much, continue south past the restaurant to the nearby waterfront. To your right is the sandy elbow of Dundarave Park where you can perch on a log and drink in the views, or walk on water via the wood-built Dundarave Pier. Head straight to the pier's tip for a stirring, nature-framed vista encompassing Point Grey (those are the towers of UBC), the forested peninsula of Stanley Park and, shimmering like a ghost in the distance, the magnificent span of the Lions Gate Bridge arching over the water. You're also likely to spot several anchored freight container ships studding the briny like mammoth apartment blocks that have been dropped in from above.

## Back story: West Van's Little Train Line

The neatly fenced-in railway line running parallel with the Centennial Seawalk now services freight as well as the seasonal runs of the Whistler Mountaineer (if you're ever on this train coming through West Van, you can expect a warm, waving welcome from locals as you pass). Built by the Pacific Great Eastern Railway (PGE) and opened in 1914, the original 20-mile/32-kilometre stretch ran from North Vancouver to Horseshoe Bay, but was intended to be the first leg of a planned freight route to Prince George. Construction of the Prince George link was mired in delays, though, and the company eventually gave up on it. Locals responded by dubbing the PGE line "Prince George Eventually" and "Province's Great Expense." Many were surprised then when the company, now owned by the provincial government, completed the Prince George extension in 1956—several decades after the plan was first presented. While the Whistler Mountaineer, which runs from North Van to the famed ski resort, is the only passenger train you'll see on the tracks today, the magnificent and fondly remembered Royal Hudson steam locomotive used to trundle tourists along here until its retirement in 1999.

● **Return to dry land and turn right along the waterfront. Weaving eastward, you're now on the Centennial Seawalk where you can expect to be serenaded by cawing seagulls dive-bombing the water. Started in 1967 as a way to stop seafront-hungry locals from trespassing across the railway tracks that run parallel to the shore, it's now West Van's de facto promenade; you'll be sharing the tarmac with wheezing joggers and friendly dog walkers in almost equal numbers. The walkway is regularly battered during storms, which explains the tangle of giant logs washed up on the formidable rocks that fortify the shoreline. Keep your eyes peeled: some of these tree trunks and craggy boulders have been transformed into little artworks—including a pair of hungry-looking crocodiles rising from the water. You'll also spot a heron weathervane soaring high on a pole: it's the first of two on this stretch.**

● **With the sea breeze licking your face, continue your Seawalk trek east. You'll pass another weathervane on your right—this one an open-mouthed fish—as well as rows** of modest-looking but pricey waterfront homes. When you come to the end of the paved walkway, turn left and stroll north up 18th St. Cross over Argyle Ave., Bellevue Ave., and Ambleside Lane.

- Turn right along Marine Dr. and walk eastward: this is the heart of the Hollyburn area, named after the old holly-bush-lined estate built by John Lawson, a wealthy West Van pioneer. It's centered on a stretch of more than 200 neighborhood shops known as Ambleside Village. Not as quaint as Dundarave but with far more stores, this is a good area to stock up on cheap fruit, stop for lunch or coffee, or just window shop.

- Alternatively, detour north up 17th St. (the next intersection) and within a couple of blocks on your right you'll come to the little West Vancouver Museum & Archives. Housed in an odd but engaging stone home (the rocks are old ships' ballast and the style mixes Arts and Crafts, Scottish Baronial, and West Coast architectural approaches) it was built for John Lawson's daughter Gertrude in 1939 and became the local museum in 1994. There's a serious focus on art in the exhibition rooms here and you can expect to see regionally important works by contemporary and historic artists like Emily Carr, B.C. Binning, and Alistair Bell.

- Return from whence you came along 17th St. (it's downhill this time, so it's much easier), and turn left along Marine Dr., resuming your eastward stroll among the shops. After 16th and 15th Sts, turn right down 14th St. and amble back to the waterfront. At the end of this short stretch on your right, you'll find the wood-sided, steeply gabled Ferry Building Art Gallery. Built in 1912 as a boat terminal, this handsome slice of pioneer heritage has since been preserved and transformed into a lively showcase for latter-day North Shore artists. Check out one of the more than 20 shows staged here annually and, if you have time, consider joining a workshop: there's a lively roster of classes, lectures, and events on-site.

- After salving your artistic side, check out the pier in front of the gallery—it's a 1990 rebuild of the original ferry dock—then continue east along this second stretch of waterfront seawall. You'll pass the Hollyburn Sailing Club on your right and within a few minutes you'll be at the edge of Ambleside Park, one of West Van's most popular outdoor hangouts. Fringed by a sandy beach, it's a great spot for a picnic, complete with a side order of breathtaking Stanley Park forest views.

● Wander east from here along the park's log-strewn beach. Ahead of you, you'll see the silhouette of a large figure, dramatically framed by the waterfront. With its arms outstretched, this First Nations welcome carving was created by the Squamish Nation and dedicated to the people of West Van in 2001. It mirrors a similar figure in a less spectacular setting just under the south side of the Burrard Bridge. From here, weave back up to Marine Dr. to catch a handy bus back to downtown Vancouver, or walk 10 minutes farther east along Marine to the Park Royal Shopping Centre.

## POINTS OF INTEREST

**Red Lion** 2427 Marine Dr., 604-926-8838

**Delaney's** 2424 Marine Dr., 604-921-4466

**Sun Spirit Gallery** 2444 Marine Dr., 778-279-5052

**Frankie's Candy Bar** 2451 Marine Dr., 604-922-8291

**The Beach House** 150 25th St., 604-922-1414

**West Vancouver Museum & Archives** 680 17th St., 604-925-7295

**Ferry Building Art Gallery** 1414 Argyle Ave., 604-925-7270

*First Nations welcome figure in Ambleside Park*

# route summary

1.  Start at the intersection of Marine Dr. and 24th St.

2.  Head west along Marine for one block.

3.  Turn left along 25th St.

4.  Cross south over Bellevue Ave. and walk to the end of Dundarave Pier.

5.  Walk back to the shoreline and turn right along the Centennial Seawalk.

6.  Follow the Seawalk east.

7.  When the paved Seawalk runs out, turn left up 18th St.

8.  Head north and cross over Argyle Ave., Bellevue Ave. and Ambleside Lane.

9.  Turn right along Marine Dr.

10. Turn left at the next intersection and head north up 17th Ave.

11. Continue north on 17th, crossing over Duchess Ave. and stopping just before the intersection with Esquimalt Ave.

12. Retrace your steps south along 17th, and turn left onto Marine Dr.

13. Continue east on Marine, then turn right along 14th St.

14. Continue south to the nearby waterfront.

15. Resume your waterfront stroll east along the paved walkway with the inlet to your right.

16. Follow the trail into Ambleside Park before returning to Marine Dr. and your bus back to Vancouver.

*West Van's Centennial Seawalk*

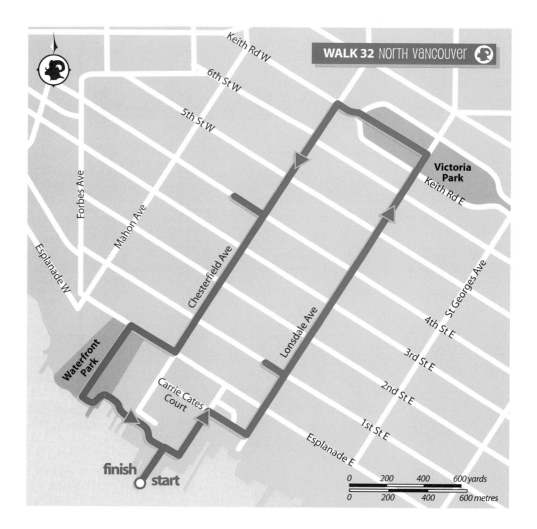

Keith Rd W

6th St W

5th St W

Forbes Ave

Mahon Ave

Esplanade W

Chesterfield Ave

Lonsdale Ave

Victoria Park

Keith Rd E

St Georges Ave

4th St E

3rd St E

2nd St E

1st St E

Esplanade E

Waterfront Park

Carrie Cates Court

finish     start

0    200    400    600 yards

0    200    400    600 metres

# 32 North Vancouver: Lonsdale Calf Buster

BOUNDARIES: **Lonsdale Quay, Lonsdale Ave., Victoria Park, Chesterfield Ave.**
DISTANCE: **1½ miles/2½ kilometres**
DIFFICULTY: **Moderate**
PARKING: **There are two parkades on the western side of the Public Market and two parking lots on the eastern side, along Carrie Cates Court.**
PUBLIC TRANSIT: **The SeaBus from downtown Vancouver's Waterfront Station stops at Lonsdale Quay.**

Eyed suspiciously as if it's on the other side of the world by some downtown Vancouverites, North Vancouver has a rich, maritime-flavored past. While its glory days as a trading port and shipbuilding center are long gone, the area is an intriguing and highly accessible spot to spend an afternoon away from the downtown hub. Originally centered on a pre-Vancouver logging settlement around Lower Lonsdale called Moodyville that was first occupied at the same time as New Westminster (this area today has a similar feel to old New West), North Van is the name of two areas in this region: the City of North Vancouver around the Lower Lonsdale area and the District of North Vancouver surrounding it. Both have their own mayors and administrations. This division is barely registered by Vancouverites who regard the whole area as one big North Van. Strolling the area on foot—be warned, it's steep in places—you'll come across colorful reminders of the past and plenty of great views across the briny to downtown Vancouver.

● Start your walk at Lonsdale Quay after taking the SeaBus across Burrard Inlet from downtown Vancouver. If you snagged a window seat at the front of the vessel, you'll have had an excellent visual introduction to North Van: mammoth tankers idling off-shore, an industrial waterfront stretching out to the right, and a forest of residential towers stepping up the foothills and nipping at the heals of the brooding Coastal Mountains. Once you hit dry land at the quay, head up the ramp and turn immediately right.

● Stroll east between the short stretch of coffee bars and ice-cream shops and within a couple of minutes you'll reach an open, boardwalk-style plaza. Check out

## BaCK STORY: THE LITTLE BOATS THAT COULD

Shimmying from downtown Vancouver's red-brick Waterfront Station, the 400-seat Burrard Beaver and Burrard Otter quickly divide the locals from the tourists. Nonchalant North Vancouverites barely register the SeaBus vessel's arrival, while wide-eyed visitors crowd the automatic entry doors, jostling for a front row traversal of Canada's busiest harbor. The pair of boxy, low-slung catamarans—plus a third scheduled to enter service any year now—first hit the waves in 1977. But they come from a long line of Burrard-crossing marine services. The first regular private ferry launched in 1900 and was taken over by the City of North Vancouver a few years later, when the route's two vessels were imaginatively renamed *North Vancouver Ferry No. 1* and *North Vancouver Ferry No. 2*—guess what the third one was called when it was added in 1936? The opening of the Lions Gate Bridge in 1938 sucked away some of this ferry traffic but the service limped on until 1958 when the last sailing took place. It would be 20 years before the regional public transit network returned to the waters with their now much-loved SeaBus twins.

the fountain in the middle: its interior is lined with a mosaic depicting aquatic wildlife and the region's main coastal landmarks. Then clomp across the wood to the waterfront railings and check out the real deal. The magnificent panoramic view from here is one of the best ways to see the downtown Vancouver skyline, shimmering like a city of glass across the water. Swivel to the right and you might spot a gaggle of cormorants perched on the corner of the SeaBus terminal, their favorite Lonsdale Quay hangout.

● Turn your back on the water, stroll straight ahead (try to avoid walking through the fountain), and push through the entrance of Lonsdale Quay Public Market. After Granville Island, it's the region's best. Highlights on the main floor include the bakery stands on the left, the jewelry, deli, and wine stores in the middle, and the fresh fish stall on the right where you can pick up some leathery salmon jerky for the walk ahead. If you need a more substantial fuel-up, head to the food court on the market's eastern flank. The Indian and Greek stalls here are recommended and you can sit outside if it's sunny enough.

- Once you've had your fill, exit through the glass doors on the side of the food court. You're now on the boardwalk snaking along the market's eastern exterior. Directly ahead of you, spreading along the waterfront, is what remains of the area's ship-building sector. Some boat repair and maintenance are still carried out here and you're quite likely to see an older BC Ferries vessel docked for a patch-up. What you won't see—they're hidden behind the sheds and cranes—are two of the original three PacifiCats. These large catamarans were built between 1998 and 2000 for $450 million to service the mainland to Vancouver Island BC Ferries route. Unfortunately they created such a large and damaging wake that they couldn't be used in the area. The resulting scandal led to the collapse of the provincial government—especially when buyers for the new ships failed to emerge.

- Head north on the boardwalk and continue to the end of the market building. Turn right onto Carrie Cates Court and stroll east. Within a few steps on your right, you'll come to the little shingle-sided Pacific Great Eastern Railway Station that serviced a long-gone freight line from the BC interior. After closing in 1928, the station had a plethora of alternative uses: in 1971, it was moved to Mahon Park to become North Van's first museum. It was moved back here in 1997 and, now restored, it houses historic displays on the area.

- Rejoin Carrie Cates Court, cross over to the left side and turn left up Lonsdale Ave. This is North Van's main drag. On the corner here is Gusto di Quattro, arguably the city's most popular Italian restaurant. Alternatively, if you're more of a beer and hearty nosh fan, try Burgoo Bistro next door. This ultra-cozy spot (especially if you're near the giant fireplace on a chilly day) specializes in comfort food like Irish stew, beef bourguignon, and shareable platters. They also make their own mead and have some choice BC brews on tap.

- Work off that mead belly by heading north up Lonsdale. It's a steep climb, so be sure your calves are ready. Both sides are lined with shops and cafés. Crossing Esplanade St., continue on to the intersection with W 1st St. On the other side of Lonsdale, you'll spot an elegant red-brick edifice dominating the corner. The street's most impressive old landmark, it was built as a bank in 1910 and had the area's first passenger elevator. It's an indicator that this was North Van's commercial heart and there was plenty of money around. Now preserved, it houses a bike repair shop.

- Turn left along W. 1st St. A few doors down on your left, you'll come to another, slightly hidden, heritage site. The blocky BC Telephone Building looks like a handsome little red-brick number, but the bricks are actually a façade laid over a concrete shell—a cutting-edge architectural innovation for the 1920s when it was built. Although it has a bygone utilitarian feel, the architects couldn't resist a few design flourishes: check out the little black-tile mosaic under the main windows.

- Return to Lonsdale Ave., turn left and continue north. Don't try too hard to resist the shops here (there's a couple of good thrift stores on the left) and consider a coffee pit stop. There are several on this stretch, suggesting that's it's either a common place for Lonsdale climbers to collapse from exhaustion or that North Vancouverites are serious caffeine addicts. Cross over W. 2nd St. and then over W. 3rd. The shops start to dissolve away here and you're left with a vista of older apartment buildings. It's okay to speed walk here since there's not much to see.

- After crossing W. 5th and W. 6th Sts. and then Keith Rd., you'll come to Victoria Park, bisected by Lonsdale Ave. Continue up the left side of Lonsdale. Within a few steps, you'll see steel hoof prints embedded in the sidewalk. Follow them onto the grass and you'll find an intriguing public artwork called *The Long Ascent*. The ironwork horse with its head hanging over a water trough here evokes the tough working life of the hardy equines who hauled goods from the foot of Lonsdale up this steep incline.

- The big climb over, stroll west through the center of the park. Once you hit the roundabout on the park's edge, turn left onto Chesterfield Ave. It's all downhill from here, so you can un-tense your muscles. Take a second to survey the excellent view over Burrard Inlet here before plunging downhill—spare a thought for the drivers who have to negotiate this stretch on icy days. There are few shops on this section but, alongside all the apartment buildings, there's a nice string of shingle-sided heritage homes along the 400 block on your right.

- Keep barreling downhill until you come to the intersection with W. 4th St. Turn right onto this street. The large old green-painted building on the corner is Presentation House Arts Centre. This rambling old complex was built in 1902 as a schoolhouse, before becoming North Van's City Hall in 1915. The city moved to a purpose-built site 60 years later and this became the home of several arts and cultural organizations.

Check to see what's on at the intimate studio theatre and spend some time in the 3rd floor art gallery where photography is the specialty. The main attraction, though, is the North Vancouver Museum & Archives. While locals have been calling for a new museum building for years, this little space is worth a visit for its eclectic array of exhibits that bring to life the area's distinctive logging, shipbuilding, and streetcar past.

● Continue downhill along Chesterfield until you reach Esplanade St. Turn right along Esplanade. Cross to the other side of the street at the next intersection. Waterfront Park is right ahead. Walk through the park to the shoreline and then follow the marked trail east. After a few minutes, you'll be back at Lonsdale Quay and the SeaBus terminal.

## POINTS OF INTEREST

**Lonsdale Quay Public Market** 123 Carrie Cates Court, 604-985-6261

**Pacific Great Eastern Railway Station** south foot of Lonsdale Ave., 604-990-3700

**Gusto di Quattro** 1 Lonsdale Ave., 604-924-4444

**Burgoo Bistro** 3 Lonsdale Ave., 604-904-0933

**Victoria Park** cnr of Lonsdale Ave, and Keith Rd.

**Presentation House Arts Centre** 333 Chesterfield Ave., 604-990-3473

**North Vancouver Museum & Archives** 209 W. 4th St., 604-987-5612

*Lonsdale Quay Public Market*

## route summary

1. Start from Lonsdale Quay SeaBus terminal.
2. Turn right toward the boardwalk plaza.
3. Head north into the Public Market.
4. Exit the market east onto the boardwalk.
5. Turn right onto Carrie Cates Court.
6. Turn left onto Lonsdale Ave.
7. Continue up Lonsdale to Victoria Park.
8. Cut west through the park.
9. Turn left and head down Chesterfield Ave.
10. Turn right onto Esplanade St.
11. Cross over to Waterfront Park.
12. Follow the shoreline east to Lonsdale Quay.

The Long Ascent

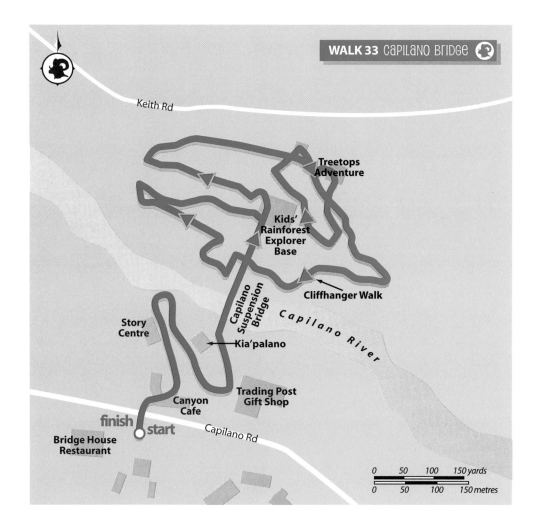

WALK 33 Capilano Bridge

Keith Rd

Treetops Adventure

Kids' Rainforest Explorer Base

Cliffhanger Walk

Capilano Suspension Bridge

Capilano River

Story Centre

Kia'palano

Trading Post Gift Shop

Canyon Cafe

finish start

Capilano Rd

Bridge House Restaurant

| 0 | 50 | 100 | 150 yards |
| 0 | 50 | 100 | 150 metres |

# 33 Capilano Suspension Bridge: Swaying With Big Doug

BOUNDARIES: **Capilano Rd., Capilano River Regional Park**
DISTANCE: **¼ mile/½ kilometre**
DIFFICULTY: **Easy**
PARKING: **There's paid parking across from the entrance on Capilano Rd.**
PUBLIC TRANSIT: **Bus 236 to and from Lonsdale Quay stops outside.**

The Lower Mainland's biggest visitor attraction, Capilano Bridge started life as a humble hemp and cedar span created by George Grant Mackay on forested land he purchased along the Capilano River in the 1880s. The First Nations locals who helped him build the folly named it the "laughing bridge" after the sound it reportedly made when it moved. Since it was a fairly precarious construction, laughing was not something anyone crossing the span actually did. The bridge soon became a popular destination for the adventurous and the curious, who had to hike up from Burrard Inlet to get here, long before the Translink bus service delivered the masses to the gates outside. After Mackay's death, the new owner replaced the fraying hemp with steel cables in 1903 and kicked the attraction up a notch with its own teahouse. Successive owners added more enticements—including gift stores, totem poles, nature trails and, in 2004, a series of elevated walkways through the trees. Despite all these flourishes, the main lure remains the bouncy span and its jelly-leg-triggering traversal. In summer, tour parties roll in relentlessly, but Capilano has a year-round life. Consider dropping by off-season (a one-day ticket covers entry for a whole year for BC residents) to partake of the site's wilderness solitude.

● **Plan your attack strategy across Capilano Rd. at Bridge House Restaurant. This cozy wooden residence was built in 1934 for the attraction's fourth owner, Archibald MacEachran, and is now a popular nosh spot for Capilano visitors. While MacEachran—the first owner to bring First Nations carvers to the site—won't be at home to greet you, you can tuck into a salmon sandwich or cream tea and watch those tour buses rolling in across the street. Once you see a gap in the convoy, pay your tab and scamper over to the main entrance.**

- After pushing through the turnstile, you'll immediately feel the presence of the large trees towering over you. Follow the red-brick walkway leftwards and you'll come to a historic display illuminating the rich history of what was dubbed the "eighth wonder of the world" by early promoters. Peruse the grainy photos of 1890s pleasure-seekers hiking 6 miles/10 kilometres through the forest from Burrard Inlet, and the crinolined Edwardian ladies clinging to the swaying span in 1905. The bridge was the extreme outdoor activity of its day, long before parachuting or bungee jumping became de rigueur.

- Continue slightly downhill to the end of this path and you'll come to a viewing platform offering your first glimpse of the bridge, bouncing between the trees over the canyon to your right. If you're a virgin Capilano crosser, this is when your legs will start to tingle.

- Swivel to your right and weave north up the incline and you'll be greeted by a small forest of totem poles arrayed around you in a ring. This area is called Kia'palano and is the center of First Nations culture in the park. The highlight is the alfresco Big House (it's actually not that big), where congenial local carvers, beaders, and weavers work and explain their crafts and totemic symbols. In summer, there are daily ceremonial dances and cultural performances here, too.

- Continue a few more steps north and you'll come to an older clutch of totems on your left. These bright, Technicolor poles are dramatically different from the more austere carvings you've just passed. Called "story poles," they were installed here in the 1930s, although new ones have been added over the years as weathering has taken its toll. The latest one, installed in 2005, relates the tale of an elderly blind man known for his good deeds who is rewarded with good fortune in his time of need by a salmon, a bear, and an eagle.

- Now it's time to exercise those jelly legs. Continue north past the story poles and the forest suddenly opens up to your left. Step up onto the wooden boardwalk and peer gingerly down on the alarmingly springy span dipping across the tree-lined canyon. If your legs are suddenly locked in non-moving mode, remind yourself that almost a million people safely cross over every year.

# Capilano Facts

The 450-foot/137-metre Capilano Bridge traverse is long enough that two Boeing 747s could fly wing-to-wing under its deck. And although it continually moves like a giant executive office toy, the span is much more secure than it looks. To safely maintain a bridge deck that bounces like a trampoline, the original hemp ropes have been substituted with steel cables and 13-ton concrete anchor blocks. The blocks apparently have the same pull as four elephants holding onto each side of the bridge. The safety of the bridge became a key concern for 1950s owner Rae Mitchell. Presumably fearing that a diet of hamburgers or the gyrations of rock-and-rollers might pull the span from its moorings, he completely rebuilt the structure in five days. No word on whether he was just trying to impress Marilyn Monroe, who visited the attraction in 1954.

- Step down from the deck, grip the rails and go for it. Remember that you're not supposed to deliberately bounce, since any movement on the wooden slats triggers a wave of undulations. If there are any teenagers heading your way, you can expect plenty of deliberate stamping, though. Once you've got used to the movement, you'll likely start to enjoy it and, about half way across, you may even peel your death grip from the cables running alongside you. This is a good spot to stop and drink in the scenery. The steep-sided Capilano Canyon will be flanking you on either side and the water will be crashing noisily across the worn rocks of the riverbed 230 feet/70 metres below. Turn north and you'll catch sight of the mountains looming above you.

- Once you've taken all your photos, continue to the other side and head up the steps, instantly restoring your legs to solid ground. You're now in the heart of the park's dark, temperate rainforest, complete with tall, flagpole-straight trees and winding walkways. First, stroll a few steps ahead on the wooden platform and you'll come to a kid-friendly interpretive display that serves as a handy introduction to the natural treasures encircling you. Within a few seconds, you'll be able to tell your sitka spruce from your western hemlock.

- Armed with your new knowledge, turn south off the platform and, when you come to a fork in the woodland pathway, take the right-hand trail. Within a few steps, you'll come to Trout Pond on your left. Continue south along this trail, passing big-fronded ferns, large pockets of skunk cabbage, and the occasional statue-still frog. You'll soon come to "Big Doug," actually a 200-foot/60-metre tall Douglas-fir tree that's been hanging around here for about 350 years.

- Just past Doug, turn right onto the gravel trail and weave north along this walkway. The damp rainforest undergrowth on your left is even denser here and within a few steps you'll come to a grand old lady that puts Doug to shame in the longevity stakes. "Grandma Capilano" may be around the same height as her sibling, but she's estimated to be more than 500 years old. Which means she was around when BC was a tree-lined natural paradise, the regional First Nations communities were thriving, and White Spot hamburgers cost just five cents.

- Continue north and you'll pass under what looks like a mini suspension bridge. A few steps later, enter the two-story treehouse-like building to your left. This is Treetops Adventure, a 650-foot/200-metre canopy walkway strung between the trees several metres above the forest floor. Follow the elevated track for a squirrels-eye view of the woodland. The cables holding up this walkway are a delicate spider's web of clever engineering attached to collars around the trees rather than to the trees themselves. The collars subject each tree to about the same amount of pressure as pressing a thumb on a tabletop.

- Once you've circled the Treetops course, you'll be deposited back near its entrance. Continue along the pathway in the direction you were originally heading. It's slightly downhill now and when you come to a fork in the trail, take the left-hand path that's signposted "Cliffhanger Boardwalk." This is a picturesque nature weave down and along the side of the canyon and then under the suspension bridge—look out for observation decks along the way. Follow the boardwalk trail to the end and you'll eventually find yourself back at ground level on the edge of Trout Pond. Turn right onto the trail and follow it north back to the end of the bridge. Cross over, then end your visit with a noodle through the giant gift shop.

# POINTS OF INTEREST

**Bridge House Restaurant** 3650 Capilano Rd., 604-987-3388

**Capilano Suspension Bridge & Park** 3735 Capilano Rd., 604-985-7474

# route summary

1. Start at Bridge House Restaurant, across the street from the park's main entrance.
2. Cross Capilano Rd. and enter the park.
3. Bear left after the entrance.
4. After the viewing platform, head north.
5. After the totem poles, turn left onto the bridge.
6. Turn left on the other side.
7. Take the right-hand trail southward around Trout Pond.
8. Turn right after Big Doug and head north on the trail.
9. Enter Treetops Adventure on your left.
10. Circle the Treetops course, then return to the trail.
11. Continue along the trail, then take the left-hand path to Cliffhanger Walk.
12. Exit Cliffhanger and turn south along the trail running parallel to Trout Pond.
13. Re-cross the bridge.
14. Bear left to the gift shop.

*Capilano Suspension Bridge*

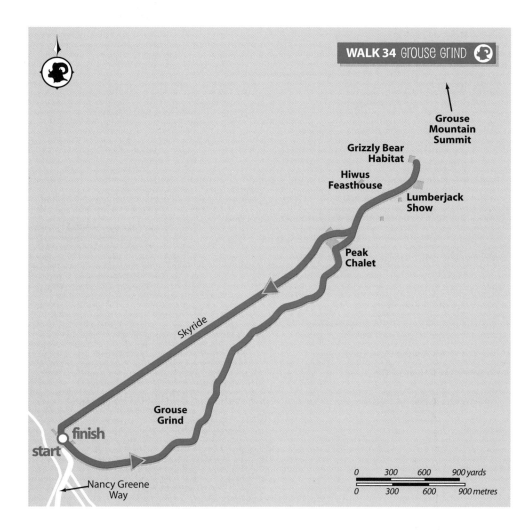

Grouse
Mountain
Summit

Grizzly Bear
Habitat

Hiwus
Feasthouse

Lumberjack
Show

Peak
Chalet

Skyride

Grouse
Grind

finish

start

Nancy Greene
Way

0    300    600    900 yards
0    300    600    900 metres

# 34 Grouse Grind: Vancouver's Alfresco Stairmaster

BOUNDARIES: **Nancy Greene Way, Grouse Mountain summit**
DISTANCE: **1¾ miles/3 kilometres**
DIFFICULTY: **Difficult**
PARKING: **There's a parking lot at the base of Grouse Mountain.**
PUBLIC TRANSIT: **Bus 236 stops at the base of Grouse Mountain, near the gondola entrance.**

Vancouver's favorite calf-punisher is a steep, rock-studded forest trek that will have your legs screaming for mercy for up to two hours (the record is 26 minutes). But the aptly titled, summer-only Grouse Grind still attracts 110,000 sweaty challengers every year. They come for the camaraderie of attacking a punishing hike with a clammy, Lycra-clad crowd that all have the same goal in mind: to get the bloody thing over with as soon as possible. The trail winds steeply and seemingly endlessly up the side of Grouse Mountain, a popular recreational peak that's 4,100 feet/1,250 metres above sea level. Once you reach the top, you'll want to collapse into a puddle, then hit the attractions that you've labored so hard to get to. While most summer visitors pay the pricey gondola fare to access these, anyone who manages to get up to the peak the hard way can enjoy them for free. Keep in mind that the Grind is officially a one-way track at peak times, so you'll have to leave the summit via the gondola: there's a special $5 fare for the down-only trip. Words of advice: wear layers that can be stripped off as you ascend, take a water bottle or two with you . . . and don't give up.

● You'll start your trek facing the gondola building just to the left of Nancy Greene Way, with the parking lot at your back. But instead of taking the easy route like the smiling visitors sweeping up the tree-bristled slope ahead of you, you'll square your jaw and cross the street east toward the fence-enclosed gateway and kneecap-popping hell. You'll know you're in the right place because the trailhead will be ringed with people rubbing their legs, stretching their muscles and bouncing up and down on the spot. You probably should do a bit of that, too.

● Push through the gate and you're on your way. Taking it slow to begin with, follow the winding, well-marked trail—or more accurately, follow the back of the person just ahead of you. You'll be passing through dense forest that obscures almost any chance of viewing the scenery around the mountain. In some ways, this makes it easier; you've no idea where you are in relation to the summit, so you just keep plugging away, hoping that the end is just over the next crag. It isn't. The trail is decked with muddy wooden slats in places but there are also lots of areas where steps are cut into rock (which can be slippery).

- After 30 minutes or so, you'll come across a large yellow sign announcing that you are at the trail's quarter point. This can be a disheartening sight—especially if it feels like you've already expended just about all your energy. The sign's second line is even more unnerving: "The remainder of the trail is extremely steep and difficult." If you're traveling with a partner, conversation will likely stop at this point as you devote all mental and physical resources to the task at hand. From here, it's vital to keep hydrating to replace the permanent sheen of sweat covering your body. Short stops are also handy, but don't rest too long or your legs might seize up.

- After about an hour, you'll be at the half-way or three-quarter-way point. This is usually the stage where sprightly youngsters start streaking past. Keep focused, though, and you'll soon be joining them at the top, although not quite as soon as your creaking knees might hope. This section is all about gritting your teeth, getting your head down, and continuing to put one wobbly leg in front of the other. The phrase, "Is it nearly over?" will be echoing through your head.

- The trees above you will suddenly start thinning as you inch up the final stretch of the trail. Don't get too relieved: the Grind has one last trick to make you curse. This section is the steepest yet and you'll be climbing almost vertically as "nature's Stairmaster" tests your weary legs one last time. The thought of finishing is a powerful incentive, though, and when you finally scramble up the rocks at the trail's end you'll be justifiably elated. Have a stretch and step over the bodies flopped out like wet fish before following the rough pathway along the east side of Peak Chalet. When you burst into the cobbled plaza area, you'll suddenly be surrounded by people who look a lot less sweaty and disheveled than you. These are the lesser mortals who took the gondola.

- Wearing your sweat like a badge of honor, head into the main entrance of the Peak Chalet on your immediate left. Stroll (or limp) through the center of the lobby to the coffee shop. You'll be surprised at how ravenous you are; pick up a restorative hot java and some chocolate fudge brownies (hey, you deserve it). Weave left from here with your goodies and push through the glass door to the balcony where you can watch the Grouse Grinders behind you stumbling bleary-eyed from the trailhead.

- Don't sit too long or your legs might turn to lead. Head back into the Chalet and poke around the gift shop or watch the colorful Theatre in the Sky movie presentation of BC scenery. Then exit the way you came in. The plaza is the center of the action on Grouse, summer or winter. In winter, this is where the mountain's well-wrapped skiers and snowboarders wind up their snowy shenanigans, often causing traffic jams for anyone trying to stroll around the area.

- Walk north from the plaza with your back to the Chalet and follow the trail that's lined with a series of mammoth wooden sculptures. Grouse's summit is dotted with these artworks, created with deft chainsaw strokes by Glen Greensides. Up to 16 feet/5 metres tall, the highlights include magnificent renderings of howling grizzly bears and eagles in flight as well as a detailed series of lumberjacks and their tools.

- Continue along the slightly uphill trail and you'll soon come to a series of canopy ziplines, the newest Grouse attraction. Attached to a harness, you'll be thrown along these lines at speed, giving you a birds-eye view of the area while you scream like a banshee. It's just the kind of thing to take your mind off your aching legs. If you can keep your eyes open, you might spot Goat Mountain and Crown Mountain, two of the nearest peaks in the Coast Mountain range, plus the ghostly, snow-capped visage of Mount Baker in Washington state. Coastwards, you'll spy the shimmering waters of Howe Sound and the tree-forested silhouettes of the Southern Gulf Islands.

- Continue northwestward and stroll farther up the mountain (don't worry, it's a gentle elevation). You'll soon come to a crescent of bench seating marking the outdoor venue of Grouse's Lumberjack Show. Running throughout the day, this is the peak's most popular summertime activity. Find a perch and you'll be treated to a lively 20-minute display of axe-throwing, wood-chopping, log-rolling, and pole-climbing.

Look out for the troublesome audience member who keeps butting in on the action; he's not quite what he seems.

- From here, it's a short hop to the peak's other big lure: the grizzly bear enclosure. Grinder and Coola, separately orphaned by their mothers, have been raised here since 2001. You'll see the pair ambling around their expansive habitat looking for food that's been strategically placed for them. Grinder is the more inquisitive and has a penchant for staring at visitors, perhaps in the same way that cartoon characters visualize people as large hams when they're hungry. Coola is the homebody and always does a good job of making his 2-foot/½-metre-deep hibernation bed from twigs and branches. Near the grizzly bear hangout, there's a smaller enclosure housing two gray wolves. Raised in captivity, these two howling carnivores have starred in several local movie productions.

- If your legs are telling you to stop, return downhill to the Chalet. Once inside, head upstairs (slowly and painfully) to the second floor and take your pick of the two eateries: the ideal way to end your Grouse trek. The Observatory restaurant is a fine dining room where you can tuck into a great array of Pacific Northwest cuisine. Since you might not be quite dressed for it, instead head to Altitudes Bistro. This laid-back, pub-style joint is a large but cozy hangout. Try to snag a window seat and you'll have a stunning view down the mountain to central Vancouver, glinting in the water beneath you—this vista is the reason Grouse is called the Peak of Vancouver. The food here is of the salmon burger and crispy chicken wings variety (the seafood clubhouse is recommended) and you can toast your success in completing the Grind with a deserved pint or two.

- When it's time to head out, pick up a $5 lift ticket from the Guest Services desk downstairs, then stroll next door to the gondola building. Aim for a spot at the front so you drink in the magnificent sea, sky, and forest panorama unfolding around you on your smooth but steep descent. It's a lot easier getting up and down Grouse this way but, as your legs are no doubt reminding you, it's not nearly as satisfying.

## POINTS OF INTEREST

**Grouse Mountain** 6400 Nancy Greene Way, 604-984-0661

**The Observatory** Grouse Mountain, 604-980-9311

**Altitudes Bistro** Grouse Mountain, 604-998-4398

## route summary

1. Start facing the gondola building to the left of Nancy Greene Way.
2. Stroll east across Nancy Greene Way to the nearby Grouse Grind trailhead.
3. Follow the steep, well-marked trail up the side of Grouse.
4. At the summit's trailhead exit, head along the east side of the Peak Chalet and turn left onto the Plaza.
5. Turn left into the Peak Chalet.
6. Exit north from the Peak Chalet.
7. Follow the wooden sculpture-lined trail northwestward to the zipline course.
8. Pass the zipline course and continue northwest to the lumberjack venue.
9. Continue north past the lumberjack venue to the bear enclosure.
10. Return southward back to the Peak Chalet.
11. Pick up your ticket and return southward down the mountain via the gondola.

*Grouse Grind*

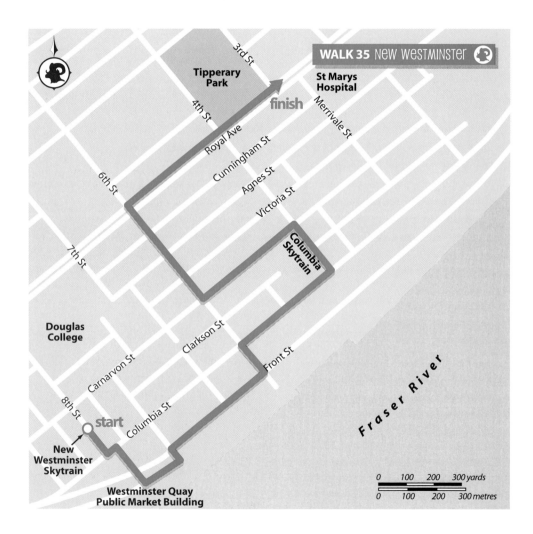

St Marys
Hospital

Tipperary
Park

3rd St

finish

Merrivale St

4th St

Royal Ave

Cunningham St

Agnes St

6th St

Victoria St

Columbia
Skytrain

7th St

Douglas
College

Clarkson St

Carnarvon St

Front St

8th St

Columbia St

start

New
Westminster
Skytrain

Westminster Quay
Public Market Building

Fraser River

0    100    200    300 yards

0    100    200    300 metres

# 35 New Westminster: BC's Other Capital

BOUNDARIES: **8th St., Fraser River, Royal Ave., Merrivale St.**
DISTANCE: **¾ mile/1¼ kilometres**
DIFFICULTY: **Moderate**
PARKING: **There's a parking lot near the casino on the waterfront and a parkade in the 500 block of Columbia St. There's also metered street parking on Columbia.**
PUBLIC TRANSIT: **The SkyTrain stops are on 8th St. and Columbia St.**

It must be tough to live in a place where the glory days have come and gone. But while contemporary New Westminster has a paint-peeled, worn-around-the-edges feel, there are some intriguing reasons to spend an afternoon here—especially if you like your history with a bit of grit. Of course it wasn't always this way. After decades of commercial success fueled by trade along the adjacent Fraser River, the colonials designated New Westminster as the first capital of the new Colony of British Columbia in 1859. Given its name by Queen Victoria, the settlement also gained the nickname "Royal City." But royals are a fickle bunch and when, in 1866, BC and Vancouver Island amalgamated, New West lost out as capital in favor of Victoria. New West continued to develop, however, and its main commercial thoroughfare, Columbia St., was one of the biggest shopping strips in the region for decades . . . until the new Trans-Canada Hwy bypassed the city in the 1960s. Nosing around the streets today, you'll find plenty of reminders of the city's rich history, especially on the colorful waterfront.

● Exit from the New Westminster SkyTrain station on 8th St. and turn right toward the waterfront. Cross over Columbia St. at the bottom of 8th and ahead of you is the old 1899-built Canadian Pacific Railway station. Now improbably converted into a Keg Steakhouse, this pretty, steeply gabled structure would easily be at home in a hobbit village. Its location marks New West's historic transportation hub. CPR trains used to roll in here, streetcars and interurban trams trundled in from Vancouver across the street, and 8th St. itself—originally named Douglas St.—was one of the first roads to link the Fraser waterfront to Burrard Inlet and the old Gastown-area settlement.

● With the pedestrian overpass here currently closed—although plans are afoot to reopen it in future—follow the walkway down the right side of the Salvation Army store. Cross Front St. and the railway tracks, heading for the landmark Westminster

Quay Public Market building a few steps ahead. Although the "River Market" closed in 2009, plans are being hatched to renovate and reopen the market in some form or another.

● If it's not open on your visit, bypass the building and make straight for the shimmering Fraser River waterfront. You'll find a wonderful boardwalk concourse lining the market's southeastern edge. Head right along the boardwalk and check out the imposing bust of Simon Fraser marking his 1808 river voyage of discovery into the heart of BC. The river that bears his name is still an active commercial thoroughfare. Gaze across the water at the industrial operations crowding the Surrey shorefront—you'll likely also see plenty of working boats taxiing past, some shepherding floating flocks of logs to the nearby Scott Paper Mill.

● Head back in the other direction along the boardwalk and you'll come across the unexpected presence of the world's tallest tin solider on your left, towering above you in all his shiny red finery. This 32-foot/9.75-metre, five-ton landmark is not just here for fun: he marks the spot where the region's first detachment of British Royal Engineers arrived on shore in 1859. They stayed for four years and laid the foundations for the colonial settling of the area by building local infrastructure and imposing order.

● Continue past the soldier's oversized boots and the boardwalk's next highlight is the impressive Fraser River Discovery Centre. Opened in 2006, then expanded and reopened in 2009, this interpretive museum tells the colorful story of the river and its role in the development of New West and the wider BC region. Spend an hour or so here and you can learn all you'll ever need to know about the gold rush, Simon Fraser and the guy in BC's Cariboo region who imported 23 camels as pack animals, only to watch them eat his cargo or run away whenever they could. Never just a dry retelling of history, there are plenty of kid-friendly buttons and touch-screens among the exhibits here.

● Back on the boardwalk, you'll spot the floating Royal City Star Casino looming over you on your right. Originally moored on the Mississippi, this red and white paddle-wheel boat has been here since 2004. Stroll alongside it as you follow the boardwalk between the boat and the side of the Fraser River Discovery Centre. When you reach the end of the wooden walkway, turn left and within a few steps you'll be at Front St. Turn right onto Front and cross to the street's left-hand side at the crosswalk. On the other side of Front, duck under the sign advertising Antique Alley.

- Shadowed by the concrete pylons supporting the overhead parking lot, this section of Front St. was transformed into an elaborate movie set for the futuristic Will Smith flick *I-Robot*. The storefronts here, many now crumbling into disrepair, were transformed into a bustling 2035 Chicago street. It's a lot less bustling today and you'll have to stroll past the intersection with Mackenzie St. to find the best of the antique shops: Not Too Shabby and Antique Alley Movie Props.

- At the end of this block, turn left onto 6th St. and make the steep, one-block climb to Columbia St. Turn right along Columbia, the commercial heart of old New West. While it's a bit shabby these days, it's easy to see that this was once an important thoroughfare, originally known as BC's Miracle Mile. Many of the old landmark buildings are still here. On your right, you'll soon pass the handsome, multi-columned façade of the 1911 Canadian Bank of Commerce Building. It's highly reminiscent of Vancouver's Waterfront Station.

  Almost next door is the Burr Theatre. Originally the Columbia Theatre, it opened in 1927 as a combined vaudeville and movie venue. The Columbia was renowned for its sumptuous auditorium, complete with a painted garden wall design, intricate trellis-work and Spanish-style iron railings—this Moorish esthetic is echoed on the building's plasterwork exterior. The theatre, now run by a non-profit society dedicated to preserving it, was renamed in recent years after Raymond Burr—the actor most famous for playing wheelchair detective Ironside—who was born in New Westminster.

- At the intersection with Church St., take the crosswalk to the other side of Columbia. Continue along this side, passing the Columbia SkyTrain station on your left. You'll soon come to the only two buildings in downtown New West that survived the 1898 fire. Dominating the corner of Columbia and 4th St. are the conjoined red-brick and plaster façades of the Burr Block and Queen's Hotel. First up is the four-story Romanesque revival Burr Block, completed in 1892. Next door is the even more handsome Queen's Hotel, built in 1887 and regarded as the city's oldest surviving commercial property. Both building exteriors have been sympathetically restored in recent years.

- Turn left and head (steeply) up 4th St. Pass Clarkson St. and then turn left along Carnarvon St. You'll be relieved to know there's a slight downhill stretch here. On the left-hand side of Carnarvon, you'll soon come to the hilltop perch of the Anglican Holy Trinity Cathedral. Wander into the grounds and check out this decidedly British-looking church, founded in 1859.

- At the next intersection, turn right and steel your calves for the four-block ascent of 6th St. Once you reach Royal Ave, take the crosswalk right in front of you and cross to the other side of Royal. Topping the gently sloping lawn ahead of you is City Hall, a blockish concrete structure built in 1953. This grand hilltop site was originally reserved for the provincial parliament buildings when New West was hoping to be the capital of the newly united BC. Check out the pair of field howitzers on the lawn, brought here from the UK onboard the *HMS Sparrowhawk* in 1866, just in case of attack.

- Continue along Royal and cross to the right-hand side at the next crosswalk. Cross 4th and 3rd Sts. and on your right you'll soon come to the clapboard, Gothic-style Irving House. Built in 1865, it's New West's oldest building. Demurely painted in shades of green, it was built for Scottish-born riverboat trader William Irving and his family, and now serves as BC's oldest house museum. Spend an hour perusing its antique-lined creaky-floored rooms: much of the ornate interior and furnishings are original and the drawing room is especially decorative. Once you've had your history fix, take any of the nearby streets along Royal and barrel back downhill to Columbia—try to stop before you hit the water. You can grab a coffee or lunch at one of the eateries here before nipping back onto the SkyTrain at Columbia station.

# POINTS OF INTEREST

**Fraser River Discovery Centre** 788 Quayside Dr., 604-521-8401

**Royal City Star Casino** 788 Quayside Dr., 604-878-9999

**Burr Theatre** 530 Columbia St., 604-523-2877

**Holy Trinity Cathedral** 514 Carnarvon St., 604-521-2511

**City Hall** 511 Royal Ave., 604-521-3711

**Irving House** 302 Royal Ave., 604-527-4640

# ROUTE SUMMARY

1. Turn right along 8th St. from New Westminster SkyTrain Station.
2. Cross Columbia St.
3. Follow the walkway along the right side of the Salvation Army store towards the waterfront.
4. Walk around the Westminster Quay Public Market building to the shoreline promenade.
5. Follow the waterfront boardwalk left until it ends.
6. Turn right along Front St.
7. Cross to the left-hand side of Front.
8. Turn left up 6th St.
9. Turn right along Columbia St.
10. Cross to the other side of Columbia at Church St.
11. Turn left up 4th St.
12. Turn left along Carnarvon St.
13. Turn right up 6th St.
14. Cross to the left side of Royal Ave.
15. Cross back to the right side of Royal Ave. at 4th St.
16. Continue along Royal, past 3rd St., to Irving House.

*Irving House*

WALK 36 STEVESTON

4th Ave
3rd Ave
2nd Ave
No 1 Rd
Railway Ave
No 2 Rd

Steveston Park

start
Moncton St
Bayview St
Westwater Dr
Trites Rd
Dyke Rd

finish

0   300   600   900 yards
0   300   600   900 metres

# 36 STeveSToN: HiSToric riverfroNT amBLe

**BOUNDARIES: 4th Ave., Fraser River, Westwater Dr., Dyke Rd.**
**DISTANCE: 1½ miles/2½ kilometres**
**DIFFICULTY: Moderate**
**PARKING: There's a large parking lot at the Gulf of Georgia Cannery.**
**PUBLIC TRANSIT: Bus 491 from downtown Vancouver stops on Moncton St., a short walk from the Gulf of Georgia Cannery.**

In-the-know Lower Mainlanders have been making summertime pilgrimages to the Steveston waterfront for years. They come for the fish and chips and a chance to stroll along the promenade and soak up a little unspoiled maritime ambiance. Recent visitors will have noticed a few changes, though. The traditional working class home of the West Coast fishing fleet has been undergoing a gentrification process in the past decade, with sections of the waterfront now housing sleek condo developments. The upside of this has been the completion of the promenade walkway: while visitors formerly stayed close to the wood-built shops and eateries around the public wharf, they can now stroll all the way from the Gulf of Georgia Cannery to the Britannia Shipyard and on to an historic farmhouse where the afternoon tea is one of the region's hidden gems. A stroll around Steveston today offers a colorful heritage amble, complete with sterling Fraser River vistas and plenty of opportunities to indulge your cravings for what may be BC's best fish and chips.

● You'll begin at the excellent Gulf of Georgia Cannery National Historic Site, located at the southern tip of 4th Ave. This fascinating 1894 wood-built complex was BC's biggest salmon canning operation until its 1979 closure. Several years later, it returned to life as a museum to relate the pioneering story of the province's fish-processing sector. Strolling the sheds—the informative free hourly tours are well worth catching—illuminates an operation where 400 employees (mostly women) worked the line, transforming fish off the boats into canned product. The ladies who handled the fish guts were known as "slimers." Poking around the old machinery and precisely preserved rooms, it feels like the workforce has just strolled off for a tea break.

● Exit the Cannery and cross east over 4th Ave. to Moncton St. Continue east along Moncton, crossing over 3rd Ave. This is the start of Steveston's shopping heart and you'll pass lots of little galleries, boutiques, and coffee shops. Recommended stops include the Riverside Art Gallery, where waterfront landscapes are a specialty, and Dave's Fish & Chips, a local dining legend serving great-value grub in an unpretentious, wood-lined setting—the batter-dipped salmon is recommended. Don't blow your appetite too early: there are plenty of other noshing options coming your way.

● Nip to the left-hand side of Moncton here and continue east past 2nd Ave. Within half a block on your left, you'll come to the small, steeply gabled Steveston Museum building, constructed in New Westminster and shipped here via the Fraser River in 1905. Inside, there's an evocative general store exhibit, complete with a working post office. Save time to peruse the archival photos of old Steveston lining the walls and make sure you head upstairs to the compact recreated bedroom and dining area: the building was originally a bank and this is where the employees lived.

● Backtrack westward on Moncton then turn left along 2nd Ave. toward the waterfront. Cross over Bayview St. and amble through the archway onto the public wharf, also known as Steveston Landing. This attractive boardwalk of seafood restaurants and souvenir shops lures legions of locals on languid summer days. If the fish and chip aromas have finally won you over, head down the ramp to the waters edge at Pajo's, a floating, family-run takeout that's a Steveston legend. They go through 500 pounds/227 kilograms of potatoes on a busy day here but it's the tempura batter on the wild halibut, salmon, and cod that will have you salivating. They also serve shrimp skewers, fish tacos, and yellow-fin tuna burgers if you fancy something a little more exotic.

● Find a perch with a view of the bobbing fishing boats to enjoy your takeout, then inch down the boardwalk's other ramp to meet the fishermen. A Steveston tradition that's been going on almost as long as the village itself, fishers sell their fresh catch right off the back of their boats, especially on weekends when there are more visitors in the village. Wandering among the salty sea dogs sitting on the their boats, you'll likely catch sight (and smell) of shrimp, tuna, salmon, and even octopus, all flash-frozen at sea before being chugged to dry land.

● Head back up the ramp to the boardwalk, stroll back through the wharf's main entrance, and turn right along Bayview St. Head east down this street for two blocks and then duck down No. 1 Rd. back to the waterfront where the boardwalk re-starts.

# THE SHIPYARD'S JAPANESE HISTORY

Among the most intriguing buildings you'll come to as you stroll the boardwalk through the Britannia Shipyard is the Murakami House, on your left. Originally built over marshland in 1885, it was home to a large Japanese family between 1929 and 1942. Asayo Murakami was brought over from Japan in 1924 to marry a Canadian but after meeting him for the first time and deciding she didn't like him, she worked at the cannery to pay off the amount spent on her passage and free herself from the match. She then met and married a boat builder and they started a small workshop operation next door. After raising 10 children in the house—the rooms have been recreated and are full of everyday items like toys and books—the entire family was unceremoniously moved to Manitoba in 1942 as part of Canada's controversial wartime Japanese internment program. Many Japanese families in BC met a similar fate and after the war only a few returned. In 2001 on her 100th birthday, several of Murakami's children came back to the former family residence to plant a garden in her honor. She died in her Alberta home at the age of 104.

Follow this boardwalk, which is markedly different from the one you've just left, eastward. Though this stretch has only been completed in recent years, it does a great job of evoking Steveston's rich maritime heritage. You'll pass a metal artwork that echoes the frame of a shipyard building, plus a short jetty that's lined with preserved machine parts. On the left of this stroll-friendly strip, you'll also see the swanky waterfront condos that are transforming this once-gritty enclave into a favored yuppie community. It's a transformation that not all the locals are happy about.

● Continuing east, you'll spot a clutch of derelict wooden piles bristling from the water on your right. These are relics of a former cannery, now just handy perches for passing herons. You'll also see the green roof of the Britannia Shipyard National Historic Site just ahead. The boardwalk takes you right though the middle of this fascinating clutch of preserved sheds, stilt houses, and workers' accommodations. Not as slick as the Gulf of Georgia Cannery, this dusty old museum complex is still highly evocative. First built as a cannery in 1889, it was converted into a shipyard in 1918 when a giant landslide along the Fraser River dramatically reduced the area's available salmon stock. The yard became the winter base and repair center for much of the West Coast fishing fleet.

- Continue a little farther along the creaky boardwalk and, on your right, enter the shipyard's largest building. Cooled by the water rippling beneath the loose-fitting floorboards, this shed-on-piles is lined with rusty tools and machines. The main room, open at one end to the water, is dominated by the *MV Fleetwood*, a sleek, arrow-shaped 1930s vessel that's being slowly restored by volunteers. This speedy boat was a rumrunner during the prohibition era and it has several bullet holes in its hull as proof of a few run-ins with navy patrol vessels.

- From the shipyard site, head south inland one block—the boardwalk trail is interrupted here—and turn right onto Westwater Dr. Continue east on Westwater until it merges with Dyke Rd. Continue east along Dyke. You'll pass the high fences and adjoining marina of the Steveston Harbour Authority on your right, hugging the waterfront. This is where commercial boats are now dry-docked and repaired. Fishing is a tough industry these days and most of the boats here now go after the priciest catch rather than the most abundant. Among the most lucrative is geoduck, a clam, which attracts top dollar on the international market.

- Stay on Dyke, cross east over No. 2 Rd., and continue along Dyke to the waterfront. The windswept views of the unspoiled shoreline here are among the area's most dramatic: locals often drive out here to catch panoramic sunset views. Continue east along Dyke and within a few minutes on the left you'll reach the reward at the end of your trek. London Heritage Farm is an authentically preserved farmhouse complex built in 1880. Now an idyllic pioneer house museum surrounded by flower gardens, it serves a great-value afternoon tea accompanied by home-baked scones, pastry fancies, and shortbread treats. Before stuffing your face, check out the detailed period rooms, recreating eras from the 1890s to the 1930s when the London family lived here. Then check them out face-to-face by perusing their portraits in the upstairs hallway: the fella with the wild beard is especially beguiling.

## POINTS OF INTEREST

**Gulf of Georgia Cannery National Historic Site** 12138 4th Ave., 604-664-9009

**Riverside Art Gallery** 1480 Moncton St., 604-274-1414

**Dave's Fish & Chips** 3460 Moncton St., 604-271-7555

**Steveston Museum** 3811 Moncton St., 604-271-6868

**Pajo's** Public Wharf, 604-272-1588

**Britannia Shipyard National Historic Site** 5180 Westwater Dr., 604-718-8050

**London Heritage Farm** 6511 Dyke Rd., 604-271-5220

## ROUTE SUMMARY

1.  Start at the Gulf of Georgia Cannery at the southern end of 4th Ave.
2.  Cross east over 4th and stroll east, on the right side, along Moncton St.
3.  Cross to the left side of Moncton at 2nd Ave.
4.  Continue east along Moncton for half a block.
5.  Return west along Moncton and turn left onto 2nd Ave.
6.  Stroll south on 2nd Ave., cross over Bayview St., and enter the public wharf.
7.  Exit the public wharf and turn right along Bayview for two blocks.
8.  Turn right at No. 1 Rd. and head back to the waterfront.
9.  Follow the waterfront promenade east to Britannia Shipyard.
10. Exit the shipyard and turn right along Westwater Dr.
11. Continue east along Westwater, which becomes Dyke Rd.
12. Continue east along Dyke.
13. Follow Dyke along the waterfront to London Heritage Farm.

*Pajo's, Steveston's favorite seafood spot*

## Appendix 1: WALKS BY THEME

### arts, architecture & culture

**Downtown** (Walk 1)
**Burrard Street** (Walk 2)
**Downtown Eastside** (Walk 5)
**Fairview** (Walk 22)
**UBC** (Walk 30)

### DINING & SHOPPING

**Yaletown** (Walk 4)
**Denman Street** (Walk 13)
**Robson Street** (Walk 14)
**Davie Street** (Walk 16)
**Mount Pleasant** (Walk 19)
**Commercial Drive** (Walk 20)
**South Main** (Walk 21)
**Granville Island** (Walk 24)
**South Granville** (Walk 25)
**Kitsilano** (Walk 28)

### NIGHTLIFE

**Granville Strip** (Walk 3)
**Gastown Bars** (Walk 8)

### HISTORY

**Chinatown** (Walk 6)
**Gastown** (Walk 7)
**West End** (Walk 15)
**Shaughnessy Heights** (Walk 26)
**North Vancouver** (Walk 32)
**New Westminster** (Walk 35)

### WATERFRONT

**Coal Harbour** (Walk 9)
**Stanley Park: Seawall** (Walk 12)
**North False Creek** (Walk 17)
**South False Creek** (Walk 18)
**Point Grey** (Walk 29)
**West Vancouve**r (31)
**Steveston** (Walk 36)

### PARKS & NATURE

**Stanley Park: Lost Lagoon** (Walk 10)
**Stanley Park: Brockton Point** (Walk 11)
**Queen Elizabeth Park** (Walk 23)
**Vanier Park** (Walk 27)
**Capilano Suspension Bridge** (Walk 31)
**Grouse Grind** (Walk 34)

# Appendix 2: POINTS OF INTEREST

## FOOD & DRINK

**Agro Cafe** 1363 Railspur Alley, 604-669-0724 (Walk 24)

**Alibi Room** 157 Alexander St., 604-623-3383 (Walk 8)

**Altitudes Bistro** Grouse Mountain, 604-998-4398 (Walk 34)

**Argo Café** 1836 Ontario St., 604-876-3620 (Walk 19)

**Beach House** 150 25th St., 604-922-1414 (Walk 31)

**Bin** 941 941 Davie St., 604-683-1246 (Walk 16)

**Black Frog** 108 Cambie St., 604-602-0527 (Walk 8)

**Blue Water Café** 1095 Hamilton St., 604-688-8078 (Walk 4)

**Bridge House Restaurant** 3650 Capilano Rd., 604-987-3388 (Walk 33)

**Brock House Restaurant** 3875 Point Grey Rd., 604-224-3317 (Walk 29)

**Burgoo Bistro** 3 Lonsdale Ave., 604-904-0933 (Walk 32)

**Cactus Club Café** 575 W. Broadway, 604-714-6000 (Walk 22)

**Café Calabria** 1745 Commercial Dr., 604-253-7017 (Walk 20)

**Café Deux Soleils** 2096 Commercial Dr., 604-254-1195 (Walk 20)

**Cafe Villaggio** 1506 Coal Harbor Quay, 604-687-6599 (Walk 9)

**Café Zen** 1631 Yew St., 604-731-4018 (Walk 28)

**Calhoun's Bakery Café** 3035 W. Broadway, 604-737-7062 (Walk 28)

**Cardero's** 1583 Coal Harbour Quay, 604-669-7666 (Walk 9)

**Cascade Room** 2616 Main St., 604-709-8650 (Walk 19)

**The Charlatan** 1446 Commercial Dr., 604-253-2777 (Walk 20)

**Chill Winston** 3 Alexander St., 604-288-9575 (Walk 8)

**CinCin Ristorante** 1154 Robson St., 604-688-7338 (Walk 14)

**Crave** 3941 Main St., 604-872-3663 (Walk 21)

**Dave's Fish & Chips** 3460 Moncton St., 604-271-7555 (Walk 36)

**Delaney's** 2424 Marine Dr., 604-921-4466 (Walk 31)

## FOOD & DRINK (CONTINUED)

**Dix BBQ & Brewery** 1871 Beatty St., 604-682-2739 (Walk 4)

**Elysian Coffee** 590 W. Broadway, 604-874-5909 (Walk 22)

**FigMint** 500 W. 12th Ave., 604-875-3312 (Walk 22)

**Fish House in Stanley Park** 8901 Stanley Park Dr., 604-681-7275 (Walk 12)

**The Foundation** 2301 Main St., 604-708-0881 (Walk 19)

**Fountainhead Pub** 1025 Davie St., 604-687-2222 (Walk 16)

**Galley Patio & Grill** 1300 Discovery St., 604-222-1331 (Walk 29)

**Gene Café** 2404 Main St., 604-568-5501 (Walk 19)

**Go Fish** 1504 W. 1st Ave., 604-730-5040 (Walk 27)

**Granville Room** 957 Granville St., 604-633-0056 (Walk 3)

**Gusto di Quattro** 1 Lonsdale Ave., 604-924-4444 (Walk 32)

**Havana** 1241 1212 Commercial Dr., 604-253-9119 (Walk 20)

**Hon's Wun-Tun House** 268 Keefer St., 604-688-0871 (Walk 6)

**Irish Heather** 217 Carrall St., 604-688-9779 (Walk 8)

**Jang Mo Jib** 1715 Robson St., 604-687-0712 (Walk 14)

**Japa Dog** northwest corner of Smithe St. and Burrard St. (Walk 2)

**Joe Fortes Seafood & Chophouse** 777 Thurlow St., 604-669-1940 (Walk 2)

**Lamplighter** 92 Water St., 604-687-4424 (Walk 8)

**Le Crocodile** 909 Burrard St., 604-669-4298 (Walk 2)

**Lennox Pub** 800 Granville St., 604-408-0881 (Walk 3)

**The Main** 4210 Main St., 604-709-8555 (Walk 21)

**Maxine's Hideaway** 1215 Bidwell St., 604-689-8822 (Walk 16)

**Melriches Coffeehouse** 1244 Davie St., 604-689-5282 (Walk 16)

**Mill Marine Bistro** 1199 W. Cordova St., 604-687-6455 (Walk 9)

**Monk McQueens** 601 Stamps Landing, 604-877-1351 (Walk 18)

**The Naam** 2724 W. 4th Ave., 604-738-7151 (Walk 28)

**New Town Bakery** 158 E. Pender St., 604-689-7835 (Walk 6)

**O'Doul's Restaurant & Bar** 1300 Robson St., 604-661-1400 (Walk 14)

**The Observatory** Grouse Mountain, 604-980-9311 (Walk 34)

**Pajo's** Public Wharf, 604-272-1588 (Walk 36)

**Pat's Pub** 403 E. Hastings St., 604-255-4301 (Walk 5)

**Paul's Place Omlettery** 2211 Granville St., 604-737-2857 (Walk 25)

**Pho Kim Penh Xe Lua** 500 W. Broadway, 604-877-1120 (Walk 22)

**Picnic** 3010 Granville St., 604-732-4405 (Walk 26)

**Prado Café** 1938 Commercial Dr., 604-255-5537 (Walk 20)

**Provence Marinaside** 1177 Marinaside Crescent, 604-681-4144 (Walk 17)

**Radio Station Café** 101 E. Hastings St., 604-684-8494 (Walk 5)

**Railway Club** 579 Dunsmuir St., 604-681-1625 (Walk 8)

**Raincity Grill** 1193 Denman St., 604-685-7337 (Walk 13)

**Red Lion** 2427 Marine Dr., 604-926-8838 (Walk 31)

**The Reef** 1018 Commercial Dr., 604-568-5375 (Walk 20)

**Robo Sushi** 1709 Robson St., 604-684-3353 (Walk 14)

**Rooster's Quarters** 836 Denman St., 604-689-8023 (Walk 13)

**Salt Tasting Room** 45 Blood Alley, 604-633-1912 (Walk 7)

**Seasons in the Park** Queen Elizabeth Park, 604-874-8008 (Walk 23)

**Six Acres** 203 Carrall St., 604-488-0110 (Walk 8)

**Slickity Jim's** 2513 Main St., 604-873-6760 (Walk 19)

**Social at Le Magasin** 332 Water St., 604-669-4488 (Walk 7)

**Steamworks Brewing Company** 375 Water St., 604-689-2739 (Walk 8)

**Steamworks Transcontinental** 601 W. Cordova St., 604-678-8000 (Walk 7)

**Stellas Tap & Tapas Bar** 1191 Commercial Dr., 604-254-2437 (Walk 20)

**Stepho's Greek Taverna** 1124 Davie St., 604-683-2555 (Walk 16)

**Subeez Café** 891 Homer St., 604-687-6107 (Walk 4)

**The Teahouse** Ferguson Point, 604-669-3281 (Walk 12)

**Templeton** 1087 Granville St., 604-685-4612 (Walk 3)

**True Confections** 866 Denman St., 604-682-1292 (Walk 13)

**Ukrainian Village** 815 Denman St., 604-687-7440 (Walk 13)

**Vij's** 1480 W. 11th Ave., 604-736-6664 (Walk 25)

## FOOD & DRINK (CONTINUED)

**Watermark** 1305 Arbutus St., 604-738-5487 (Walk 28)

**The Whip** 209 E. 6th Ave., 604-874-4687 (Walk 21)

**Winking Judge** 888 Burrard St. St., 604-684-9465 (Walk 2)

**Yaletown Brewing Company** 1111 Mainland St., 604-688-0064 (Walk 4)

## HOTELS

**Empire Landmark Hotel** 1400 St., 604-687-0511 (Walk 14)

**Fairmont Hotel Vancouver** 900 W. Georgia St., 604-684-3131 (Walk 1)

**Granville Island Hotel** 1253 Johnston St., 604-683-7373 (Walk 24)

**Listel Hotel** 1300 Robson St., 604-684-8461 (Walk 14)

**Opus Hotel** 322 Davie St., 604-642-6787 (Walk 4)

**Shangri-La** 1128 W. Georgia St., 604-689-1120 (Walk 2)

**Sylvia Hotel** 1154 Gilford St., 604-681-9321 (Walk 13)

**Westin Bayshore** 1601 Bayshore Dr., 604-682-3377 (Walk 9)

## ENTERTAINMENT & NIGHTLIFE

**Art Club Theatre Company** Granville Island Stage 1585 Johnson St., 604-687-1644 (Walk 24)

**Carousel Theatre** 1411 Cartwright St., 604-669-3410 (Walk 24)

**Celebrities Nightclub** 1022 Davie St., 604-681-6180 (Walk 16)

**Chan Centre for the Performing Arts** 6265 Crescent Rd., 604-822-9197 (Walk 30)

**Commodore Ballroom** 868 Granville St., 604-739-4550 (Walk 3)

**Edgewater Casino** 750 Pacific Blvd South, 604-687-3343 (Walk 17)

**Firehall Arts Centre** 280 E. Cordova St., 604-689-0926 (Walk 5)

**Frederic Wood Theatre** 6354 Crescent Rd., 604-822-2678 (Walk 30)

**Orpheum Theatre** 884 Granville St., 604-665-3050 (Walk 3)

**Plaza Club** 881 Granville St., 604-646-0064 (Walk 3)

**Royal City Star Casino** 788 Quayside Dr., 604-878-9999 (Walk 35)

**Scotiabank Theatre** 900 Burrard St., 604-630-1407 (Walk 2)

**Stanley Theatre** 2750 Granville St., 604-687-1644 (Walk 25)

**Theatre Under the Stars** Malkin Bowl, 604-734-1917 (Walk 10)

**Waterfront Theatre** 1412 Cartwright St., 604-685-3005 (Walk 24)

**Yale Hotel** 1300 Granville St., 604-681-9253 (Walk 4)

## MUSEUMS & Galleries

**Artworks Gallery** 225 Smithe St., 604-688-3301 (Walk 4)

**BC Sports Hall of Fame** 777 Pacific Boulevard, 604-687-5520 (Walk 4)

**Bill Reid Gallery of Northwest Coast Art** 639 Hornby St., 604-682-3455 (Walk 1)

**Britannia Shipyard National Historic Site** 5180 Westwater Dr., 604-718-8050 (Walk 36)

**Contemporary Art Gallery** 555 Nelson St., 604-681-2700 (Walk 4)

**Crafthouse Gallery** 1386 Cartwright St., 604-687-6511 (Walk 24)

**Douglas Reynold's Gallery** 2335 Granville St., 604-731-9292 (Walk 25)

**Equinox Gallery** 2321 Granville St., 604-736-2405 (Walk 25)

**Federation of Canadian Artists Gallery** 1241 Cartwright St., 604-681-8534 (Walk 24)

**Ferry Building Art Gallery** 1414 Argyle Ave., 604-925-7270 (Walk 31)

**Gallery of BC Ceramics** 1359 Cartwright St., 604-669-3606 (Walk 24)

**Gulf of Georgia Cannery National Historic Site** 12138 4th Ave., 604-664-9009 (Walk 36)

**Heffel Fine Art Auction House** 2247 Granville St., 604-732-6505 (Walk 25)

**JEM Gallery** 225 E. Broadway, 604-879-5366 (Walk 19)

**London Heritage Farm** 6511 Dyke Rd., 604-271-5220 (Walk 36)

**Monte Clarke Gallery** 2339 Granville St., 604-730-5000 (Walk 25)

**Morris and Helen Belkin Art Gallery** 1825 Main Mall, 604-822-2759 (Walk 30)

**Museum of Anthropology** 6393 N.W. Marine Dr., 604-822-3825 (Walk 30)

**Museum of Vancouver** 1100 Chestnut St., 604-736-4431 (Walk 27)

**North Vancouver Museum & Archives** 209 W. 4th St., 604-987-5612 (Walk 32)

**Old Hastings Mill Store Museum** 1575 Alma Rd., 604-734-1212 (Walk 8)

**Pendulum Gallery** 885 W. Georgia St., 604-250-9682 (Walk 1)

## MUSEUMS & GALLERIES (CONTINUED)

**Riverside Art Gallery** 1480 Moncton St., 604-274-1414 (Walk 36)

**Steveston Museum** 3811 Moncton St., 604-271-6868 (Walk 36)

**Sun Spirit Gallery** 2444 Marine Dr., 778-279-5052 (Walk 31)

**Vancouver Art Gallery** 750 Hornby St., 604-662-4719 (Walk 1)

**Vancouver Maritime Museum** 1905 Ogden Ave., 604-257-8300 (Walk 27)

**Vancouver Police Centennial Museum** 240 E. Cordova St., 604-665-3346 (Walk 5)

**West Vancouver Museum & Archives** 680 17th St., 604-925-7295 (Walk 31)

## EDUCATIONAL & CULTURAL CENTERS

**Coal Harbour Community Centre** 480 Broughton St., 604-718-8222 (Walk 9)

**Emily Carr University** 1399 Johnston St., 604-844-3800 (Walk 24)

**Nature House** Lost Lagoon, 604-257-6908 (Walk 10)

**Presentation House Arts Centre** 333 Chesterfield Ave., 604-990-3473 (Walk 32)

**Roundhouse Arts & Recreation Centre** 181 Roundhouse Mews, 604-713-1800 (Walk 4)

**Vancouver Public Library** 350 W. Georgia St., 604-331-3603 (Walk 14)

## LANDMARKS & MONUMENTS

**BC Place** 777 Pacific Boulevard, 604-669-2300 (Walk 9)

**Brenchley House** 3351 Granville St. (Walk 26)

**Burr Theatre** 530 Columbia St., 604-523-2877 (Walk 35)

**Canada Place** 999 Canada Pl., 604-775-7200 (Walk 1)

**Canuck Place** 1690 Matthews Ave. (Walk 22)

**Carnegie Centre** 401 Main St. (Walk 5)

**Chinese Benevolent Association Building** 108 E. Pender St. (Walk 6)

**City Hall (New Westminster)** 511 Royal Ave., 604-521-3711 (Walk 35)

**City Hall** 453 W. 12th Ave., 604-873-7011 (Walk 22)

**Dal Grauer Substation** 950 Burrard St. (Walk 2)

**Dominion Building** 207 W. Hastings St. (Walk 5)

**Electra** 970 Burrard St. (Walk 2)

**Frederick Kelly House** 1393 The Crescent (Walk 26)

**General Motors Place** 800 Griffiths Way, 604-899-7400 (Walk 17)

**Irving House** 302 Royal Ave., 604-527-4640 (Walk 35)

**MacDonald House** 1388 The Crescent (Walk 26)

**Marine Building** 355 Burrard St. (Walk 1)

**McRae Mansion/Hycroft House** 1439 McRae Ave. (Walk 26)

**Nichol House** 1402 The Crescent (Walk 26)

**'O Canada' House** 1114 Barclay St., 604-688-0555 (Walk 15)

**Old Auditorium** 6344 Memorial Rd. (Walk 30)

**Pacific Great Eastern Railway Station** south foot of Lonsdale Ave., 604-990-3700 (Walk 32)

**Pantages Theatre** 152 E. Hastings St. (Walk 5)

**Roedde House** 1415 Barclay St., 604-684-7040 (Walk 15)

**Rosemary** 3689 Selkirk St. (Walk 26)

**Sam Kee Building** 8 W. Pender St. (Walk 6)

**St. Paul's Hospital** 1081 Burrard St., 604-682-2344 (Walk 2)

**Victory Square** corner of W. Hastings St. and Cambie St. (Walk 5)

**Vogue Theatre** 918 Granville St., 604-688-1975 (Walk 3)

**Wall Centre** 1088 Burrard St., 604-331-1000 (Walk 2)

## Places of Worship

**Christ Church Cathedral** 690 Burrard St., 604-682-3848 (Walk 1)

**First Baptist Church** 969 Burrard St., 604-683-8441 (Walk 2)

**Holy Trinity Cathedral** 514 Carnarvon St., 604-521-2511 (Walk 35)

**St. Andrew's Wesley United Church** 1022 Nelson St., 604-683-4574 (Walk 2)

## SHOPPING

**Bacci's** 2790 Granville St., 604-733-4933 (Walk 25)

**Barefoot Contessa** 1928 Commercial Dr., 604-255-9035 (Walk 20)

**Bibliophile Book Shop** 2010 Commercial Dr., 604-254-5520 (Walk 20)

**Chocoatl** 1127 Mainland St., 604-676-9977 (Walk 4)

**Dutch Girl Chocolates** 1002 Commercial Dr., 604-251-3221 (Walk 20)

**Duthie Books** 2239 W. 4th Ave., 604-732-5344 (Walk 29)

**Eugene Choo** 3683 Main St., 604-873-8874 (Walk 21)

**Frankie's Candy Bar** 2451 Marine Dr., 604-922-8291 (Walk 31)

**Front & Company** 3772 Main St., 604-879-8431 (Walk 21)

**Granville Island Public Market** 1689 Johnston St., 604-666-6477 (Walk 24)

**Gravity Pope** 2205 W. 4th Ave., 604-731-7673 (Walk 28)

**Hill's Native Arts** 165 Water St., 604-685-4249 (Walk 7)

**HMV** 1160 Robson St., 604-685-9203 (Walk 14)

**House of McLaren** 125 Water St., 604-681-5442 (Walk 7)

**John Fluevog Shoes** 65 Water St., 604-688-6228 (Walk 7)

**Kids Market** 1496 Cartwright St., 604-689-8447 (Walk 24)

**La Grotta Del Formaggio** 1791 Commercial Dr., 604-255-3911 (Walk 20)

**Lazy Susan's** 3647 Main St., 604-873-9722 (Walk 21)

**Little Sister's Book & Art Emporium** 1238 Davie St., 604-669-1753 (Walk 16)

**Lonsdale Quay Public Market** 123 Carrie Cates Court, 604-985-6261 (Walk 32)

**Lucky's Comics** 3972 Main St., 604-875-9858 (Walk 21)

**Lululemon Athletica** 1148 Robson St., 604-681-3118 (Walk 14)

**Marquis Wine Cellars** 1034 Davie St., 604-684-0445 (Walk 16)

**Meinhardt Fine Foods** 3002 Granville St., 604-732-4405 (Walk 25)

**Minna-No-Konbiniya** 1238 Robson St., 604-682-3634 (Walk 14)

**Motherland Clothing** 2539 Main St., 604-876-3426 (Walk 19)

**Pulp Fiction** 2422 Main St., 604-876-4311 (Walk 19)

**Purdy's Chocolates** 2705 Granville St., 604-732-7003 (Walk 25)

**Red Cat Records** 4307 Main St., 604-708-9422 (Walk 21)

**Regional Assembly of Text** 3934 Main St., 604-877-2247 (Walk 21)

**Robson Street Public Market** 1610 Robson St., 604-682-2733 (Walk 14)

**Save-On-Meats** 43 W. Hastings St., 604-683-7761 (Walk 5)

**Smoking Lily** 3634 Main St., 604-873-5459 (Walk 21)

**Ten Lee Hong Enterprises** 500 Main St., 604-689-7598 (Walk 6)

**Travel Bug** 3065 W. Broadway, 604-737-1122 (Walk 28)

**Twigg & Hottie** 3671 Main St., 604-879-8595 (Walk 21)

**Umbrella Shop** 1550 Anderson St., 604-697-0919 (Walk 24)

**Wanted – Lost Found Canadian** 436 Columbia St., 604-633-0178 (Walk 5)

**West End Farmers Market** Nelson Park, 1100 block of Comox St. (Walk 15)

**Wonderbucks Trading Company** 1803 Commercial Dr., 604-253-0510 (Walk 20)

## ParKS & GarDeNS

**Bloedel Floral Conservatory** Queen Elizabeth Park, 604-257-8584 (Walk 23)

**Creekside Park** corner of Pennyfarthing Dr. and Creekside Dr. (Walk 27)

**Cultural Harmony Grove** under east side of Burrard Bridge (Walk 27)

**Dr. Sun Yat-Sen Classical Chinese Garden** 578 Carrall St., 604-662-3207 (Walk 6)

**Nitobe Memorial Garden** 6804 S.W. Marine Dr., 604-822-6038 (Walk 30)

**Pigeon Park** corner of W. Hastings St. and Carrall St. (Walk 5)

**Shaughnessy Park** The Crescent (Walk 26)

**Victoria Park** corner of Lonsdale Ave., and Keith Rd. (Walk 32)

## attraCTIONS & aCTIVITIES

**Aquabus Ferries** 1333 Johnson St, 604-689-5858 (Walk 18)

**Capilano Suspension Bridge & Park** 3735 Capilano Rd., 604-985-7474 (Walk 33)

**Children's Farmyard** near Pipeline Rd., 604-257-8531 (Walk 10)

**Fraser River Discovery Centre** 788 Quayside Dr., 604-521-8401 (Walk 35)

## attractions & activities (continued)

**Granville Island Brewing** 1441 Cartwright St., 604-687-2739 (Walk 18)

**Grouse Mountain** 6400 Nancy Greene Way, 604-984-0661 (Walk 34)

**H.R. MacMillan Space Centre** 1100 Chestnut St., 604-738-7827 (Walk 27)

**Harbour Air** W. Waterfront Rd., 604-274-1277 (Walk 9)

**Harbour Cruises** North Foot Denman St., 604-688-7246 (Walk 9)

**Jericho Sailing Centre** 1300 Discovery St., 604-224-4177 (Walk 29)

**Miniature Railway** near Pipeline Rd., 604-257-8531 (Walk 10)

**Science World** 1455 Quebec St., 604-443-7443 (Walk 17)

**Second Beach Swimming Pool** Stanley Park Dr., 604-257-8371 (Walk 12)

**Vancouver Aquarium** 845 Avison Way, 604-659-3474 (Walk 11)

**Vancouver Lookout** 555 W. Hastings St., 604-689-0421 (Walk 7)

**Vancouver Rowing Club** 450 Stanley Park Dr., 604-687-3400 (Walk 11)

## miscellaneous

**Burrard Civic Marina** 1655 Whyte Ave., 604-733-5833 (Walk 27)

**Cannabis Culture Headquarters** 307 W. Hastings St., 604-682-1172 (Walk 5)

**Chinese Consulate General** 3380 Granville St. (Walk 26)

**Federal Fisheries Wharf** near the foot of Pennyfarthing Dr. (Walk 27)

**Ocean Construction Supplies** Johnston St., 604-261-2211 (Walk 24)

**Spruce Harbour Marina** 1015 Ironwork Passage, 604-733-3512 (Walk 18)

**Student Union Building** 6138 Student Union Blvd. (Walk 30)

# INDEX

# about the author

John Lee was born and raised a few miles north of London in the pub-strewn city of St. Albans, before heading to university (okay, polytechnic) in Leicester. Eager for overseas adventure, he next finagled his way into Western Canada's University of Victoria to study politics before teaching English in Tokyo and then taking a life-changing trek on the Trans-Siberian Railway. By the time the train trundled into Moscow, he had decided to abandon all reason and become a full-time freelance travel writer. More than 10 years later, he's still doing it. An adopted Vancouverite for most of that time, John's travel writing has appeared in more than 125 major newspapers and magazines around the world and his trips have taken him from New Zealand's Fox Glacier to the pubs of Galway and the barbecue pits of Texas. Since 2004, he's also been a *Lonely Planet* guidebook author and has written 14 books for the company. For more information on what he's up to, visit **www.johnleewriter.com.**